ETHICS BEYOND WAR'S END

ETHICS BEYOND WAR'S END

ERIC PATTERSON
Editor

GEORGETOWN UNIVERSITY PRESS
Washington, DC

© 2012 Georgetown University Press. All rights reserved. No part of this book may be reproduced or utilized in any form or by any means, electronic or mechanical, including photocopying and recording, or by any information storage and retrieval system, without permission in writing from the publisher.

Library of Congress Cataloging-in-Publication Data

Ethics beyond war's end / Eric Patterson, editor.
  p. cm.
Rev. essays from a conference held in Apr. 2010 at Georgetown University.
Includes bibliographical references and index.
ISBN 978-1-58901-888-4 (pbk. : alk. paper)
1. War—Moral and ethical aspects. 2. Just war doctrine. I. Patterson, Eric, 1971–
JZ6392.E75   2012
172'.42—dc23
                                                              2011036279

This book is printed on acid-free paper meeting the requirements of the American National Standard for Permanence in Paper for Printed Library Materials.

15 14 13 12   9 8 7 6 5 4 3 2 First printing

Printed in the United States of America

For our family's next generation:
Tristan, Kristina, Elisabeth, Spencer, Caleb, Samuel, and Jane

CONTENTS

PREFACE — ix

INTRODUCTION — 1
ERIC PATTERSON

1. MORAL RESPONSIBILITY AFTER CONFLICT — 17
   The Idea of *Jus Post Bellum* for the Twenty-First Century
   JAMES TURNER JOHNSON

2. THE AFTERMATH OF WAR — 35
   Reflections on *Jus Post Bellum*
   MICHAEL WALZER

3. *JUS ANTE* AND *POST BELLUM* — 47
   Completing the Circle, Breaking the Cycle
   GEORGE R. LUCAS JR.

4. IN MY BEGINNING IS MY END — 65
   ROBERT ROYAL

5. A MORE PERFECT PEACE — 77
   Jus Post Bellum and the Quest for Stable Peace
   ROBERT E. WILLIAMS JR.

6. ETHICS IN THE TIMES OF WAR — 97
   PAULETTA OTIS

7. JUST WAR AND AN ETHICS OF RESPONSIBILITY — 123
   JEAN BETHKE ELSHTAIN

8. ENDING THE US CIVIL WAR WELL — 145
   Reconciliation and Transitional Justice
   DAVID A. CROCKER

9. JUSTICE AFTER WAR 175
Toward a New Geneva Convention
BRIAN OREND

10. "JUST PEACE"
An Elusive Ideal 197
MARK EVANS

CONCLUSION 221
Toward a Twenty-First Century *Jus Post Bellum*
ERIC PATTERSON

CONTRIBUTORS 231

INDEX 237

PREFACE

THIS BOOK BEGINS WITH A QUESTION, "Where is the *jus post bellum*?" It was 2004 and the setting was a month-long seminar for scholars on "War and Morality: Rethinking the Just War Tradition" on the campus of the US Naval Academy at Annapolis. My doctorate was less than two years old and most of my colleagues in the room had been publishing on ethics and war for years—even decades. The first scholar I asked replied, "Good question." There was an awkward pause. "I don't think there is one." It turns out that many were flummoxed by the question, although one senior philosopher pointed me to the new work by a Canadian scholar named Brian Orend.

The fact that we could spend a month talking about the morality of going to war (*jus ad bellum*) and the morality of how war is fought (*jus in bello*) without discussing the morality of conflict settlement and postconflict (*jus post bellum*) should be startling to the outside observer. However, for just war thinkers there has been and remains plenty of work to do simply applying just war theory to the ever evolving battlescape, which today includes global terrorist networks, armed humanitarian intervention, the use of nonlethal weapons (lasers, heat-rays, high-decibel machines), piracy, rogue states, preventive and preemptive war, private military contractors, robots and drones, and the like.

My own idea for a parsimonious framework with policy relevance was first published in 2005 and is the basis for the book *Ending Wars Well: Just War Thinking and Post-Conflict*. The basic model is that a war must end with some form of *order;* the dilemma we see today in Africa and Central Asia is that there is political disorder, and that disorder is more than insecurity—it is the conflation of a lack of domestic security, governance and institutions, and regional security across borders. Without order there can be no politics. The second part of the model is *justice*: We all want to see aggressors pay and victims be vindicated, but I have argued that justice must not destabilize the order. Draconian reparations, ICC indictments, or reneging on amnesties is likely to destabilize a tenuous peace. However, justice is possible in some cases, as illustrated by Nuremberg, Tokyo, the trial of Saddam Hussein, and Rwanda's *gacaca* courts. Finally, order and justice can be the first steps to, and be reinforced by, *conciliation*. Conciliation, or reconciliation in some cases, is extremely rare in political life, but it is the material for long-term peace and security as we see in the Franco-German relationship.

With this framework in mind, and a burgeoning interest in the morality of late- and postconflict developing particularly in the United States following the invasions of Afghanistan and Iraq, I hosted a one-day conference specifically on *jus post bellum* at Georgetown University in April 2010. Some of the participants were a part of the 2004 conference at Annapolis and we were all fortunate at the depth and breadth of the symposium, which included some of the very best thinkers on just war theory in North America. This book is a result of the essays developed in advance of the conference and which were subsequently revised in its aftermath.

Many thanks are thus in order. First, I sincerely appreciate the participation of the conference participants and contributors to this volume. I thank Thomas Banchoff, director of the Berkley Center for Religion, Peace, and World Affairs at Georgetown University, for providing resources to make the conference possible. Berkley Center staff, most notably Melody Fox Ahmed, Annie Hunt, and Abby Waldrip, supported the event and my team of research assistants contributed in numerous ways: Caryl Tuma, Joseph Shamalta, Ilan Cooper, Vanessa Francis, Elizabeth Royall, and Jonathan Barsness. I appreciate Richard Brown and the staff of Georgetown University Press for their confidence in the book. Finally, I am grateful to my family for their support in yet another writing project, and I dedicate my work on the project to my children, nieces, and nephews.

INTRODUCTION

ERIC PATTERSON

In October 1944 British Prime Minister Winston Churchill flew to Moscow to meet with Soviet leader Josef Stalin. Part of their discussion centered on British and Soviet spheres of influence following an Allied victory over the Axis powers. Churchill nonchalantly jotted on a piece of paper his suggested percentages of British and Soviet spheres of influence: 50–50 in Hungary and Yugoslavia, 90 percent for the Russians in Romania, and 75 percent in Bulgaria, whereas the Brits were to have 90 percent influence in Greece. Churchill pushed the paper across the table to Stalin, who ticked off the various countries one by one: Romania, Bulgaria, Greece, Hungary. Stalin then returned the sheet to Churchill. The prime minister recorded in his biography that the following exchange ensued:

Churchill: Might it not be thought rather cynical if it seemed we had disposed of these issues so fateful to millions of people, in such an offhand manner? Let us burn the paper.
Stalin: No, you keep it.[1]

Is this all that there was to it? Was the end of the Second World War in Europe really decided over brandy, without regard for wider issues of colonies, oil, or the looming German question? What about the unresolved business of the Treaty of Versailles from World War I, not to mention other players such as Japan, China, and the United States?

Today we tend to look back on that as a golden period, a so-called great war for civilization. We refer to its American participants as the Greatest Generation. Historians hail Churchill, Franklin Roosevelt, and members of the Truman administration as the leaders who prosecuted a war against barbarity and handed us a new world order in the aftermath. However, many of the postwar achievements—the political rehabilitation of Germany and Japan, the Marshall Plan, the Truman Doctrine, the Bretton Woods System, the inauguration of the United Nations—were ad hoc. They were often experimental quick fixes to the dilemmas of international politics of the time, and they were not tethered to robust strategic and ethical analyses that provided a long-term future picture of what international relations might look like at war's end. Certainly, some planning did occur on specific issues, but neither Churchill, Roosevelt, Harry Truman, Clement Attlee, Dean Acheson, General George C. Marshall, nor any other major figure as far as we know utilized a formal ethical framework to think ahead to the long-term issues of justice and security at war's end beyond immediate victory over the Axis powers, securing Europe and the Pacific, and prosecution of the enemy's senior leadership.

Nevertheless, in retrospect, the late- and postwar decisions of the Allied leadership illustrate three critical principles. First, after war's end there had to be robust, enduring *order*. Churchill and Stalin, as veteran observers of an earlier world war, understood that better than anyone, and they began secretly discussing their spheres of influence as early as 1943. They recognized that the settlement of World War I led to disorder: a bankrupt Europe; a seething, starving Germany; American isolationism; and the absence of agreement among the Great Powers—such as that which kept the peace between them for nearly a century following the 1815 Concert of Vienna. What was needed was level-headed—or cold-blooded—calculations of international security rooted in political realism, not the fanciful idealism of the League of Nations and the Kellogg-Briand Pact (which had outlawed war in 1927). International security would only be secure if pragmatic actions were taken to found the peace: spheres of influence, buffer zones, a divided Germany, and powerful national militaries. After the war ended, many practical steps were implemented as new conditions arose to bolster security and avert new wars from breaking out, from continued military occupation to new alliances such as the North Atlantic Treaty Organization (NATO).

Second, the Allied Powers were particularly concerned with *justice*. The Nazis were particularly heinous, having not only violated international law in aggressing their neighbors but by practicing what today we call ethnic cleansing and genocide. In 1945 the Allies chartered an International Military Tribunal to prosecute leaders of the German war effort. Made up of four judges from each of the four victorious Allied powers, the Tribunal at Nuremberg ultimately passed 25 death sentences, 20 life sentences, 97 lesser prison terms, and acquitted an additional 35 individuals. The postwar German government prosecuted hundreds more.[2]

Nuremberg symbolized the rule of law and morality, however imperfectly applied, as indispensable to a just and durable peace. Robert Jackson, the lead Allied prosecutor and a member of the US Supreme Court, argued that "the wrongs which we seek to condemn and punish have been so calculated, so malignant and so devastating that civilization cannot tolerate their being ignored because it cannot survive their being repeated."[3] The Nuremberg trials, as well as their counterparts in Tokyo, set the stage for wider international commitments to justice-in-war in the terms of the United Nations Charter and especially in the 1949 Geneva Conventions.

Third, Washington and London were keenly concerned with issues of *conciliation*. With the Soviet colossus looming as the next European predator, the Allies desperately needed national reconciliation in France following the Vichy era, a unified Italy tilted westward, and conciliation between the two historic antagonists, Germany and France, in order to counterbalance the Soviets. Furthermore, over time the occupations of Germany and Japan would need to evolve into partnerships with former adversaries on behalf of common security.

None of this is to say that the Allies had a strategic or moral framework of order, justice, and conciliation that resulted in NATO, the Marshall Plan, and enduring international institutions. Most of these specific policies and programs evolved as the need arose in the period of flux from 1945–49. But, national leaders the world over deeply believed in the primacy of international order and supported some efforts at justice and conciliation.

The purpose of this book is to go beyond the ad hoc, short-term thinking characteristic of the ending of most wars. Whether the focus is World War II or later conflicts from Korea to Angola to Iraq, the issues remain the same: How to achieve security? Is there space for justice? Is reconciliation possible? This volume attempts to answer such questions from the perspective of just war theory. More specifically, the chapters extend the just war tradition to late- and postconflict issues, privileging considerations of order, justice, and conciliation.

Understanding the Just War Tradition

Classical war theory includes the many centuries of debate, scholarship, and application of moral principles to the dilemmas of historical battlefields. In fact, just war principles such as "right intention" and "just cause" date back at least to the Roman era in the writings of Ambrose (governor of Milan) and Augustine (bishop of Hippo). They were applied by Western churchmen, philosophers, and legal thinkers during the reaction to Islamic conquest, the Crusades, the era of Portuguese and Spanish imperial expansion, and now the present. In the early modern era, a secular version of just war theory developed in what Hugo Grotius called the "law of nations," and just war principles provide building blocks for the modern state system (e.g., legitimate authority and sovereignty) as well as the laws of armed conflict (e.g., proportionality, discrimination).

The heritage of just war theory is a classical and Christian philosophical milieu, but this is not to say that there are not parallels to be found in other cultures.[4] Nonetheless, in its traditional presentation, the just war tradition provides statesmen, philosophers, and soldiers policy and moral guidance on two key issues: the conditions under which it is moral to go to war (*jus ad bellum*) and the ethics of how war is fought (*jus in bello*). Early just war theorists such as Thomas Aquinas laid the foundation, arguing that the just decision to use military force (*jus ad bellum*) was based on three criteria: *legitimate authority* acting on a *just cause* with *right intent*. A contributor to this volume observes, "over time prudential criteria were added to the original *jus ad bellum* trio: *likelihood of success, proportionality of ends, last resort,* and *comparative justice*. The prudential items are additional practical criteria for judging the wisdom and morality of employing violence."[5] Of course, politicians the world over have long argued the righteousness of their cause in order to justify the use of military power, but does this mean that all such ethical claims are a sham? No. Rather, the lip service to morality is an important signal that warfare and politics are not separate from normative considerations.

In addition to the *jus ad bellum* criteria governing the resort to force, *jus in bello* provides ethical guidance on restraining the use of the military instrument in the course of conflict, balancing issues of military necessity and campaign objectives with moral regard for human life and property. Restraint means using tactics proportionate (*proportionality*) to battlefield objectives while limiting harm to noncombatants (*discrimination*).

The Neglected Dimension: Just Postwar Thinking

For the better part of two millennia, just war thinking ended with little formal attention given to the ethics of the postconflict environment (*jus post bellum*). This is not to suggest that the just war tradition is simplistic or arcane: it must continually be reapplied in novel contexts. Augustine and Aquinas could little imagine nuclear weapons or unmanned submersible vehicles, but their principles remain remarkably sturdy when thoughtfully applied to changing political systems and the innovations of the battle space. But most strategists and just war thinkers ended with some version of B. H. Liddell-Hart's maxim "the end of war is a better state of peace." They did not extend their analysis to systematic investigation about how to ensure that war's end results in enduring peace, what the character of that peace might look like, or examine the linkages between war's causes and policies regarding the postconflict environment.

Why is this the case? Why has the venerable just war tradition neglected *jus post bellum*? There are many possible reasons why justice at war's end has been neglected, at least until very recently. The most obvious reason is that, historically, war was seen as occurring between two governments (sovereign powers). At conflict's end, even a government that had lost territory tended to maintain sovereignty, with its accompanying principle of nonintervention. In other words, at war's end everyone went home: It was nobody's business what the state did within its delimited territory—even if that state was weak or despotic.

A second reason that *jus post bellum* was neglected is that the tradition's earliest motivations were quite different from those that motivate much contemporary just war writing. For example, in the fourth century Augustine defended the morality of Christians to serve in government, including law enforcement and the military, when there were strong antistate and pacifist tendencies among Christians due to mandatory worship of the emperor and public persecution. Just war thinking was just a small element of Augustine's larger project: Consideration of how legitimate authority in a fallen world could and should approximate the ideals of the City of God. Consequently, Augustine, like the Greek philosophers before him, wrote extensively on political philosophy, privileging political order (Pax Romana) over disorder (the Vandals, Huns, and Goths who destroyed Rome) as a moral good. Thus government officials had a moral obligation to buttress order by preventing wrongdoing, righting wrongs, and punishing wrongdoers. This was true for both local criminals and predatory neighboring regimes. Augustine's approach informed the next thousand years of just war thinking, but today his philosophical assumptions are often overlooked. The same neglect is true of the broader philosophical bases of other just war scholarship through the centuries: Aquinas, the Spanish neo-Scholastics, Grotius, and dozens more rooted their just war thinking in a larger discussion of the moral objectives and limitations of pursuing "the good life." Without this wider set of considerations, we are left with the typical just war blogging prevalent today: narrow discussions of military tactics and armaments divorced from political and moral theory.

A third reason that just war thinking did not develop a comprehensive *jus post bellum* is because many political theorists recognize that governments were almost always in a state of war, either a "hot" ongoing conflict of actual combat, or a "cold" war of tension, strategic diplomacy, and commercial competition against known adversaries. Thomas Hobbes sardonically summarized this best:

> For war consisteth not in battle only, or the act of fighting; but in a tract of time, wherein the will to contend by battle is sufficiently known: and therefore the notion of time, is to be considered in the nature of war; as it is in the nature of weather. For as the nature of foul weather lieth not in a shower or two of rain; but in an inclination thereto of many days together: so the nature of war, consisteth not in actual fighting; but in the known disposition thereto, during all the time there is no assurance to the contrary. All other time is peace.[6]

Hobbes, an Englishman accustomed to gloomy weather, did not argue that states exist in a general condition of peace most of the time. Quite the opposite: His quip "all other time is peace" is sarcastic, meaning that states in anarchy (with no central authority) are always in a state of war.

In short, if the forecast in international relations is for rain, theorists will continue to focus their attention primarily on dealing with the rain rather than on how to handle the rare sunny day. So, too, just war theorists devoted their attention to the ethics of war because conflict and competition were seen as the eternal status quo.

Another reason that just war thinking neglected *jus post bellum* has to do with the tradition's fundamental purpose: restraint. Just war theory's purpose was never to provide a moral carte blanche for warfare (holy war), nor did it pretend that a nonviolent world was possible or responsible (pacifism). Instead, just war theory's purpose was to call for responsible action while imposing limits, recognizing the moral obligation of leaders to defend and promote order, security, and justice in a fallen world. Indeed, the political ethic of responsibility inherent in the just war tradition expected, and continues to expect, that sovereigns (governments) rule their dominions with justice after the fighting has stopped. In other words, the just war tradition historically did not need a *jus post bellum* because there were robust religious, moral, and philosophical teachings—from the Old Testament to Aristotle to Aquinas—about the ethics of righteous governance. There was no need for a doctrine of *jus post bellum* when there was moral tradition, such as chivalry and feudal obligation, governing how sovereigns were to act in peace.

There is at least one other reason that the just war tradition lacked a comprehensive *jus post bellum*, and that has to do with the secularization and formalization of the tradition into what Michael Walzer calls the "legalist paradigm."[7] Since the late nineteenth century, just war thinking has become a pillar of international law and the foundation of the war convention, but, as tends to happen in international law, those principles become fixed and inflexible. Indeed, in many ways, the just war tradition of moral reflection largely stagnated for generations until well after World War II, when individuals like Paul Ramsey and Michael Walzer breathed life into it as a prudential form of ethical inquiry on tough cases like global nuclear deterrence, the so-called supreme emergency faced by adolescent Israel attacked on all sides, and the tribulations of the Vietnam War. Ironically, however, international law outpaced just war thinking in the area of postconflict with the historic trials at Nuremberg and Tokyo and the establishment of the United Nations as a collective security organization to ward off threats to international peace and security following the Second World War. However, the promise of 1945 quickly evaporated with the Cold War and new problems—from atomic attack to counterinsurgency—called for the more thoughtful stretching kind of moral calculus available within just war theory. So too did the questions of military humanitarian intervention in places like Bosnia, Rwanda, and more recently Darfur, or the question of preemptive or preventive attack to halt weapons of mass destruction or potential genocide.

In each of these cases, the focus has returned attention to the ethics of the decision to go to war (*jus ad bellum*) and how war is fought (*jus in bello*), while the development of a framework for ending wars well—through either moral statesmanship, philosophy, or international law—remained stunted.

Hence, this book. This volume is a compendium of new, cutting-edge thinking on how the just war tradition applies to post conflict. The world needs such critical and creative thinking for a number of reasons that blare daily from the headlines. Soldiers and strategists need a framework for *jus post bellum* because they increasingly are called upon when Phase IV Operations (postconflict reconstruction and stabilization) degenerates into Phase 0 Operations (preconflict). In other words, when the peace is insecure or unjust, it can lead to renewed or intensified conflict, as happened in Iraq in the second half of 2003. The same is true when the so-called peace settlement actually settles very little, causing postconflict grievances and friction that inevitably results in a gorier bloodbath, be it World War I's flawed Treaty of Versailles or the fragile 1992 Arusha Accords that provided a mere eighteen-month respite before the 1994 Rwanda genocide.

In both types of cases we need prudential thinking about the ethical and practical dilemmas of postconflict and the political will to undergird the peace. We also need just postwar thinking in the area of military humanitarian intervention. Since the end of the Cold War, the international community has been increasingly willing to devote military power to chaotic arenas of insecurity, from West Africa to East Timor. When it comes to legal punishment, there are juridical instruments for *jus in bello* violations, namely prosecution such as those carried out by the international criminal tribunals for Rwanda and the former Yugoslavia, the International Criminal Court, or the Genocide Convention. Justice is an important objective. What we lack, but need, is a wider framework for considering postconflict, from issues of traditional security to longer-term efforts at transitional justice and conciliation.

Furthermore, our interests compel us, in a globalized world, to connect the dots: to realize the connections between postconflict instability in West Africa and US petroleum interests, between instability in Africa's Great Lakes and Chinese demand for raw materials, between massive refugee flows and immigration patterns in the Mediterranean. Moreover, our deepening commitments to human rights make these issues all the more pressing.

In short, just war thinking at war's end should provide a framework for political and military leaders to think through pragmatic, ethical responses to late- and postconflict scenarios in specific cases. Just postwar theory reminds us of the limits—from financial ones to moral ones—on state behavior and should remind us of the consequences, both intended and unintended, of our action or inaction. The expanded security horizon of the twenty-first century demands our attention to postconflict situations beyond our immediate vision. In sum, there is no simplistic fix-all formula for postconflict, no sophomoric moral checklist to indicate that if x, then y is just. Rather, this book provides approaches rooted in just war thinking that can be applied on a case-by-case basis and thus are useful for policy experts and national leaders in their considerations of war's causes, how war was fought, and a pragmatic yet ethical vision for a secure future that is built, bit by bit, into aspirational yet actionable policy.

Outline of the Book

Over the past five years a few scholars have begun extending the just war tradition to what happens at the end of war, but, unfortunately, the massive investment in postconflict operations and so-called reconstruction and stabilization operations, from Africa to Iraq and Afghanistan, has lacked a general rooting in the just war tradition. True, Western militaries continue to be guided by the principles of *jus ad bellum* and *jus in bello*, but there is little formal application of just war thinking to war's end. This book begins to close this gap by bringing together the leading scholars of just war and postconflict from the social sciences and philosophy. The chapters that follow address a number of key themes. First, what are the normative and theoretical assumptions necessary for a robust, useful approach to ending wars well? For example, a theory of justice at war's end should provide a framework for considering the causes of the conflict—including the culpability of political leaders who made the decision to wage war—as well as violations of the laws of armed conflict such as rape and looting. Models must account for the cyclical nature of contemporary conflict: situations when the postconflict sires the next conflict, as happened in Rwanda. The second theme of this book is how to apply these normative and theoretical ideas to the real-world task of developing and implementing peace settlements. Some chapters specifically contrast the ideas underlying real-world cases where postconflict settlements failed to found a just and durable peace with other cases that have proven more resilient (e.g., the US civil war, ongoing conflict in Colombia). A third theme of the book is how governments and practitioners move beyond modest—though nevertheless tough-to-implement—security goals of order to implement broader strategies of postconflict justice and reconciliation, particularly in hard cases like the Balkans and Afghanistan.

The book begins with a chapter by just war historian James Turner Johnson that addresses the question of moral responsibility after armed conflict throughout the long tradition of Western just war scholarship. Johnson argues that classical just war theory did consider the aftermath of war in some cases, but that this was generally conceived of as simply one element of a larger project to understand the right ordering of society. More specifically, a concept found in the writings of classical just war thinkers such as Augustine and Aquinas is *tranquillitas ordinis*, referring to the tranquility that stands as the moral ideal for politics itself, and which comes into being only when there is a proper order characterized by justice.[8] Of course, such order, justice, and peace can never be fully achieved, except in the City of God—but this should not lead to despair or paralysis of action. Instead, the fact that these good ends can never be fully achieved means that the obligation to strive for them continues. Thus, classic just war thinking saw armed force as a possible tool in the practice of politics, and this practice was always aimed at trying to get closer and closer to the ideal. Johnson extends this to the changing nature of contemporary conflict, particularly with regard to questions of the responsibility of victors to order and justice at war's end.

The next several chapters apply the just war tradition to some of the intractable problems of modern postconflict, such as the responsibility of occupiers, the unique dilemmas of intrastate insecurity following civil war, and the cyclical nature of contemporary conflict where there is little peace, merely interregnums between outbreaks of violence. Michael Walzer observes that traditional understandings of just war regard "just outcome" as merely a return to the prewar status quo without taking into account the ethical implications of that status quo. The status quo conceptualization of "just outcome" sets a low threshold for justice and often results in the perpetuation of authoritarian or predatory regime. Walzer contends that the existence of insidious regimes, large-scale genocide, and pressing humanitarian disasters should provoke, at the very least, a reexamination of traditional just war thinking, especially when it comes to the postconflict responsibilities of occupation. But Walzer cautions that extending just war thinking to justify regime change and democracy promotion is a problematic and potentially naïve stroke of idealism that often disregards local particularities and specific historical or cultural concerns.

George Lucas argues that *jus post bellum* can "complete the temporal circle" of concerns to prepare properly for war, enter into it justly, conduct it appropriately, and bring it to an end in a fashion that ensures greater probability of lasting peace. More specifically, his chapter demonstrates the link between "right intention" in classical just war theory not only with the goal of restoring peace, but (following Immanuel Kant) of ensuring that a termination of hostilities aims at reestablishing a just civil society, showing respect for the basic needs and rights of citizens, and restoring the rule of law with the goal of making future wars less likely. *Jus post bellum* addresses the responsibility of nations and their armed forces to ensure that military personnel are fully apprised of these responsibilities, ensuring not only that war-fighters conduct themselves accordingly during conflict, but in so doing, ensure that a just peace and an authentic end to hostilities is achievable. This is true of ongoing conflicts in Afghanistan and Iraq, where everything from poor planning to injustices perpetrated at Abu Ghraib prolong conflict and shape perceptions of the postwar environment.

Robert Royal argues that ending wars well usually entails beginning them well. He explores the connections between war aims and just war tenets such as "just cause" and "reasonable chance of success" (*jus ad bellum*) in an effort to break out of narrow military goals to wider considerations of the ethics of national security strategy. This chapter explores more wide-ranging and subtle considerations about what constitutes success in a just war. However, Royal also cautions against expecting too much from military actions that are, by their very nature, limited in what they can accomplish. Other considerations—restoring civilian conditions, good government *post bellum*, preventing the return to the conditions that called for violence or intervention in the first place—are needed in the deliberations about whether or not to go to war, but they also need to be recurring and ongoing considerations throughout the war in preparation for the postconflict environment.

Perhaps the most difficult type of conflict to finally and satisfactorily bring to conclusion is civil war. The intractability of such conflict is due in part to the zero-sum nature of the local security dilemma: If one side gives up its weapons under the peace deal, there is no protection should the other side renege—they are neighbors. We have witnessed the bitter fruit of this logic in Sudan, Rwanda, Congo, Angola, Afghanistan, Sri Lanka, Mozambique, and elsewhere over the past generation. Robert Williams's chapter quotes General William Tecumseh Sherman, himself a veteran of a tragic civil war: "War's object is a better state of peace." How does this notion of a better state of peace apply to intrastate war? Williams asks what the emerging understanding of *jus post bellum* in interstate wars can offer to the quest for stable peace in the aftermath of intrastate wars. For instance, how can the codification of treaties and regional "zones of peace" in international life be applied to intrastate wars? Williams looks at the trade-offs made between moral war aims (*jus ad bellum*, especially just cause) and the political realities of late conflict and settlements in civil wars, and ultimately argues that emerging *jus post bellum* principles should focus on the objective of stable peace and provide guidance toward that end.

American military strategists divide war into a series of stages or phases. Contemporary doctrine defines those phases of conflict as Phase 0, shaping the preconflict environment; Phase 1, deterring aggression from occurring; Phases 2–3, seizing the initiative and dominating the battlespace; Phase 4, stabilizing postconflict insecurity; and Phase 5, enabling civil authority so that the military can draw down and long-term peace under civilian government is established. Pauletta Otis's chapter analyzes the ethical principles found in just war theory as they are practiced and applied during the different phases of war, particularly in wars occurring in highly religious contexts. Otis argues that it is not simply the initial determination to go to war, or how to fight it, or how to end war that should be the concern of just war theorists, but all of the phases: planning, mobilization, conflict, demobilization, stability and support, nation building, and peacemaking. Ethical principles and practices influence each discrete phase and have cumulative effects on successive phases, ultimately nurturing or eroding the conditions for long-term peace and security.

Jean Bethke Elshtain examines questions of justice in postconflict. What responsibilities are borne by the state or group of states that prevail in a military conflict? What does the victor owe to the vanquished? This is a complex question within the just war tradition given that tradition allowed for "just punishment" as part of an end-of-war settlement. Resentment and hatred were to be eschewed, but the assumption was that there are forms of punishment that are entirely appropriate. In more recent years, however, the view seems to have taken hold that punishment be reserved for a small number of relevant perpetrators and to assume that the general populace of the country one has fought are also victims; hence they are exempt from punishment and, instead, become beneficiaries of the continued engagement of the victors with their own country. Elshtain critically examines this presumption of just punishment and how it has developed since Nuremberg, ultimately articulating an "ethic of responsibility" vis-à-vis the defeated nation or group of states.

Policymakers and scholars have begun to contemplate issues of punishment, reparations, and postconflict justice under the rubric of "transitional justice."[8] Transitional justice critically considers how countries or regions should reckon with past wrongs and make (or fail to make) transitions to a better future. Argentina and Chile, South Africa and Uganda, Cambodia and the Philippines are only a few of the places that have taken up transitional justice challenges. David Crocker's chapter compares the just war tradition with transitional justice as well as with a framework he calls "amnesty, reintegration, and reconciliation," or AR2, which has a stronger emphasis on reintegrating excombatants and building long-term peaceful relations among former adversaries.[9] Crocker uses this theoretical postconflict lens to evaluate the end of the US Civil War as documented by historian Jay Winik, and the issues of national political reconciliation, the end of hot war, and the longer-term flashpoints of unresolved racial justice and interracial democracy. The US Civil War is a compelling case for consideration, particularly for US government officials, because of the potent tensions between Lincoln's vision of a national reconciliation and the demise of slavery, and the long-term moral limitations of amnesty and political Reconstruction in the South.

Brian Orend's provocative chapter is titled "Justice After War: Toward a New Geneva Convention." This chapter considers two models of post-war justice: revenge and rehabilitation. Orend argues that a moral end to war (*jus post bellum*) consistent with the other goals of just war theory (*jus ad bellum* and *jus in bello*) will focus on rehabilitation rather than revenge. By codifying the reconciliation model in an international treaty, Orend hopes to set minimal guidelines for *jus post bellum* and ensure that reconciliation, not revenge, is the goal of postconflict operations. Orend's model of postconflict rehabilitation rejects sanctions and compensation payments because they harm innocent civilians in the defeated country. Instead, he argues for investing in a defeated aggressor, to help it rebuild and to help smooth over the wounds of war, and in some cases forcing regime change leading to the creation of a new, better, nonaggressive, and even progressive, member of the international community—as occurred in West Germany and Japan following World War II. Orend's chapter is particularly timely not only because it looks at US-led efforts of rehabilitation in Germany and Japan, but also because he extends the analysis to US-led efforts to reconstruct and rehabilitate Iraq and Afghanistan.

Finally, philosopher Mark Evans considers the implications of *jus post bellum*, calling a just peace "an elusive ideal." He begins by observing that both the ultimate goal of a *just* war and the rectificatory moral imperative present in the aftermath of an *unjustified* war are governed by the same ideal: a "just peace." It is an elusive ideal not only because a just peace so often seems difficult to achieve in postconflict situations, but also because its theoretical meaning and import can be hard to pin down. The latter aspect of its elusiveness in particular could impugn the utility—and perhaps threaten the very coherence—of a theory of *jus post bellum*. Evans provides a conceptual mapping of just peace, demonstrating that many of the disputes in what is really the nascent theorizing of *jus post bellum* in general are deep controversies over this concept of just peace. In the end,

Evans is critical of narrow conceptions of just peace, calling for an expansive *jus post bellum* characterized by transitional justice, human rights, and reconciliation.

Conclusion

The authors in this book agree that moral reflection at war's end is not only an ethical imperative but a strategic and humanitarian one as well. *Jus post bellum* can inform policymaking because it is wars that end well which, over the course of decades, end up promoting domestic and international security. Over the long haul they cost less in terms of slain soldiers, military spending, and taxation on the citizenry. That is not to say they are cheap—often careful postconflict operations are extremely costly for a period of years, as in postwar Europe and Japan—but they can root a politically and morally satisfying environment of security. Furthermore, efforts to end wars well will, in many instances, attempt to overcome the conditions that result in gross humanitarian crises such as the lingering civil wars in Afghanistan, Sudan, and the Balkans. However, the chapters that follow point out the challenges of postwar justice, and a range of approaches consonant with just war theory and related fields including transitional justice and conflict resolution, all of which attempt to employ prudential, ethically sound models for ensuring postconflict security.

Notes

1. Geoffrey Roberts's "Stalin's Wars: From World War to Cold War, 1939–1953," *Journal of Cold War Studies* 10, no. 3 (2008), 179–81; Winston Churchill's *Memoirs of the Second World War*, abridged version (New York: Mariner, 1991).

2. See Eugene Davidson, *The Trial of the Germans: An Account of the Twenty-Two Defendants before the International Military Tribunal at Nuremberg* (Columbia, MO: University of Missouri Press, 1997); Joseph E. Persico, *Nuremberg: Infamy on Trial* (New York: Penguin, 1995); Drexel A. Sprecher, *Inside the Nuremberg Trial* (Lanham, MD: University of America Press, 1999).

3. Sprecher, *Inside the Nuremberg Trial*, 103.

4. For an introduction to this, see James Turner Johnson's essay "Debates over Just War and Jihad: Ideas, Interpretations, and Implications across Cultures" in Eric Patterson and John P. Gallagher, eds., *Debating the War of Ideas* (New York: Palgrave-Macmillan, 2009).

5. James Turner Johnson, *Morality and Contemporary Warfare* (New Haven, CT: Yale University Press, 1999), 34.
6. Thomas Hobbes, *Leviathan*, Edwin Curley, ed. (Indianapolis, IN: Hackett, 1994), chapter 13, paragraph 8.
7. Michael Walzer, *Just and Unjust Wars*, 3rd ed. (New York: Basic Books, 2000).
8. David A. Crocker, "Reckoning with Past Wrongs: A Normative Framework," *Ethics & International Affairs* 13, no. 1 (1999), 43–64; "Punishment, Reconciliation, and Democratic Deliberation," *Buffalo Criminal Law Journal* 57, no. 2 (2002), 509–49; "Reckoning with Past Wrongs in East Asia," in Mike Mochizuki and Charles Burress, eds., *Memory, Reconciliation, and Security in East Asia* (Stanford: Stanford University Press, 2012).
9. Michael Moser, "The 'Armed Reconciler': The Military Role in the Amnesty, Reconciliation, and Reintegration Process, *Review* (November–December 2007), 13–19. See also Maj. John J. McDermott, "Reconstruction as a Case Study in Flawed Conflict Transformation" (Fort Leavenworth, Kansas: School of Advanced Military Studies, United States Army and General Staff College, 2008), and "Reconstruction and Post-Civil War Reconciliation," *Military Review* (January–February 2009), 67–76.

CHAPTER I

MORAL RESPONSIBILITY AFTER CONFLICT

The Idea of *Jus Post Bellum* for the Twenty-First Century

JAMES TURNER JOHNSON

JUST WAR THINKING is commonly described today as having two main elements: the *jus ad bellum*, which deals with the question of moral responsibility in the resort to the use of force, and the *jus in bello*, which deals with moral responsibility in how such force is actually used during an armed conflict. It may be argued that this way of sorting the issues leaves out another important question: that of the nature of moral responsibility after an armed conflict has ended. Some recent writers have accordingly argued that a third element is needed and should be developed in just war thinking, to which many of them have given the name *jus post bellum*. This line of analysis and argument raises three distinct issues, all of which are important: the connection between concern for the *post bellum* environment and just war thinking; the relevant history of moral, political, and military thought and practice regarding responsibilities after the end of an armed conflict; and the question of how to think about such responsibilities not only in the narrow context of the parties to the conflict but in the larger frame of the common good of the region in which the conflict has taken place, of other societies related to those involved in the conflict by cultural ties, and of the international order as a whole. This chapter addresses these issues.

Understanding the Just War Frame Correctly

First, what of the connection between concern for the aftermath of the use of armed force and just war thinking? Is the problem of moral responsibility after an armed conflict a new problem for just war thinking? To answer this sort of question requires attention to the nature of the idea of just war in itself. Recent discourse on morality and war includes many contemporary varieties of thinking with deep differences among them but which nonetheless are all advanced as forms of just war reasoning, as well as various positions critical of just war reasoning, each of which has its own conception of what such reasoning is. It is clearly important to make sure that thinking about morality and the use of armed force be focused on the realities of contemporary armed conflict and the contexts within which contemporary uses of armed force arise, but if such thinking is to be considered as just war reasoning, it is best to calibrate it by reference to the parameters defined and carried in the historical just war tradition.

This historical tradition has taken shape around a robust and long-lived definition of the idea of just war in terms of three fundamental moral requirements: that armed force must be undertaken only under the authority of a person or persons in a position of sovereign rule, and thus with responsibility for maintaining and protecting the goals of political community of order, justice, and peace; that armed force be used only when there is a just cause, understood in terms of defense of the common good as defined by such order, justice, and peace, for the redress of wrong done, or for the punishment of wrongdoers; and that armed force be used only with a right intention, avoiding the desire to dominate, unyielding animosity, the love of destruction and killing, and so on in favor of restoring peace or establishing it anew where there had been no peace. This understanding of just war—more properly, this understanding of when it is justified for a sovereign to employ armed force, and the responsibilities entailed—coalesced in Western thinking between the canonist Gratian's *Decretum*, from the mid-twelfth century, and Thomas Aquinas's *Summa Theologiae*, roughly a century and a quarter later. This conception remained robustly intact right up into the era of the Reformation, and it was on its basis that such thinkers as Grotius laid the foundations of the modern understanding of international law.[1] The best way to conceive what the idea of just war is about—its fundamental content and implications for moral conduct in the use of armed force—is by reference to this historical tradition of just war.

Let us be sure to observe that while today's familiar typology would label these moral requirements—sovereign authority, just cause, right intention including the end of peace—as part of the *jus ad bellum*, this term was never used during the centuries from Gratian to Grotius. Rather, as Aquinas's succinct discussion of these ideas makes clear, they are what defines when a war is just; they define *bellum justum*, just war. Specific canonical rules existed in this period requiring avoidance of harm to noncombatants and avoidance of certain weapons deemed too destructive to be morally used, but where the definition of just war was concerned, these were not included. What was going on? The answer has two facets.

First, there was a separately developing tradition focused specifically on the conduct of men under arms. This was the chivalric code, the *loi d'armes*—rendered in English as the law of arms and later the law of war, and in the Latin of the late medieval period as the *jus in bello*. As I have shown in my historical work on the just war tradition, this came together with the earlier tradition of *bellum justum* during the era of the Hundred Years War to form a fuller conception of just war, one which developed in greater detail the shape of moral conduct in the justified employment of armed force. So the first part of the answer to my question of what was going on in the initial coalescence of the just war idea is to admit that there was also this second line of development, coalescing somewhat later, that had to do specifically with conduct in the use of armed force.[2] When this came together, it made the earlier definition of *bellum justum* seem more specifically about the justified resort to such force. This was also the judgment of later generations, and the term *jus ad bellum* was coined to refer to this part of the broader idea of just war.

But for those involved in shaping the classical conception of *bellum justum*, it had to do with the entire spectrum of the use of armed force, not just the question of the justification of resort to such force. One sees this in every one of the three moral requisites that defined the classic just war idea. The authority of the sovereign is required, as only the sovereign, being responsible for the common good of all within the society, stands above the particular interests of everyone else. This is explicit in the canonists: Only the sovereign is in a position to be able to be a fair judge among competing private interests.[3] But looked at closely, this idea that sovereignty implies responsibility for the common good extends beyond the sovereign's own society to the order, justice, and peace of other societies as well: thus it is both a right and a responsibility of legitimate sovereigns to put down and punish tyranny, and to assist in establishing order, peace, and justice in societies that had been oppressed by tyranny. So at a closer look, the classic just war requirement of sovereign authority for the use of armed force is a much richer and stronger concept than what is typical of much present-day just war thinking, where the requirement called by such names as "legitimate authority" or "competent authority" is often demoted to an inferior place below just cause (so that, perhaps, the moralist gets to determine just cause) and functions as little more than part of a checklist or an item on a sign-off sheet.[4] The conception of the responsibilities of sovereigns underlying the classic just war requirement of sovereign authority for the resort to armed force clearly extends beyond the mere fact of setting the use of force in motion to implications for how such force is used and its effects after its actual use has ended.

Similarly, the classic just war conception of just cause has fundamentally to do with establishing justice: restoring that which has wrongly been diminished or taken away and exacting punishment on those responsible for the wrongdoing.[5] These are concerns that are not limited to the period when force is actually being used; the classic idea of just cause also points at the need to maintain the justice won by the use of force.

Finally, there is the matter of right intention, with its two faces. For the medieval writers on just war, the necessity of avoiding wrong intentions (defined in the list provided in Augustine's *Contra Faustum*) has to do with maintaining personal morality: While the use of force itself is morally neutral, use of force with wrong intention puts one in a state of sin, and therefore after participation in battle warriors were required to confess any wrong intentionality they had had and do penance for it before being admitted back into the full sacramental life of the church.[6] As Bernard Verkamp has cogently argued, this provided psychological as well as moral readjustment aimed at reintegrating those who had taken part in war back into postwar society.[7] This remains an important element of concern for the nature of life after an armed conflict has ended. As for the second face of the classic just war requirement of right intention, the end of peace, the implications of requiring that peace be the fundamental driving purpose behind any just resort to armed force are far-reaching. Peace, as conceived here, is not simply the absence of war; it is a state of affairs interconnected with the establishment and maintenance of a just order, and the just use of force must aim at this end. Nor is this end simply the conclusion of the active use of force, as much contemporary opinion would have it; for medieval just war theorists the idea of end still had the meaning of the Greek *telos*, which referred to the desired fulfillment and completion of the process in question, and the process in the case of just war is the establishment of a peace characterized by order and justice. Augustine, on whom the medieval just war writers relied heavily, was unwilling to call the peace desired as the end of political efforts, including the just use of armed force, by the term *pax*; he reserved this conception of peace for the experience of rest in the City of God, for those fortunate enough to have received it by divine grace. But the term he used for the peace at which earthly political striving should aim, *tranquillitas ordinis*, has its own richness, referring to the tranquility that stands as the moral ideal for politics itself, and which comes into being only when there is a proper order—namely, one characterized by justice.[8] Of course such order, justice, and peace can never be fully achieved; that is the message carried by the term *tranquillitas* instead of the term *pax*, which refers to an achieved end, the state realized only in the City of God. But that God offers this end as his gift does not mean that in the earthly life there is no moral responsibility to serve the ends available here, including those of the good society. That these good ends can never be fully achieved means that the obligation to strive for them is a continuing one. So again, classic just war thinking had to do with the use of armed force as a possible tool in the practice of politics, and this practice was always aimed at trying to get closer and closer to the ideal.

When we consider it closely, classic just war thought sets a high bar for a contemporary conception of responsibilities after an armed conflict. Just as the classic conception of just war includes both what came to be designated *jus ad bellum* and *jus in bello*, it also includes what is now being called *jus post bellum*.

A final remark on the matter of the relationship of just war thinking to the question of moral responsibility after an armed conflict has ended: a considerable strand in contemporary just war thinking begins with the idea that the use of armed force is itself always morally problematic; the most prominent example of this way of thinking is the US Catholic bishops' placing a "presumption against war" at the beginning of their moral conception of war and everything connected to it.[9] This is a dirty-hands conception of the morality of using armed force: The aim must be to avoid using such force, or, if it is being used as an unhappy exception in a given case, to end that use as soon as possible. I think that the classic just war theorists had a far better grasp of the morality of the use of force in relation to the realities of life in this world: that there is evildoing, that there are people who engage in it, and that sometimes the use of armed force is the only way to stop them, restrain them for the future, and perhaps punish them for what they have done in the past, as a way of providing what is too frequently today referred to as closure but is in fact simple distributive justice. To talk about responsibility after an armed conflict has been formally ended it is also necessary to talk about the possibility of the use of armed force in that aftermath, as an element in restoring the affected society to a bearable and sustainable level of stability, well-being, and the possibility of productive relationships among its members. What would Bosnia have been like after the Dayton agreements had there been no IFOR, and what would it be like today if there had not continued to be some military presence there to continue to protect the struggle to achieve peace? The dimensions of what may be required in any given case are inherently difficult to grasp, and this argues for flexibility in the use of force in whatever case is at hand. To take another example, it remains unclear whether the new Iraqi government will prove successful in satisfying its responsibilities, or whether the Iraqi armed forces will prove able to maintain the order necessary to turn back the forces aiming at destruction and chaos. In such a context, with the achievement of the desired goals still uncertain, there may remain a need for United States armed forces, and to think of our moral responsibility there simply in terms of getting all our forces out of Iraq entirely misses the point. One can reach this realization from several routes; my point here is that consideration of the implications of the classic idea of just war is among those routes.

The History of Thinking about, and Dealing with, the Aftermath of War

I have argued in the previous section that concern for what happens after an armed conflict has ended is already strong in classic just war thought. In the history between the formation of this conception of just war and our own time there have been other lines of development leading to similar conclusions, and there have also been developments leading in exactly the opposite way.

Let me first consider the practice of war. In the Middle Ages the nature of war was limited not only by the ideals of chivalry and the canonical rules of the church, but also by far more realistic constraints. It is certainly good to have moral prohibitions against direct, intended harm to noncombatants and creation of disproportionate destruction, but it was easier to honor such restraints when armies themselves were a relatively small part of the population as a whole and depended on that larger population as their economic base. War was a part-time affair, both because of the impossibility of campaigning during much of the year but also because the warriors needed to be at home to oversee their properties and seek to ensure their continuing productivity. Most of the time war was about disputes over property and the revenues generated from the disputed areas, and it was emphatically not in the interest of belligerents to employ scorched-earth tactics or to treat the population of the disputed areas badly, for after the war these would add to the political, economic, and military strength of the victor. The actual weapons employed during this period were difficult to use and, in the case of siege machines, arduous to transport. And so on. Concern for a positive state of affairs after a conflict was thus built into the system of warfare and of political and economic life as a whole.

The gradual growth of armies of common men, first supplementing and then displacing armies based on knights and their immediate retainers, did not fundamentally upset these realities about war. Nor did the introduction of firearms, for early firearms depended on the same pools of resources and labor that were needed for the weapons they displaced. The first genuine challenge to this way of war was the post-Reformation wars of religion, which equated struggles over territory with struggles over religious allegiance and introduced the practices of counterpopulation warfare and scorched-earth tactics. In the frame of religious motivation, what mattered most after the war was over was not the economic productivity of the land fought over or the lives of the people who lived there, but the establishment of right religious allegiance. The result was a kind of war with much more widespread and devastating impact on the people in the areas affected and, especially in northern Europe during the Thirty Years War, a level of destruction that not only wiped out large portions of the population but also rendered the land unproductive and all but uninhabitable. In reaction, the negotiations that mark the end of this century of conflict, the Peace of Westphalia at the end of the Thirty Years War, redefined the political order so as to attempt to bracket out the possibility of future wars over religious allegiance. In the following century and a half, the era of the so-called sovereigns' wars, the practice of war once more took on the character it had had before the advent of religiously motivated wars, one which by its nature respected the well-being of areas and populations fought over after a conflict was concluded.

But then came the Napoleonic revolution in warfare, which introduced the idea of the nation in arms, including large national armies and a conception of civilian society as directly involved in supporting the armed struggle. Backing this up was a revolutionary ideology that functioned in the same way that religious adherence had functioned in the wars of the post-Reformation era. By the early nineteenth century the technology of war had already changed to make for more destructive capability, but as the century developed and the Industrial Revolution gained force, both the economics of sustaining, equipping, and transporting armed forces and the destructive power of their weapons increased. The efforts to restrain war by law and by common agreement among nations that took shape in the latter nineteenth century (including such landmarks as the 1856 Paris Declaration, the Lieber Code, the first Geneva Convention, the 1868 St. Petersburg Declaration, and the 1899 Hague Declarations) were a reaction against this, and the lines of this reaction continued to develop throughout the twentieth century up to the present time.[10] Renewed attention to the idea of just war, which historically traces to the debates over nuclear weapons and the Vietnam War, is also a reflection of this changed nature of war.[11] Interestingly, the focus in all of this has been heavily on war conduct—efforts to limit or outlaw the use of certain kinds of weapons, efforts to protect civilians from being targeted—and though implications for the well-being of a war-torn area and its people can be drawn from these efforts in many cases, this was not their primary focus. In any case, the effect of legal and moral efforts at restraint in war is not nearly so great alone as it would be if the conception of war and its purposes—as well as the technologies available—were oriented in the same direction, as they had been in earlier times.

There is also a correlation between the conception of how to pay the costs of war and concern for establishing well-being after a war is done. For centuries the practice of war included spoliation—taking enemy property and even enemy persons as profit. Grotius's discussion of what is allowed in war and after war (*On the Laws of War and Peace*, Book Three) provides a handy window on the practices of his own time and his understanding of what had been customary before.[12] While he prescribed moderation, he assumed the continuing right of despoiling beaten enemies, a right that extended up to ruling over them if their own ruler or rulers had been conquered or driven out. But moderation for him was key: For the reasons given above, the practice of war up to his time generally made it in the belligerents' interest not to abuse the right of despoiling the enemy, and the limited capabilities available to armies tended to the same end. But by the latter part of the nineteenth century, coincident with the change in the nature of war I have noted above, this custom of war had escalated to the idea that the loser in a war should pay the victor's costs in the war, and perhaps also pay punitive damages. Perhaps the most important exemplification of this way of thinking was the heavy obligation of reparations placed on the losing side in the Treaty of Versailles after World War I. Up through the eighteenth century, broadly speaking, sovereigns made war, and they were the ones who could be made to suffer if they lost. But after the democratization of war that began under Napoleon, it could seem reasonable to hold an entire society to account when their armed forces were defeated in war. The result in the case of the reparations imposed after World War I are well known: Germany, in particular, was bankrupted and held in penury, which led to stresses that aided the rise of Communism and National Socialism, and in the latter case to the rise of Hitler's dictatorship and to World War II. This history is a powerful argument against the practice at Versailles. By contrast, the economic rebuilding of Germany and Japan after World War II undergirded political rebuilding and strengthened regional security, creating positive results from which both victors and vanquished, as well as the rest of the world, have continued to benefit.

It is important to note that nothing in the established customs of war, nor in the agreements formally concluding this war, imposed an obligation on the victors to rebuild the vanquished. The terms of unconditional surrender in each case seemed, indeed, to imply the opposite, and the example of Versailles reinforced the worst implications. But the policy choice to rebuild the defeated societies instead reflected the mix of moral (humanitarian) and self-interested motives I have identified above in other connections.

The ending of an armed conflict, however, often comes about not through clear-cut victory but as a result of negotiated agreements that impose their own specific obligations on the parties to the conflict. In some cases these may be in conflict with other conceptions of responsibility after the shooting stops. For example, the reestablishment of a system of justice may imply setting up procedures for identifying war criminals, holding them to account, and punishing them—yet the prospect of doing so may complicate or prevent ending a conflict through negotiated agreement, as some of the principals in such negotiations may be likely targets for war crimes proceedings. Each case is different, and at best general principles in each case must be interpreted for it.

Finally, in the examination of historical correlations that is the business of this section, there is the matter of the implications that accompany the idea that there is a right of humanitarian intervention, with armed force if necessary, in societies where serious abuses of fundamental human rights are taking place. This idea traces from the largely moral debates over the responsibility of other nations to intervene in the armed conflicts in former Yugoslavia, Somalia, Rwanda, and elsewhere during the 1990s to the report of the International Commission on Intervention and State Sovereignty (ICISS), *The Responsibility to Protect*, in 2001, to the still expanding body of commentary initiated by this report and the debates surrounding it.[13] A direct connection can be drawn between the argument for intervention to stop and perhaps punish serious violations of basic human rights and the idea that such intervention implies action to remedy the harm done by such violations and restore full respect for human rights in the aftermath of the intervention. Indeed, the argument for intervention seems importantly to depend on the idea that there is a general responsibility both for individual states and for the international community to maintain and nurture respect for fundamental human rights. But as the debates have shown, this is a complicated subject, and no general consensus has yet formed as to what this might mean. Intervention across state borders against the will of the state, even for robust humanitarian purposes, continues to be a prima facie violation of territorially defined state sovereignty, and the protection this rule offers to states in general is not to be easily given up. The territorially defined conception of sovereignty came into being and has lasted as the norm in international relations because in principle (and most of the time in actuality) it helps to produce and maintain within and among states a stable order, a system of justice, and peaceful relationships—the goals of politics as classically conceived and as reflected in just war tradition. Still, the level of agreement thus far reached that intervention by force may be warranted, or perhaps even obligatory, to respond to ongoing egregious violations of basic human rights carries with it the closely related conception that there is a broad global responsibility for well-being in all nations of the world, and that this extends to a responsibility to restore a society harmed by such violations, as well as by the conflict that ended them.

The debate over such interventionary use of armed force began in the 1990s, of course, responding to the conflicts I have mentioned. But also from the 1990s there is the case of the Iraqi invasion, drastic spoliation, and annexation of Kuwait, and the use of armed force under United Nations auspices to remove Iraq and restore Kuwaiti sovereignty. After this conflict there was assistance for the restoration of Kuwait, but no talk of restoration to Iraq for harm done by the coalition forces engaged in driving its army out of Kuwait. Rather, Iraq was punished by various means. As this example shows, the idea that a nation responsible for aggression should pay a cost for it is still very much with us; this suggests that there are real limits to the idea that the victor and perhaps others have a responsibility to restore a society damaged by armed conflict.

Responsibilities and Their Limits

We are, of course, now in a new century, but the complicated debates continue, as do the lessons to be drawn from the past discussed above.

For the United States, but also for others, the concerns tend to be focused particularly by the military actions in Iraq and Afghanistan. In both cases the United States has shown in policy and action its commitment to maintaining the sovereignty of these countries, to democratic political institutions and processes, to social reconciliation, and to economic rebuilding, just to name some of the most important goals of the restoration of social well-being. Yet as the case of Iraq shows, there seem to be significant limits to what such responsibility entails. First, military force alone cannot make possible the achievement of these goals, though it is clearly necessary for the purpose of deterring and punishing the continuing insurgency and maintaining social order. The end of peace that just war tradition sets as the proper goal in order for the use of armed force to be just is not in fact a goal that such force by itself can bring into being: All it can do is help to establish the conditions. Second, strong public opinion in both countries wants the United States to end its presence in Iraq. When loud arguments are made against the presence of US military forces there, they turn out also to be arguments for a limited responsibility for the postconflict well-being of Iraq. It is now the stated policy of both the United States and the Iraqi governments that the ultimate responsibility for such well-being has now shifted to the Iraqis themselves. This is part of the meaning of sovereignty. But this shift is also in some tension with all that is implied by the end of peace and the goal of societal well-being. Third, competing responsibilities are always present in the real world, and capabilities are never infinite but must be managed with prioritization and compromises so as to seek to ensure the best results—or at least results that can be lived with. Combat-related stresses on US forces put a limit on thinking about what American responsibility for Iraqi society implies in real terms; so do the military needs in Afghanistan, so does the state of the US economy, and, not least, so does opposition to use of US military force, both domestic and foreign. The picture is not a simple line drawing; it is more like a pointillist painting, where each dot of color has its own essential importance, and all of the dots are necessary to the painting as a whole.

Elsewhere I have argued that close attention to competing obligations is necessary in every given situation when one addresses the question of use of military force for intervention in cases of grave humanitarian need, including for the purpose of ending grave violations of fundamental human rights, punishing those responsible for the violations, and restoring the violated social order.[14] Here, in the broader context of thinking about responsibility after an armed conflict, I would apply the same lines of reasoning.

First, there is the matter of the tension between a government's responsibility for the well-being of its own society and its responsibility toward a society in which it has been involved in armed conflict. In such a case, it is good to remember, both societies will have been affected by the conflict, and even if the effects are felt differently and are of different magnitudes or degrees, they are real on both sides nonetheless. In classic just war terms, the idea of sovereignty as implying responsibility for such well-being is focused principally on the sovereign's own people. The model behind this thinking is the responsibility the head of a family has for the well-being of that family, an idea that is found in both classical civilization and the Hebrew Bible. In simple terms, the idea is that responsibility for those closer in relation is greater than for those farther away. For just war thinkers from the Middle Ages through at least the early modern period, this was understood as a model rooted in natural law. While the idea of natural law has fallen out of fashion today, the understanding of levels of responsibility continues to be important. Though individuals may find good moral reasons to engage in personal self-sacrifice for others, this does not translate into a rationale to require members of these individuals' families or of their societies to engage in such self-sacrifice, or to carry one's personal sacrifice so far as to manifest neglect in that person's responsibilities to the people in these groups. Moral logic here has a considerable overlap with realism.

But at the same time, responsibility to care for the well-being of one's own—one's own family, one's own country—clearly extends to care for the larger communities in which one's family and one's country are situated, and on whose well-being their own depends in myriad if often complex ways. So to say, in effect, that responsibility for the well-being of others begins at home is not to say it ends there, but rather to say that such responsibility places finite limits on the responsibilities one owes to others.

The relationship between these two kinds of responsibility differs according to the circumstances of each case. At the beginning of this chapter I put the matter of concern for responsibilities after the end of an armed conflict as including the question of how to think of those responsibilities not only in the narrow context of the parties to the conflict but of the larger frame of the common good of the region in which the conflict has taken place, of other societies related to those involved in the conflict by cultural ties, and of the international order as a whole. The particular mix of responsibilities differs in each of these contexts. Exactly how has been the subject of much moral and political reflection for centuries, and continuing difference is to be expected. Yet in my own judgment the mix must be one that provides for participation in ensuring that people in societies torn by armed conflict not only have their basic physical needs cared for but are assisted in rebuilding the infrastructures, institutions, and relationships that will enable them to resume taking care of those basic needs and all the others that interact complexly to form a society's well-being. Some societies will have preserved these in some form even through an armed conflict; in such cases, the issue for others is to strengthen them and seek to make sure the goods thus provided are available to all and distributed justly. In other cases, the devastation that has been caused by armed conflict is analogous to that experienced by communities hit by natural disasters such as tsunamis, earthquakes, and hurricanes, but worse in that the relationships on which a well-functioning society depends may have also been torn apart by enmity, and in that the harm to social well-being from armed conflict may go on for years, while natural disasters, awful as they may be, do their worst and are then over.

At the core of the just war idea is the perception that the use of armed force in a given circumstance is justified by the good it can do. The just war idea is not a dirty-hands conception of armed force in which use of such force is always assumed to be bad but can be overruled in certain dire situations; nor is it a lesser evil conception in which the evils war brings are balanced against any good it does by eliminating greater evils. In the former case the main responsibility of any society that employs armed force would seem to be to end that employment as soon as possible, regardless of what this may entail for the societies involved. In the latter case the extent of responsibility after conflict is determined by the calculation of greater and lesser evils. Just war thinking is different; it is about using armed force to establish order, justice, and peace, and dealing with the evils war necessarily brings with it is part of the good at which it aims.

What of the question of fault? The classic conception of just war is straightforwardly about responding to some fault, understood as a disordering of justice, so as to remedy it. The end of peace makes this not just a punitive conception, but a restorative one. To be justified, the use of armed force must carry with it the responsibility to see how it comes out, and to try to make it come out well. This is a very different understanding from that of war guilt applied at Versailles and the reparations imposed as a result. It is also a very different understanding from that of persons opposed to any and all uses of force as necessarily bad, so that resort to the use of armed force is itself the fault that has to be remedied. It recognizes that in a world in which justice is all too often threatened or disordered, armed force may be needed to set things right. But the effort to do so may extend after an armed conflict has ended. The end sought for remains; yet the role of the use of armed force shifts and other means of serving justice, and thus securing the end of peace, become central. In this environment the other actors I have identified above all have a role to play: other societies in the region of the conflict, who have a direct interest in seeing a stable, just, peaceful society among their neighbors; those with significant cultural ties to the affected populations, who have a similar interest expressed in different terms; and the broader international community of societies, which depends on the well-being of each individual society for the well-being of the whole. Part of the restoration of societies torn by conflict has to do with dealing with fault, but in the aftermath of conflict the way to this end is through judicial, political, and social institutions, and armed force properly has only a supportive role in these, maintaining the order and sometimes providing basic resources that make their development possible.

One of the most interesting developments in just war tradition is the introduction of the idea called simultaneous ostensible justice by both Vitoria and Grotius.[15] This was, for both of them, a recognition that in many—perhaps most—actual armed conflicts both sides, as best they can tell, believe themselves to be fighting justly. For these early modern theorists in the tradition of just war, recognizing this pattern allowed them to make a more forceful argument for fighting humanely—that is, for them, fighting according to the limits established in just war tradition. They thus countered the argument that those fighting unjustly have no rights—an argument that Grotius confronted particularly in the guise of the arguments for religious war, whose results he saw clearly. The argument I have made for the nature of responsibility after conflict is similar: It is a distributed responsibility that includes responsibilities of the direct parties to the conflict both toward their own societies and to one another's societies, but does not stop with these parties alone. It also includes the broader communities I have described, who have a common interest in facilitating human well-being.

Recognizing such responsibility and the reasons for it, moral and material, is not to specify particular kinds of action for particular kinds of parties that would cover all situations. Not only would this be impossible to do in any detail because of the diversity of situations, but trying to define the responsibilities in this way would necessarily get in the way of drawing out the implications of the broader moral and political considerations that already point to such responsibility. For this reason I am no fan of the term *jus post bellum*, because the term *jus*, literally "law," seems to imply that reflection on responsibilities after an armed conflict can be reduced to specific rules. It may be possible to draw up such rules specifying certain kinds of behavior after certain conflicts, but this should be the result of decisions made on the basis of moral and political considerations of the conditions in each situation. Responsibility after armed conflict is real, but its nature should be assessed anew for each concrete case.

Notes

1. I describe the historical coalescence and development of just war tradition in detail in James Turner Johnson, *Ideology, Reason, and the Limitation of War* (Princeton, NJ: Princeton University Press, 1975).

2. See further Johnson, *Ideology, Reason, and the Limitation of War*, 64–80; James Turner Johnson, *Just War Tradition and the Restraint of War* (Princeton, NJ: Princeton University Press, 1981), 131–50.

3. Cf. Gratian, *Decretum*, Part II, Causa 23, Question II, introduction and Canon 1, in Gregory M. Reichberg, Henrik Syse, and Endre Begby, eds., *The Ethics of War: Classic and Contemporary Readings* (Hoboken, NJ: Wiley-Blackwell, 2006), 113.

4. On the implications of the sovereign's responsibility for the common good see Thomas Aquinas, *Summa Theologiae*, II/II, Q. 40, Article 1, *I answer that*, and Q. 42, Article 2, *Reply Objection 3*, in Reichberg, Syse, and Begby, eds., *The Ethics of War*, 177, 186. For my own fuller discussion of this matter see James Turner Johnson, "Aquinas and Luther on War and Peace," *Journal of Religious Ethics* 31 no. 1 (Spring 2003): 3–20; see particularly Section 2. On the rendering of the authority criterion as competent authority

see National Conference of Catholic Bishops, *The Challenge of Peace* (Washington, DC: United States Catholic Conference, 1983), 84.

5. See, for example, the selections from Gratian cited in note 3 above and Aquinas cited in note 4. In this locus Aquinas appeals to the authority of Augustine: "Wherefore Augustine says (*Questions. In Hept.*, q. X, *super Jos.*): 'A just war is wont to be described as one that avenges wrongs, when a nation or state has to be punished, for refusing to make amends for the wrongs inflicted by its subjects, or to restore what it has seized unjustly.'"

6. Again, Aquinas (*Questions. In Hept.*, q. X, *super Jos.*) quotes Augustine on this: "Hence Augustine says in *Contra Faustum* (XXII, 74): 'The passion for inflicting harm, the cruel thirst for vengeance, an implacable and relentless spirit, the fever of revolt, the lust of power, and such like things, all these are rightly condemned in war.'"

7. Bernard J. Verkamp, "Moral Treatment of Returning Warriors in the Early Middle Ages," *Journal of Religious Ethics* 16, no. 2 (Fall 1988): 223–49.

8. For Augustine on the distinction between earthly and ultimate peace and on the goods involved in earthly peace, see the selections from Augustine's writings in Reichberg, Syse, and Begby, eds., *The Ethics of War*, 77–80.

9. National Conference of Catholic Bishops, *The Challenge of Peace*, iii, 22, 26.

10. For the Lieber Code, see *General Orders No. 100 (1863): Instructions for the Government of Armies of the United States in the Field* (Washington, DC: US War Department, 1863), excerpted in Reichberg, Syse, and Begby, eds., *The Ethics of War*, 566–71. For the other agreements see Adam Roberts and Richard Guelff, eds., *Documents on the Laws of War*, third edition (Oxford: Oxford University Press, 2000), 47–66.

11. The major landmark works in the recovery of the idea of just war include two books by Paul Ramsey, *War and the Christian Conscience* (Durham, NC: Duke University Press, 1961) and *The Just War* (New York: Scribner, 1968), Michael Walzer's *Just and Unjust Wars* (New York: Basic Books, 1977), and the US National Conference of Catholic Bishops' *The Challenge of Peace*. Ramsey's two books focus heavily on the nuclear debate, though he also treats the Vietnam War in *The Just War*; Walzer's work comes out of the context of the Vietnam debate, though it ranges more broadly over issues in the ethics of war; and the Catholic bishops' pastoral focuses centrally on the matter of nuclear weapons, their possession, and their possible use.

12. See Reichberg, Syse, and Begby, eds., *The Ethics of War*, 421–37, for excerpts.

13. International Commission on Intervention and State Sovereignty, *The Responsibility to Protect* (Ottawa: International Development Research Centre, 2001).

14. See James Turner Johnson, *Morality and Contemporary Warfare* (New Haven, CT: Yale University Press, 1999), 102–16.

15. See Johnson, *Ideology, Reason, and the Limitation of War*, 185–95, 231–32.

CHAPTER 2

THE AFTERMATH OF WAR

Reflections on *Jus Post Bellum*

MICHAEL WALZER

New Thinking in Just War Theory

As A DISTINCT CATEGORY, *jus post bellum* is not part of classic just war theory. But it isn't entirely missing from the theory either. The original idea was probably that *post bellum* justice was included in the criteria for *ad bellum* justice. The inclusion would have been twofold: first, a war can only be considered just if there is a strong possibility of success, and in order to judge that possibility, political leaders must have some idea of what success would look like. And, second, the requirement of a just intention means that whatever is taken to constitute success has to be not merely possible but also morally defensible; it has to be, if only in prospect, a just outcome. So arguments about what would come after the war were a crucial part of the arguments about whether the war should or should not be fought in the first place. *Ad bellum* anticipated *post bellum*.

But there is another sense in which the just outcome of the war is supposed to be anticipated in its beginnings. The standard understanding of aggression holds that it is a violation of the status quo ante. The world was at peace, in such and such an arrangement of states and borders—which was presumed to be just insofar as it was established, conventional, widely accepted, and also insofar as its stability made for regional (or global) peace. The aggressor violently disrupts this arrangement, moving an army across the existing border, and then a just war restores the arrangement and the border. Justice after the war is the same as justice before the war. The idea of reparations gains its force from this understanding. The breaking of the old order has to be repaired. Though the violence of the aggression and the human damage that it produced cannot be undone, we can compensate the surviving victims and rebuild the ruined cities. We insist that the aggressor state make things, as much as it can, just like they were before. And that, on this view, which I take to be the classic view, is the definition of a just outcome.

It is worth noting that the early modern idea of a political revolution derived from this conception of a just war. The tyrant started the revolutionary process by breaking the established constitutional order, attacking his subjects, and violating their rights. Tyranny was understood as a kind of aggression. The people, organized perhaps by the lesser magistrates of the realm, justly defended themselves and restored the constitution. The movement was circular, ending where it began. A revolution that didn't end in a restoration would not have revolved completely.

Just war and revolution are deeply conservative ideas, though what they aim to conserve is the peacefulness of the status quo ante—not its particular political arrangements, which may indeed need to be changed, but only through normal politics, not through war. There are always state leaders who believe that their country's borders aren't where they should be or that the division of colonial possessions and spheres of influence or the access to natural resources is fundamentally unjust. That may or may not be so (the status quo is usually unjust, though not in the way state leaders believe it to be); in any case, just war theory holds that war is not a permissible remedy. When Francisco de Vitoria said that the only justification for war is "an injury received," he meant a recent injury that violated the existing conventions and arrangements, not an injury received a hundred years before that had long ago been incorporated into the existing conventions and arrangements.[1] Territorial irredentism was no more an excuse for war than imperial ambition. Violent disruptions of the status quo were, almost by definition, unjust.

The 1991 Gulf War provides a nice example of the classic understanding of *post bellum* justice: restoration for both sides; reparations for one side. The first Bush administration thought that its war was justly concluded when Kuwait was liberated from the Iraqi occupation—and Saddam Hussein, his aggression defeated, was still in power back in Baghdad and able to pay reparations to Kuwait. Justice did not extend to regime change. It did extend to the imposition of restraints on the Iraqi regime, but the purpose of those, or at least their initial purpose, was to make the old border safe. This was a contested view at the time, especially because President Bush had called for rebellions against the Baghdad regime, and when these occurred and were savagely suppressed he did nothing to help the rebels. Still, stopping the war after the liberation of Kuwait was in accord with the classic view of a just ending and a just peace.

There is much to be said for this view: Think of how many lives would have been saved if the Korean War had ended as soon as American and South Korean forces had repelled the North Korean invasion and restored the old boundary—however unsatisfactory that boundary was. Or imagine what the Middle East would look like today had Israel, after winning the Six Day War in 1967, immediately restored the Gaza Strip to Egypt and the West Bank to Jordan. In both these cases, the ambition for a better peace than the status quo ante produced outcomes that were (and remain) arguably worse.

One might say, as Avishai Margalit has recently suggested, that the actual goal of just war theory is not a just peace but "just a peace"—that peace itself, as it existed before the war began and as it might exist after the war ends, is the actual goal, without regard to its substantive justice.[2] Given the awfulness of war, peace is what just warriors should seek. But is this, in fact, just any peace? Suppose that the aggressor state wins the war and establishes a peace that is not like the status quo ante but is still peace in the literal sense: the absence of war. Do we have to accept this kind of peace, or oppose it only politically, or is it morally permissible or even necessary to renew the just war at the first opportunity? How long does it take before the new peace constitutes a status quo that it would be unjust to disrupt? We need some understanding of how peace and justice connect in order to answer these questions. I would suggest that the connection must be strong but minimalist—so as to sustain the recognition that peace itself is a value at which we can justly aim and sometimes live with, even if it is unjust. But in this chapter I am going to assume the victory of the just warriors and ask what their responsibilities are after victory. Sometimes, I want to argue—but not all the time—they must aim at an outcome that is different from the status quo *ante* and that is more than just a peace.

Restoration and reparation may be right for the victims of aggression but may not be the right way to deal with the aggressor regime, which they leave intact and in power. What if the act of aggression is inherent in the nature of the regime—as in the case of Nazi Germany? No one on the Allied side imagined that the war could end justly with Hitler still in power, even if his government then paid reparations to all its victims. The 1939 status quo was nobody's goal; the Allied commitment to a just peace in Europe took precedence over the old European conventions and arrangements, and this meant military occupation and regime change for Germany. Though these weren't entirely new ideas, World War II made them into defensible versions of *jus post bellum*.

The experience of Nazism also provided another argument for regime change. It seems astonishing today, but there were lawyers in Britain and the United States who argued in 1945 that the Nazi leaders could be put on trial for crimes against Poles and Russians but not for crimes against German citizens. "The killing and persecution of German Jews," Gary Bass reports in his historical study of war crimes trials, "seemed protected by German sovereignty."[3] Not justified by sovereignty, but protected from international scrutiny and indictment. That argument was rejected in the run-up to Nuremberg and again at the actual trials. State officials are not answerable only to their own courts when they massacre their own citizens. Other states can—and I would argue that they should—intervene to stop the killing, and the officials responsible for the killing can then be brought to justice before international courts. The movement of military forces across an international frontier to stop a massacre is not aggression; it is more like law enforcement. We refer to it as humanitarian intervention, and it should be obvious that its goal can't be to stop the killing and leave the killers, or the killer regime, in power. Had African or European states acted to stop mass murder in Rwanda in 1994, for example, they would have had to overthrow the party of Hutu Power, which ruled the country—and then they would have had to find other rulers. An intervention in Darfur in 2007 or 2008 would have had to replace the Khartoum government, at least in Darfur. In the case of humanitarian intervention, *jus post bellum* involves the creation of a new regime, which is, minimally, nonmurderous. And it is more than likely that the creation of a new regime will require some period, perhaps an extended period, of military occupation. These possibilities raise the question of *jus post bellum* in a new way.

Was Saddam Hussein's savage suppression of Shi'ite and Kurdish rebels protected by Iraqi sovereignty? Or did *post bellum* justice in 1991 require a march on Baghdad and the overthrow of the Baathist regime? I didn't think so at the time, though it does seem in retrospect that regime change and occupation could more easily have been justified in the circumstances of 1991 than in those of 2003. But that is not the argument that I want to pursue here. I only want to insist that the classic view of *post bellum* justice is now subject to revision whenever we encounter inherently aggressive and murderous regimes. The identification of these encounters will be contested, but these are contests that we cannot avoid.

Similar questions arise in antiterrorist wars like that of the United States in Afghanistan. The invasion of Afghanistan has led to a long-term American military presence in the country—after what looked like, but wasn't, a quick military victory. In Afghanistan (and in Iraq too), the creation of a new regime did not come, as planned, after the war was over but in its midst. What does *post bellum* justice mean when wars don't end? What are the obligations that come with staying on and fighting on in these circumstances? And what are the obligations that determine the timing and character of getting out? These are new questions to which I have no clear answers.

Jus Post Bellum and Obligation

Jus post bellum is an aspect of justice generally, and like justice generally, it imposes obligations on its subjects. Before I discuss what these obligations are, I want to address the issue of subjection itself: On whom do the *post bellum* obligations fall? Consider a historical case: In Cambodia in 1974, a maniacal left-wing regime was systematically murdering its own people. The government of Vietnam sent its army across the border to overthrow the regime and stop the killing. No doubt it had geopolitical reasons for doing this, in addition to the obvious moral reasons, but whatever the mix of its motives, stopping the killing was a good thing to do. China, by contrast, along with many other states (indeed, along with all other states) did nothing to stop the killing. China sat and watched. And yet, after the invasion, the Vietnamese had further *post bellum* obligations in Cambodia, and the Chinese did not.

This is an odd, though familiar, feature of moral life. People who do good in the world have more obligations than people who don't do anything. Volunteer for some worthy task, and you are quickly entangled in a web of obligations; you hardly have a minute to yourself, while the men and women who never volunteer for anything can do what they like with their evenings. The case is the same with states as it is with individuals. Once the Vietnamese had sent an army into Cambodia for the best of reasons, to save human lives (whatever their other reasons), they were bound to keep on saving lives in Cambodia. They had to secure and maintain some kind of law and order and establish a nonmurderous government to replace the one they had overthrown. And when they didn't act selflessly to do that, but served their own interests by setting up a puppet government, they were rightly subject to strong criticism.

Among just war theorists there is some uneasiness about states that remain neutral in wars between an aggressor and a victim (think of Sweden in World War II)—and perhaps also about states, like China in my example, that remain passive in the face of mass murder in a neighboring country. Still, in international law, neutrality and passivity are rights that come along with sovereignty. And if sovereignty by itself doesn't seem a sufficient cover for inaction, many political theorists and moral philosophers would recognize the same right-not-to-act on the ground that states cannot be obligated to put the lives of their citizens at risk, just as individuals are not bound to put their own lives at risk to save the lives of strangers. Therefore, it is only the state that makes the positive *ad bellum* decision that acquires the positive *post bellum* obligations. If we assume that the positive decision is just, then, once again, doing the right thing brings with it the obligation to do many more right things. There is no escaping the dire consequences of good behavior—though I should add that bad behavior, in contrast to doing nothing at all, also brings obligations in its wake, as the idea of reparations suggests.

Of course, if all *ad bellum* decisions were made multilaterally, the dire consequences would be shared; *post bellum* justice would be a collective responsibility. But this is not possible in practice, since the forms of multilateral decision making available in contemporary international society are notoriously unreliable. Neither the Security Council nor the General

Assembly of the UN, for example, would have backed the Vietnamese decision to invade Cambodia. And, similarly, the Indian decision to invade East Pakistan (now Bangladesh) would never have been authorized by the UN; nor would the Tanzanian decision to invade Uganda and rescue its people from the murderous regime of Idi Amin. And yet these were just—and, it seems to me, morally necessary—invasions. When a massacre is in progress, unilateral military action may not be the best response, but it is often the only possible response. And then the state responsible for the invasion and the rescue will also be responsible for the political and social reconstruction of the invaded country.

We can imagine an arrangement by which the second of these responsibilities could be taken on by states that had been unwilling to take on the first. They weren't prepared to fight and put their soldiers at risk, but they might be prepared to participate in the work of peacekeeping and reconstruction. Even if the *ad bellum* decision was unilateral, *post bellum* decision making could be multilateral. Of course, the state that had risked its own soldiers' lives might think that it was entitled to make all the decisions in the occupied country, starting with the security decisions. On the other hand, occupation and reconstruction are costly undertakings, and the intervening state might be eager to share those costs and therefore willing to share some of its decision making power. It might look for help, however, and find that other countries feel no obligation to help—after all, they didn't invade someone else's country. How might we go about freeing the rescuers from the ongoing burdens of the rescue? If we believe that multilateralism leads to a better version of *post bellum* justice, we will have to make it a political project.

Does it lead to a better version? Are obligations formally accepted by many states more likely to be fulfilled than unilateral obligations? There are well-known collective action problems here: Each state thinks that the others should do more, or it thinks that it can shirk its obligations because the others are already doing enough, or one state's withdrawal or failure to perform brings the whole effort down, as each of the others refuses to pick up its share. The work of a single state might go better, especially if, in exchange for material support, it accepted some form of international regulation—as in a trusteeship system, if there were such a system. That too would be a project, and a difficult one, given the history of trusteeship under the League of Nations. And it might seem especially hard not only to insist that intervening states have acquired obligations, but also that performance of those obligations should be monitored by an international organization. Nonetheless, it isn't a bad idea.

Justice after War's End

What are the obligations of *post bellum* justice? I have described reparations as the obvious obligation of the aggressor state. Reparations can be extracted forcibly by the victors; they can also be the subject of negotiations not so much between winners and losers as between the victims and their heirs, on the one side, and the aggressors and their heirs, on the other (consider the negotiations between Israel and Germany after World War II). The heirs come into it because of the post-ness of the justice: *Jus post bellum* is, in part at least, justice for children. It is important to recognize that reparations are a form of collective punishment, since the burden is distributed through the tax system to all the members of the aggressor state including those who opposed the aggression and those who were too young, as the Bible says, "to know their right hand from their left." The collectivism is simply the consequence of citizenship, and I think that it can be justified—though the enslavement of those same people, forced to work for the victims of their state, would not be justified. We penalize innocent people, including children, in the aggressor state in a constrained way, in order to benefit innocent people in the state that was unjustly attacked. And that is *jus post bellum*: not perfect, but as good as it can be.

But I am more interested here in the newer obligations that go along with occupation and reconstruction. These can be extensive and demanding, but they also have limits, and it may be useful to start with those. The limits are of two sorts, practical and moral. States are not bound to do (or to try to do) what they are not able to do. The probability of success, which plays a critical role in *jus ad bellum*, plays the same role in *jus post bellum*. The United States is not obligated to create a Swedish-style social democracy in Afghanistan (I am not claiming that that was ever our intention) for the simple reason that we can't do that. Obligations are closely connected to capabilities. Often states try to do more than they can do because what they can do isn't exciting enough to win the support necessary for doing it. Or, they pretend to be aiming at great but impossible achievements in order to cover their real, interest-driven goals. In any case, impossibility is a critical limit, and if we recognize it we will be more capable of making realistic choices and of criticizing partisan and aggrandizing projects.

The moral limits of *post bellum* obligations have their primary source in the people to whom the obligations are owed—the people who have been rescued, for example, by the military intervention or the people whose brutal and aggressive regime has been overthrown. The intervening state can't then impose its version of a just politics without regard to their version. It isn't bound to do what its own citizens think is best. The local understanding of political legitimacy is a critical constraint on what just warriors can attempt. But it isn't an absolute constraint. During the occupation of Japan after World War II, the Americans pretty much wrote a constitution for the Japanese; this was certainly achieved with consultation, but without much readiness to bow to Japanese political or social norms. One of the clearest examples of not bowing was the inclusion of an article that mandated gender equality—which had no place in Japanese political culture as it then was. But since the constitution created a democratic regime and since it allowed for its own amendment, this seems to me a legitimate imposition. We might even say that the existing local norms and some minimal conception of human rights are competing constraints on what the intervening state can do.

The local norms are critically important because the goal of regime change is a regime that can govern without the massive use of coercive power. It must be politically strong enough to survive the withdrawal of the state and army that set it up; its legitimacy must be recognized by its citizens; it must be able to collect taxes and provide the services that its citizens expect. These are constraining requirements. They rule out puppet governments that will be forever dependent on the firepower of a foreign army—like those created in Eastern Europe after World War II. But they also rule out certain kinds of idealistic politics, when the ideals are ours but not theirs.

The positive obligations of just warriors after they overthrow an aggressive or murderous regime and stop the killing begin with what we can think of as provision. They have to provide law and order, food and shelter, schools and jobs. Of course, they will do this, insofar as they can, through local agents—members of the old civil service and the old army who weren't involved in the crimes of the genocidal regime and also internal opponents of the regime and returning exiles. But ultimate responsibility belongs to the occupying forces. The American army in Iraq in 2003 was radically unready to take on this responsibility after the overthrow of the Baathist regime. We can take this unreadiness as a useful example: It was a clear violation of the norms of *jus post bellum*. This is true whatever the justice of the invasion and however the war was fought. *Post bellum* justice is independent of *ad bellum* and *in bello* justice—in the same way as these latter two are independent of each other. An unjust war can lead to a just outcome, and a just war can lead to an unjust outcome.

Once immediate necessities are provided, the critical obligation of the invading and occupying forces is political reconstruction. The obligation is the same whether a single state has supplied the forces, or a coalition of states, or an international agency. It is a difficult obligation because what is required is the creation of a regime that can dispense with its creators—that can, literally, order them to leave. The goal of reconstruction is a sovereign state, legitimate in the eyes of its own citizens, and an equal member of the international society of states. As soon as that goal is reached, the occupying forces will probably be asked to leave, and they should leave. It will be a test of their virtue, and of the justice of the occupation, that they have not created a puppet government and that they make no claim to permanent military bases or to economic privileges and contracts unavailable to other states. Though they can aim at a friendly government (it is hard to imagine them doing anything else), this must be a friendly government fully capable of acting in its own interests.

Should they aim at a democratically elected government? I want to say yes to this question, not because democracy is the best regime (though I think it is), but because it has historically been the regime least likely to turn on its own people. I can imagine ways less formal than elections to produce a responsible government—in a tribal society, for example, customary forms of consultation may still be robust and effective. But democracy is generally to be preferred for the sake of its inclusiveness. Modern democracy includes everyone, men and women, rich and poor, majorities and minorities, and so it offers greater protection than a regime of oligarchs, patriarchal chiefs, or clerics of the dominant religion. Protecting women—or, better, empowering them so that they can protect themselves—is especially important, since they are often the first civilian victims of war and the last beneficiaries of reconstruction. Giving them the vote is only a first step, but it is an important step toward guaranteeing their security.

Jus post bellum is most importantly about social justice in its minimal sense: the creation of a safe and decent society. But it is also about justice in its other sense—about doing justice to the perpetrators of tyranny, aggression, mass murder, and ethnic cleansing. I have already alluded to the Nuremberg precedent for the establishment of international tribunals—followed with mixed results in cases like the former Yugoslavia, Rwanda, and Sierra Leone. "Do justice even if the heavens fall" is not a good idea in the aftermath of war; *jus post bellum*'s first aim, as I have been arguing, is to stop the heavens from falling. Sometimes a clear judicial repudiation of mass murder and the punishment of the murderers is the best way to forge a secure peace. Sometimes security might require amnesties and public forgetfulness. Sometimes, the simple exposure and acknowledgment of crimes may point the way to reconciliation. In these life and death cases, the idea of just a peace takes precedence over a just peace—though we should certainly try to bring the two together.

Finally, there are certain lingering obligations that may affect the timing and character of getting out. The invading and occupying forces must make sure that the new regime is in fact nonmurderous, committed to defend and capable of defending the most vulnerable of its citizens. And they must make sure that the men and women who cooperated with the occupation in any capacity will be safe in its aftermath—and if any of them are not safe, they must be given the opportunity to leave with the occupying forces and be taken in by the occupying state. This obligation holds whether the intervention and the occupation were just or unjust. The French after the Algerian war were bound to take in the Harkis (Arab soldiers who fought in the French army), and the Americans after Vietnam were bound to take in the so-called boat people—indeed, the people who took to the boats should have been helped to leave before they had to resort to that. John Rawls's argument about privileging the worst-off in domestic society has an analogy here: We must attend to those most at risk when ending the occupation of a foreign country.

War is a time of killing and being killed. The crucial requirement of *jus post bellum* is the preservation of life. That is the minimalist reason that I have given for trying to set up a democratic regime, and it is the reason for everything else that invading and occupying armies must do—for the provision of necessities, for special attention to vulnerable minorities, for movement toward gender equality, for something as close as possible to justice for war criminals and murderers. There is work here that foreign forces can do, but ultimately the work has to be taken over and sustained by the locals. The post in *jus post bellum* is not of indefinite duration. Moral and political requirements must be met over whatever time it takes. But the shorter the time, the better.

Notes

1. Francisco Vitona, *Political Writings*, edited by Anthony Pagden and Jeremy Lawrence (Cambridge: Cambridge University Press, 1991), 324.
2. Avishai Margalit, *On Compromise and Rotten Compromises* (Princeton, NJ: Princeton University Press, 2011), chapter 1.
3. Gary Bass, *Stay the Hand of Vengeance: The Politics of War Crimes Tribunals* (Princeton, NJ: Princeton University Press, 2000).

CHAPTER 3

JUS ANTE AND *POST BELLUM*

Completing the Circle, Breaking the Cycle

GEORGE R. LUCAS JR.

Just Wars and Irregular Wars

NATURE OFFERS TWO VERSIONS of what the noted astronomer Sir Arthur Eddington called the "arrow of time"—namely, physical processes that are either irreversible or reversible. Irreversible processes embody the linear vector that Eddington himself had in mind with this phrase. They are linear in that they have a definite temporal direction, a concrete origin, some well-defined temporal duration, and a terminus, and, consequently (as the eminent English-American philosopher A. N. Whitehead put it), a "perpetual perishing." Indeed, as Whitehead remarked, "time itself is a perpetual perishing"—a metaphor that seems especially apt for war.[1]

But nature also exhibits other processes that are enduring, repetitive, cyclical, ongoing, and hence reversible. Temporally speaking, as the equally eminent German philosopher Hegel observed regarding their circularity, these processes "have no beginning and no end," a metaphor that, in darker moments, seems equally apt for war.[2] War presents itself as linear: a vector with an origin, a duration, a terminus, and with damage done over its temporal duration that often seems irreversible. War's effects cannot be undone, and in that sense they seem linear. But wars that do not end well threaten to beget new wars that, as progeny of the old, perpetuate a cycle of violence and destruction that is unending. It is that never-ending cycle of violence that poets and theologians have lamented since antiquity.[3]

The justification of war follows (or seems to follow) the logic of linearity and irreversibility. Historically, that logic pronounces on war's origins and on its finite duration, constraining the permissible actions of its participants. The first set of these concerns is directed primarily toward political leaders and policymakers concerning when, if ever, it would be permissible to resort to war in defense of a nation or, more troublingly, to further its political objectives or resolve its conflicts with adversaries (*jus ad bellum*). The second, somewhat less systematic question is addressed primarily to military leaders and military personnel empowered to wield the sword in pursuit of their nation's policies and objectives. It concerns the limitations or constraints on their behavior, particularly the specific means and manner in which they may or may not be permitted to resort to the use of deadly force during wartime (*jus in bello*). Precisely because it is composed of specific and contextual advice, rather than abstract principle, *jus in bello* has been somewhat haphazardly and unsystematically enshrined in treaties, conventions, and otherwise in the settled customs or traditional practices within the profession of arms.[4]

Until recently, however, explicit attention was less often paid to war's ending and aftermath (*jus post bellum*), or, apart from those ancient lamentations, to its tendency to perpetuate an unending cycle of violence. Only within the past decade, in fact, has a third mode of discussion emerged, grounded in more careful attention to specific details of proposals that were heretofore taken merely as statements in opposition to war (as well as expressions of profound dissatisfaction with just war doctrine itself) by the German Enlightenment philosopher Immanuel Kant.[5] Attributed primarily to the careful analysis of Kant's specific pronouncements on war by Canadian scholar Brian Orend, what is now widely termed *jus post bellum* concerns how wars are to be justly concluded, how peace is to be made, treaties negotiated, reconciliation affected, responsibility affixed, punishment administered or amnesty granted, and especially how devastated victims and nations are to be reconstructed and rehabilitated, all (in Kant's systematic vision) in order to make future wars less likely.[6]

Not surprisingly, the rise of interest in *jus post bellum* is concurrent with the rise to primacy of irregular warfare (or hybrid war) in this century, a development that further complicates all the foregoing traditional demarcations.[7] The Swiss jurist and political philosopher Emer de Vattel was responsible for this nomenclature, and it was meant to call attention to a departure from the norm of war as addressed in law.[8] Regular warfare (*guerre réglée*) consists of armed conflict between the uniformed military representatives of established nations, carried out according to natural law or sanctioned custom.[9] It is that which international law, including the Law of Armed Conflict (LOAC) principally addresses. Irregular war, by contrast (also referred to as MOOTW, or military operations other than war), was thought to consist in the occasional foray of military forces into ancillary and decidedly secondary activities like peacekeeping, law enforcement, and military interventions for humanitarian purposes including disaster relief, to all of which conventional LOAC or humanitarian law was much less clearly applicable.

In this decade, in particular, the exception has become the rule. Like it or not (and most military personnel like it not at all), irregular war is likely the only sort of war that nations and their militaries will be called upon to fight.[10] Developing new rules for these new kinds of wars adds a substantial dimension to present understandings of constraints on the use of military force in furtherance of otherwise-legitimate political objectives.[11] In regular or conventional war, for example, the custom long enshrined in international law is to demarcate sharply between the two traditional concerns of cause and conduct. Nations and their leaders and statesmen collectively declare war. That decision constitutes no part of the soldier's function or responsibility. The nation and its leaders should be accountable for their overall declaration and its consequences, while soldiers, regardless of the side for which they fight, are understood to be rightly held responsible in law only for their individual conduct in carrying out those broad orders. This division of moral responsibility is the cornerstone of what Michael Walzer first characterized as "the war convention."[12]

Irregular warfare undermines that convention. If the boundaries between cause and conduct are reasonably clear in conventional warfare, they are inherently less so in irregular conflicts, generating a host of legal and moral anomalies.[13] Critics of America's irregular wars in Iraq and Afghanistan, for example, have pointed to what they term an asymmetry in *jus in bello* that arises with respect to soldiers and their conduct whenever their leaders' cause for war is found to be morally unsustainable.[14]

Because the justification for engaging in such hostilities is inherently tenuous (and seldom a straightforward case of self-defense or response to aggression), principles like proportionality and double-effect, taken in the war convention to determine culpability or permissibility of tactical actions, must be calculated differently. Combatants representing nations whose cause for irregular warfare cannot be sustained, for example, have no *moral* right to kill alleged enemy combatants, regardless of whether such killing is otherwise found proportional to their military objective or not, or even whether it would otherwise be excused traditionally under existing international humanitarian law (e.g., by the doctrine of double effect, or DDE). That is, their nation's and leaders' moral errors regarding cause morally taint the soldiers' conduct of those unjust activities as well. This serves to undermine another cornerstone of the war convention, the "moral equality of combatants."[15]

In quite a different sense, irregular war oscillates unpredictably between routine combat and security or constabulary operations.[16] When simply engaged in providing security as part of a postwar occupation force, for example, soldiers are more constrained in their permissible use of deadly force and hence inherently more liable to risk of harm themselves than they are during regular combat. Failure to recognize and adjust to these changing circumstances, the COIN manual explains, may undermine the justice of the intervening nation's cause through the individual soldier's (the "strategic corporal's") actions, a situation that is all but in the most extreme cases inconceivable under conventional circumstances.[17]

Another troubling characteristic of irregular war is the tendency of combat operations themselves to shift unpredictably between routine *in bello* conditions, *ex bello* efforts to extricate the intervening forces from active hostilities, and *post bellum* activities entailing security operations and provisional reconstruction of the host nation.[18] In hybrid war (of which Afghanistan and the Taliban, at present, constitute an excellent illustration), a hot conflict between conventional adversaries is often interspersed with what otherwise seems to be a long-standing postwar occupation by NATO and coalition troops. Traditional conceptions of military necessity and proportionality that intrude upon the principle of distinction and noncombatant immunity during wartime no longer apply in the *ex bello* or *post bellum* circumstances. In the context of rebuilding a war-shattered nation—as well as extricating one's own occupation troops from it—more restrictions are placed upon the use of force by occupation forces, and their efforts morph from conventional fighting to peacekeeping, stability, and the prevention or avoidance of conflict and civilian casualties. While this *post bellum* feature of humanitarian intervention and other forms of irregular war are now increasingly acknowledged, they are far from well understood. Any attempt to encompass new rules for irregular war conflicts must surely come to terms with the questions concerning how we are to understand war's terminal phase, as posed in this most recent development in just war theory.

The Concept of *Jus Post Bellum*

In the preface to this volume, as well as in his earlier works, Eric Patterson criticizes conventional just war theorists, including Michael Walzer, for having largely neglected the problem of war's aftermath.[19] He considers, and rejects as inadequate, a number of prevailing attitudes that contribute to this neglect, and even traces and addresses active resistance to encompassing war's aftermath within the purview of legitimate moral and legal reflection. One major exception to this trend, Patterson notes, is the work of Canadian human rights and international law scholar Brian Orend. In his own work, however, Orend himself credits Kant with having initiated the discussion (in contrast to classical just war theorists) of what Kant likewise saw as the serious but neglected problem of *jus post bellum*: the need to establish justice and the rule of law and restore a functioning civil society *in the aftermath* of war. While such end-game efforts occur in the aftermath of all wars (as noted above), it is precisely these efforts at reconstruction and rehabilitation that constitute the essence of irregular warfare and COIN.

In a subsequent book, a critique of Walzer, Orend showed that this third distinctive category of just war theory is mentioned, but largely neglected, in Walzer's own analysis.[20] Both of his initial two books demonstrated that just war doctrine must henceforth be understood to consist of three (rather than merely two) parts, each corresponding to war's beginning, prosecution, and end: *jus ad bellum*, the justification of *entering into* war; *jus in bello*, the military conduct of adversaries *during* war; and *jus post bellum*, the obligations of war's victors to its victims to establish a just and lasting peace sufficient to prevent the onset of future conflict. Orend demonstrated that *jus post bellum* is not merely an afterthought, but a preeminent and overriding obligation for which belligerents are responsible in the interest of justice. No war can be termed truly just, and no belligerents exonerated for their participation, in which there is not from the outset a manifest intent (revealed in policy and practice) to ensure a stable peace that provides for both long-term security and the protection of basic human rights in that war's aftermath. This, Orend argues, is part and parcel of the full import of right intention in classical *jus ad bellum*. He makes frequent and favorable reference to the US Marshall Plan in Europe, and the reconstruction of Japan after World War II, as illustrations of the importance of this principle.[21]

In sharp contrast to the majority of contemporary just war theorists (Walzer included), Orend persistently emphasizes that the three dimensions of just war discourse are not neatly separable, and must not be compartmentalized. One cannot discuss *jus ad bellum* in abstraction, distinct from the expectation that combatants, proposing to defend or enforce justice, must employ only just means in the realization of just ends (*jus in bello*). This intention must precede and thoroughly infuse combat, even as the intention to restore peace with justice and to repair a society's ability to sustain and protect its citizens (*jus post bellum*) must infuse both deliberations about war and the subsequent conduct of it. War's onset, its conduct, and its aftermath flow seamlessly together, and policymakers as well as combatants are drawn together into a web of moral responsibility for war's advent and outcome.

Once again, although Orend's principal observations about *jus post bellum* address the problem of war and conflict generally, his discoveries have been found especially pertinent to the analysis of irregular war. Orend himself offers praise to American and British military forces in Iraq, as well as to Canadians in Afghanistan, for grasping the importance of just conduct to an irregular war's ultimate justification, through their unprecedented emphasis on noncombatant immunity and the need for restraint and economy of force as well as for their sincere efforts to investigate and prosecute their own military's periodic lapses.[22]

Regarding rules of engagement during *jus post bellum*, in the aftermath of more conventional hostilities undertaken for otherwise morally justifiable ends we might reasonably expect (and a minimally just state should consistently demand) that its own military forces commit themselves to respecting the most basic elemental rights of noncombatants in the enemy state. This commitment must be sustained through education and training leading up to deployment, and reinforced consistently during the period of deployment. This is especially important when, as in humanitarian interventions or regime change, the opposing state and its rank-and-file citizens do not themselves constitute the enemy in any meaningful sense.

Far from constituting a lofty or unrealistically high standard, this principle is simply a demand for consistency of purpose.[23] Commitment to noncombatant immunity as well as to restraint, proportionality, and the economy of force are not abstract ideals, nor are they reducible to uncomprehending or cynical compliance with the requirements of international law. Instead, adherence to such principles essentially defines the intervening state's or coalition's commitment to minimal justice in the first place, from which it derives its authority to wield the sword in defense of justice. By marked contrast, it is *not* the putative justice of their cause, but the sustained and intentional injustice of their means, that identifies and morally de-legitimates the tactics of both terrorists and so-called rogue states.[24]

Orend's account of *post bellum* sometimes suggests a tripartite discrimination that parallels the temporal distinction of war's phases: a beginning, a duration, and an end.[25] This suggests a comfortable linearity with a preferred temporal direction that is irreversible, with phases of war that entail a clear demarcation and with a clear discrimination between the different agents distinctly responsible for each. If intended, such a tidy temporal ordering is mistaken. We have seen that the concerns of *jus in bello* in irregular war infuse considerations of its beginning (whether to embark upon humanitarian intervention or regime change, for example). Prospects for *jus post bellum* likewise affect how the war is conducted: whether, for example, it can be rightly prosecuted at all, as well as when, or at what point, conventional rules of armed conflict must be modified or replaced by those more appropriate to a security-providing force engaged in reconstruction (more along the lines of the rules of engagement of a domestic constabulary than a conventional military). These phases of irregular war do not flow unidirectionally. As I noted above, they tend to oscillate or cycle unpredictably. There is no preferred arrow of time in an irregular war.

Despite his tidy tendency to forefront a univocal temporal order as the basis for his distinction, however, Orend actually does a good job of showing how the three considerations interact dialectically and continuously, with right intention in *jus ad bellum*—the aim of peace—being the governing consideration. The larger point to be considered, as Australian philosopher Antony Coady puts it, is "simply that a war that is fought without a considered view to bringing about a legitimate peace has a morally defective rationale that taints its legitimate beginnings and its ongoing processes."[26]

Coady, in turn, identifies three distinct considerations that need to be addressed, practically and procedurally, all of which might rightly be thought to fall under the rubric of *jus post bellum*. These are:

(a) How to end a war justly. (Here Coady raises and discusses important questions to do with the role of negotiations, the preservation of enemy political structures to enable peace negotiations, the problems raised by policies of unconditional surrender, and so on.)
(b) How to deal with postwar conditions for the treatment of the defeated side by the victorious side, of the sort described in this volume by Mark Evans, as constituting extended *jus post bellum*. Coady identifies three subconcerns in this area:
    1. Rebuilding and reconstruction issues. How should the victors treat the defeated armed forces, the infrastructure of the defeated country, the government? What difference should the ideology of the victors make?
    2. The question of punishment and reparations and the relation of this to peace and reconciliation processes.
    3. The difficult roles of the military as occupiers, peacemakers, or peacekeepers (what I have referred to above as the dilemma of the occupation force, performing its roles of reconstruction and security such as that of domestic constabulary).
(c) And finally, how to deal justly with one's own troops after the war (physical and psychological war injuries, veterans' benefits, and the like, a category that Orend identifies as internal *jus in bello*).[27]

Coady recognizes that it may seem paradoxical that "just victors should acquire obligations to restore the circumstances of the unjust, defeated enemy," but argues nonetheless in support of this *post bellum* responsibility.[28] First, many if not most of the opponent's citizens will not themselves bear guilt for causing the war. Yet much collateral damage will have been created to those civilians' property, health, and livelihood. Even if this damage is somehow justifiable in context, it needs to be repaired; Coady argues that, if possible, it should probably be repaired by those who inflicted it. In addition, it is reasonable to expect that third-party nations not involved in the war themselves nonetheless also bear some moral obligations to help, just as such nations do in the wake of natural disasters.[29] Coady concludes that "a central aim in the ending of a war for those who are fighting a just war should be that of leaving the peoples of the surrendering enemy nation in a position to contribute to an independent political life for themselves after the war," even if that stable life turns out to be much different than what they experienced prior to the war.[30]

Jus Ante (as well as *Post*) *Bellum*

What we might term "just intentionality" informs a law-abiding and rights-respecting nation's decision to wage war, and its subsequent conduct of hostilities. This generates, in turn, a general asymmetry not so much in tactics (such as terrorism) as in the general attitude, sense of purpose, and day-to-day intentionality and behavior of the law-abiding and rights-respecting combatants. This asymmetry is revealed in the restraint shown by the just nation's or just coalition's warriors and warfighters in *jus in bello* and *jus post bellum* phases. It is this asymmetry in behavior and intentionality that allows us to discriminate with confidence between the warrior and a mere murderer, as well as between legitimate acts of war and terrorism and similar criminal activities. It is this intentional and behavioral asymmetry that dismisses as nonsense the oft-heard claim of relativists and advocates of realpolitik, that "one man's terrorist is another man's freedom fighter."

This underlying principle of asymmetry and the overall accompanying conception of just conduct of combatants in wartime is a crucial if confusing feature of irregular war. As such, it must be taught, emphasized, and reinforced with unmistakable clarity in the education and training of legitimate military forces. The moral requirement of making this distinction and preparing warriors to uphold it in their conduct constitutes an important fourth dimension of the new rules for new wars: namely, *jus ante bellum*, the proper education and training of moral warriors fit to undertake the rigorous new moral and legal requirements of irregular war.[31]

Jus ante bellum, properly considered, must be included in any comprehensive doctrine of *jus post bellum* in order to address the question of just military preparedness.[32] By doing so, we complete the circle of relevant considerations: the head of the presumed linear vector turns to join its tail, revealing the underlying *conceptual circle* of just war considerations. This category of just war doctrine encompasses the appropriation of resources for military preparedness, training, and education of troops; provisions to develop requisite military leadership; appropriate management and oversight of military and defense apparatus; and the general preparation for future war.

Kant's injunction in all these respects was to abjure them, along with standing armies altogether, as a preliminary condition for peace.[33] The preparation for future war is a guarantee of war, he believed, and perpetuates (rather than breaks) the unending cycle of violence. Kant did allow for what he termed "voluntary, periodic military training of citizens so that they can secure their homeland against external aggression," but it might otherwise be surmised from his overall line of reasoning that the very act of training and equipping a large army brings the temptation, if not the necessity, to use it other than as a true last resort.[34] Many at present, I suspect, would plausibly argue that more than Kant's citizen-militia is both permissible—and to some extent desirable—for the protection of human rights.[35] No nation that followed Kant's policy strictly would be in a position to come to the aid of victims of genocide in Rwanda or Darfur. Especially with the advent of irregular war as the principal military responsibility arising from both natural disasters and political state failure, incidents of genocide, and the rise of terrorism as a tactic pursued by nonstate actors, Kant's original *jus post bellum* proposals seem insufficiently robust to address such contemporary challenges.

For this reason, scholars like Harry van der Linden and Roger Wertheimer now propose to add this important new fourth dimension to these discussions.[36] What van der Linden, for example, calls just military preparedness focuses on how militaries are to be recruited, equipped, trained, and deployed. He tentatively identifies a number of basic criteria for proper policy and procedure in this respect—such as resisting the weaponization of space, nuclear proliferation, or any other kind of proliferation of threats (including, perhaps the threat of cyber warfare)—all oriented toward the underlying objective that military preparedness "should accord with its general purpose of using military force *only* for the sake of protecting people against massive human rights infringements caused by large-scale armed violence."[37] In both Wertheimer's and van der Linden's accounts the obligation falls heavily upon minimally just states to train their military personnel with this general purpose in mind; their education should focus on autonomy and professionalism, and include the ability to participate in (or dissent from) moral decision making concerning the initiation and execution of military force. It likewise entails that the militaries be fully representative of, and their membership drawn from, those whom they serve and protect, and that a nation's leaders make every effort to seek out and accord proper respect to the unvarnished, uncensored expert professional advice of experienced military leaders concerning the feasibility of war and preparations for war.

Of particular importance to this overall project is the proper education (rather than merely training) of military personnel themselves. This should be oriented toward achieving a mature understanding of their proper professional role as enforcers of international law and defenders of basic human rights.[38] Such an understanding would help make it less likely that individual military personnel would commit war crimes, to be sure. But it would also ensure that they would have the intellectual wherewithal and leadership capacities to resist either unjust orders or participation in unjust wars, and that their most senior leadership, likewise, would have both the judgment and the moral courage to lead them in these respects as true senior professional mentors, ensuring that the practices of the profession conform to appropriate norms of professional conduct.

While Wertheimer and van der Linden are extremely critical of US policy in these respects, a more positive and supportive account of the required infrastructure for professional military education, especially in the areas of leadership, law, and ethics, infuses the work of the NATO-based Military Ethics Education Network (MEEN) in Europe. Under a grant from the UK-based Leverhulme Trust, this network of military ethics scholars has attempted a thoroughgoing survey and account of educational practices in their respective nations' military academies dealing with military education and the preparation of future officers. Their group efforts have persistently addressed the need for what they call ethical interoperability—that is, commonly shared norms of military conduct among international coalition military forces from a variety of countries and cultures, collaborating on peacekeeping and humanitarian operations throughout the world.[39]

This emphasis upon the proper preparation of military leaders for combat leadership through emphasizing the protection of the basic human rights of noncombatants and vulnerable victims of war and humanitarian atrocities does not, however, begin to address the larger questions of defense policy, weapons procurement, troop deployment, military financing, and the appropriate formulation of grand strategy that van der Linden's just military preparedness addresses. With respect to all of these, van der Linden demands that the United States abandon its own grand strategy of global force projection as a necessary precondition of just military preparedness.

I harbor residual suspicions, however, concerning what would no doubt seem a popular policy proposal. I suspect that simply asking the United States to abandon its current force projection policy would be akin to asking the Los Angeles police to withdraw from violence-prone and contested areas of that city in which their own continuing presence is sometimes criticized and resented. This analogy is apt, and deserves serious reflection. The LAPD are not popular; their officers have, in numerous well-publicized (and even photographed) incidents, violated the most basic rights of criminal suspects, and on occasion have made terrible and cruel errors of judgment with respect to the local populace. Many residents of those areas might accordingly (as with the US military in Afghanistan and Iraq) "want them out of Watts," so to speak. But the LAPD, comprised largely of decent men and women, consistently repudiates these errors on the part of its representatives and tries to improve its ability to engage in effective community policing (which could be considered a close domestic analogue of counterinsurgency). If the police simply left, most local inhabitants would be much worse off. We would not suddenly enjoy perpetual peace in Watts or in the rest of Los Angeles.

Instead, we would quickly experience massive outbreaks of Mexican-style drug wars, domestic equivalents of Somali pirate hijackings, and suffer in general from perpetual violence, instability, and criminal conspiracies.

This, of course, is precisely the problem at present in Afghanistan. What might be a better (in the sense of more desirable) grand strategy is to replace *unilateral* US force projection with NATO-sponsored or UN-sponsored global force projection, the international equivalent of a ubiquitous domestic police presence as the ultimate guarantor of law, order, and personal security. The UN option, however, simply will not happen, and, under the limitations of present capacities, would largely prove incompetent, if not corrupt. The common NATO strategy has become more problematic after first the Dutch at Kandahar and now the German contingent at Kunduz showed themselves unequal to the tasks of discriminating police work and counterinsurgency in Afghanistan, in a manner that increasingly threatens the very existence of NATO itself.[40] This is why the *jus ante bellum* efforts at forging and strengthening ethical interoperability are of overriding importance for any comprehensive notion of *jus post bellum* and just war doctrine overall.

Conclusion

I began this chapter with a kind of mythopoetic commentary on war and the nature of time. If there is any seriousness to the latter, it is the observation that there is some kind of preparatory state, as well as postlude, to acts of violent conflict resolution. The orderly linear march up to and into war that serves as the underlying conceptual framework of classical just war doctrine is inaccurate.

It is not simply that leaders must judge when to wage wars, or soldiers how to fight them. It is not even that everyone involved must worry about how to clear up the mess afterwards. One must also ask: How are leaders to be prepared to know how to judge the cause and implications of war? How are soldiers supposed to know how to fight, and how to end hostilities? Does not the aftermath of one war frame the interstices in which lessons are learned, concepts taught, and capacities developed to handle conflict more adequately in the future—and, hopefully, to avoid it altogether or minimize its destructive impact when it cannot be avoided? How is all that education to occur?

Alongside the development of appropriate policy for managing conflict and avoiding confrontation, building institutions of civil society, and procuring equipment, hardware, and resources for national defense, I have argued that a fully developed conception of *jus post bellum* also includes the demand for a right intention to both fight and conclude wars with justice. This demands that warriors and a nation's military forces be properly equipped and educated to their principal purpose of defense—not merely of their own homeland, but of the liberties and basic rights of vulnerable victims of injustice everywhere. As wars, especially so-called irregular wars, are increasingly fought over such issues and for the protection of such victims (or for the apprehension or deterrence of their oppressors), this conception completes the circle of temporal considerations in just war doctrine. Just war theory requires that fighting forces be adequately prepared for their mission of justice and law enforcement; it requires that force be employed only for such purposes; that warriors conduct the ensuing hostilities with proportionality, discrimination, restraint, and respect for war's victims; and that as soon as possible, hostilities be concluded with justice and that security, safety, and equitable governance and law enforcement be reestablished. Completing that circle aims at breaking the cycle of perpetual violence and war.

The very discovery and emphasis on *jus post bellum* signifies a kind of deeper reflection on the nature of war and conflict that it is the responsibility of just nations and peoples to foster. This reflection that I am calling *jus ante bellum* forms a necessary cornerstone in the development of leaders capable of responding to conflict with justifiable exercises of force in the protection of rights and enforcement of the law. Such reflection is the milieu in which warriors are selected, educated, and prepared to use force judiciously and fight unavoidable wars justly. Such reflection teaches both leaders and warriors how to end wars well, and avoid war's worst consequences in the future.

Notes

1. More than especially apt in Whitehead's case, as he himself eschewed the fashionable pacifism of the time, over which he broke with his student and collaborator Bertrand Russell. He subsequently suffered the loss of his eldest son, Eric Alfred Whitehead, killed in action with the Royal Flying Corps over the Forêt de Gobain defending London from

German air attack on March 13, 1918. The dedication of Whitehead's magisterial *Principles of Natural Knowledge* (Cambridge: Cambridge University Press, 1919) contains this eulogy to his son: "[He gave] himself that the city of his vision may not perish. The music of his life was without discord, perfect in its beauty."

2. Circles are, of course, recurring metaphors in hermeneutical philosophy, and abound in Hegel's work, especially the *Phenomenology* and the *Science of Logic* (1812): e.g., in the former work, truth is portrayed as the cyclical temporal process of historical becoming: "the coming-to-be of itself, the circle that presupposes its end as its goal and has its end for its Beginning" (preface, para. 18).

3. The eminent classicist Donald Kagan perfectly captures this repetitive, cyclical feature of war from ancient times in his elegant work *On the Origins of War, And the Preservation of Peace* (New York: Random House, 1995).

4. James Turner Johnson, *Morality and Contemporary Warfare* (New Haven, CT: Yale University Press, 1999).

5. E.g., in the seventh thesis of the "Idea for a Universal History with a Cosmopolitan Intent" (1784); at the conclusion of "Speculative Beginning of Human History" (1786); in Kant's rejoinder to Moses Mendelssohn in "Theory and Practice" (1793); and most especially throughout his commentary on Rousseau's revisions of the famous project of the Abbè St. Pierre, *Zum ewigen Frieden* ("Toward Perpetual Peace," 1795).

6. Brian Orend, *War and International Justice: A Kantian Perspective* (Waterloo, Ontario: Wilfred Lauier University Press, 2000).

7. In the Joint Operating Concepts of the US Department of Defense, for example, the designation military operations other than war has since been replaced by a somewhat more refined, tripartite distinction between irregular warfare (IW), major combat operations (MCO), and stabilization, security, transition and reconstruction operations (SSTRO) such as humanitarian intervention and disaster relief. Irregular war itself is defined as "a violent struggle among state and nonstate actors for legitimacy and influence over the relevant populations. IW favors indirect and asymmetric approaches, though it may employ the full range of military and other capabilities, in order to erode an adversary's power, influence, and will." The most recent term to describe the complex interplay between conventional and unconventional operations is hybrid war. These distinctions are somewhat artificial and for the most part poorly drawn and even more poorly described. The message, however, is clear: the United States and other allied and coalition governments will face criminal and terrorist attacks of unconventional sorts, employing a variety of tactics and weapons, aimed largely at civilian populations rather than enemy governments or their military forces, and aimed at creating insecurity among the populations that are destabilizing to their respective governments. The joint doctrine is aimed at defining and formulating strategic responses to a variety of such conflicts. Available at www.dtic.mil/futurejointwarfare/concepts/iw_joc1_0.pdf.

8. Emer de Vattel, *The Law of Nations, or the Principles of Natural Law, Applied to the Conduct and to the Affairs of Nations and of Sovereigns*, trans. Charles G. Fenwick (Washington, DC: Carnegie Institution, 1916 [1758]).

9. It is essentially Vattel's notion that is subsequently codified in General Orders No. 100 (the Lieber Code) and subsequently in the first Hague Conventions (1899/1907),

enshrining the formal, legal definition of regular war as hostilities carried out between sovereign states with equal rights under the law, a status that extends to their own lawful combatants engaged in armed hostilities consistent with the constraints of international humanitarian law, or the law of armed conflict (LOAC).

10. G. R. Lucas, "'This Is Not Your Father's War'—Confronting the Moral Challenges of 'Unconventional' War," *Journal of National Security Law & Policy* 3 (2009): 329–40; Lucas, "Forward," *Ethics Education and Irregular Warfare*, eds. Don Carrick James Connelly and Paul Robinson (London: Ashgate Press, 2009).

11. David Petraeus, *U.S. Army Counterinsurgency Field Manual*, eds David H. Petraeus and James F. Amos (Washington, DC: Department of the Army, 2006), 3–24; Michael Gross, *The Moral Dilemmas of Modern War* (New York: Cambridge University Press, 2010); G. R. Lucas, *Jus in Bello for Nonconventional Wars* (CA: International Studies Association 49th Annual Meeting, 2008); Lucas, "New Rules for New Wars: Jus in Bello for Irregular War," in *Theory and Methodology of Ethical Conduct during Asymmetric Warfare*, eds. Howard Adelman and David Dewitt (New York: United Nations University Press, in press).

12. Michael Walzer, *Just and Unjust Wars*, 3rd ed. (New York: Basic Books, 2000 [1977]).

13. Darrel Mollendorf, "Jus ex Bello," *Journal of Political Philosophy* 12 (2008): 123–36; Jefferey Reiman, "Ethics for Calamities: How Strict Is the Moral Rule against Targeting Non-Combatants," in *Empowering Our Military Conscience: Transforming Just War Theory and Military Moral Education*, eds. Roger Wertheimer (London: Ashgate Press, 2010).

14. C. A. J. Coady, *Morality and Political Violence* (Cambridge: Cambridge University Press, 2008); Jeff McMahan, *Killing in War* (New York: Oxford University Press, 2009).

15. Roger Wertheimer, "Reconnoitering Combatant Moral Equality," *Journal of Military Ethics*, 6 (2007): 60–74.

16. Petraeus, *U.S. Army Counterinsurgency Field Manual*.

17. G. R. Lucas, "Inconvenient Truths: Moral Challenges to Combat Leadership in the New Millennium," 20th Annual Joseph Reich Sr. Memorial Lecture (2007), available at www.allacademic.com/meta/p_mla_apa_research_citation/2/5/3/5/9/p25359, accessed September 7, 2007. This reference is to Marine General Charles C. Krulak's well-known description in "The Strategic Corporal: Leadership in the Three Block War," *Marines Magazine* (January 1999), available at www.au.af.mil/au/awc/awcgate/usmc/strategic_corporal.htm.

18. Mollendorf, "Jus ex Bello," 123–36.

19. Eric Patterson, "*Jus Post Bellum* and International Conflict: Order, Justice, and Reconciliation," in *Re-Thinking the Just War Tradition*, eds. Michael W. Brough, John W. Lango, and Harry van der Linden (Albany: State University of New York Press, 2007), 35–52; Patterson, *Just War Thinking* (Lexington, MA: Lexington Press, 2007).

20. Brian Orend, *Michael Walzer on War and Justice* (Cardiff: University of Wales Press, 2000).

21. Brian Orend, *The Morality of War* (Petersborough, ON: Broadview, 2006).

22. Orend, *The Morality of War*.

23. G. R. Lucas, "The Reluctant Interventionist: The Critique of Realism and the Resurgence of Morality in Foreign Policy" (CA: American Philosophical Association, 1999); Lucas, "From Jus ad Belllum to Jus ad Pacem: Rethinking Just War Criteria for the Use of Military Force for Humanitarian Ends," *Ethics and Foreign Intervention*, eds. Donald Scheid and Deen K. Chatterjee (New York: Cambridge University Press, 2004), 72–96.

24. Jean Bethke Elshtain, *Just War against Terror: The Burden of American Power in a Violent World* (New York: Basic Books, 2004).

25. JPB; e.g., Orend, *Morality of War*, 35–53.

26. Jessica Wolfendale, *New Wars and New Soldiers: Military Ethics in the Contemporary Worlds*, eds. Jessica Wolfendale and Paolo Tripodi (London: Ashgate Press, 2011).

27. C. A. J. Coady, "The *Jus Post Bellum*," in *New Wars and New Soldiers: Military Ethics in the Contemporary World*, eds. Jessica Wolfendale and Paolo Tripodi (London: Ashgate Press, 2011).

28. Coady, "The *Jus Post Bellum*."

29. Coady is quite critical, however, of the praise heaped by Orend, in particular, on the examples of West Germany and Japan, which, he complains, "are endlessly cited favourably in contemporary debates about the virtues of imposed 'reconstruction' following unconditional surrender." Coady finds, in contrast, that there are reasons to be skeptical about the idea that unconditional surrender, occupation, and external reconstruction by Western allied powers was a major contributor to the successful restoration of those two societies. Coady cites a recent review of the economics and politics of postwar reconstruction which argues that in the case of Germany, "ultimate success was achieved not because of the occupation but despite it" (Christopher J. Coyne's *After War: The Political Economy of Exporting Democracy*, 130).

30. Coady, "The *Jus Post Bellum*."

31. Martin L. Cook, *The Moral Warrior: Ethics and Service in the U.S. Military*, eds. George R. Lucas, Jr. (Albany: State University of New York Press, 2004); Roger Wertheimer, "Essays by Michael Walzer, T. O. Scanlon, George Lucas, et alia," *Empowering Our Military Conscience: Transforming Just War Theory and Military Moral Education* (London: Ashgate Press, 2010).

32. Harry van der Linden, "From Hiroshima to Bagdad: Military Hegemony versus Just Military Preparedness," *Philosophy after Hiroshima*, eds. Edward Demenchonok (New Castle: Cambridge Scholars Press, 2011).

33. E.g., "Preliminary Article Three" in "Perpetual Peace."

34. The US State Department in the 1990s, for example, was very critical of the Weinberger-Powell doctrine on the grounds that the US had never actually deployed the military under it, and therefore asked why we should pay for all this. They wanted recourse to the military option to be more available, at that time, in setting foreign policy. I suspect, in hindsight, that many who held this view during the Clinton administration in the 1990s have rethought it considerably in the aftermath of the ensuing administration. They got what they asked for, in a sense, with President George W. Bush, and one suspects they are not altogether happy with the results.

35. Jean Bethke Elshtain, *Just War against Terror*.

36. Harry van der Linden, "From Hiroshima to Bagdad: Military Hegemony versus Jus Military Preparedness"; "Questioning the Resort to U.S. Hegemonic Military Force," in *The Moral Dimensions of Assymetrical Warfare: Counter-terrorims, Western Values, Military Ethics*, eds. Ted van Baarda and Desirée Verweij (Leiden: Brill Academic Publishers/ Martinus Nijhoff, 2009), 31–46; "Just War Theory and U.S. Military Hegemony," in *Rethinking the Just War Tradition*, eds. M. W. Brough, J. W. Lango, and H. van der Linden (Albany: State University Press, 2007), 53–71; Wertheimer, "Reconnoitering Combatant Moral Equality," 60–74; Wertheimer, *Empowering Our Military Conscience: Transforming Just War Theory and Military Moral Education*. See also Lucas, "This Is Not Your Father's War," 239–340, and "Forward."

37. Among other things, in van der Linden's account, this would entail that any just society's military preparedness would have to be properly balanced against other legitimate concerns of citizens for their collective security, such as education and health care.

38. G. R. Lucas, "'Forgetful Warriors.' Neglected Lessons on Military Leadership from Plato's Republic," in *The Ashgate Research Companion to Modern Warfare*, eds. George Kassimeris and John Buckley (London: Ashgate Press, 2010).

39. MEEN, *Ethics Education in the Military*, eds. Don Carrick, James Connelly, and Paul Robinson (London: Ashgate Press, 2008); MEEN, *Ethics Education for Irregular Warfare*, eds. Don Carrick, James Connelly, and Paul Robinson (London: Ashgate Press, 2009). See the account of the work of this group, and the need for enhanced ethical interoperability among NATO member-nation militaries, found at the conclusion of my NATO 60th anniversary banquet speech in February 2009 (Lucas 2009). See also the two concluding chapters in Wertheimer (2010).

40. G. R. Lucas, "Military Ethics Education: Toward What End?" UK Defence College Ethics Symposium (Shrivenham, UK: 2009).

CHAPTER 4

IN MY BEGINNING IS MY END

Robert Royal

Near Bayeux, France, the site of the massive D-Day invasion of World War II, there is a small British cemetery. It holds the remains of British soldiers who fell a generation earlier, liberating France during the First World War. A Latin inscription on the monument translates approximately as "To the fallen conquered who liberated their conquerors from conquest." When I visited it was unclear whether the monument was built by the British, which seems more plausible, or the French, which would have been a bit gauche. Nevertheless, it expresses gratitude to the fallen inhabitants of an island, England, conquered a thousand years earlier by the ancestors of the modern French, who had returned to free them from German occupation. It is a noble sentiment that tries to place the recent sacrifices and deaths into the mutual history of the two countries—no hard feelings about Napoleon and Waterloo, in other words. Of course, the ignored third nation, Germany, was not merely defeated but punished in multiple ways, particularly by heavy reparations, with the Treaty of Versailles. Not much more than a decade after the Bayeux monument was built, those reparations helped give rise to great suffering and unrest among the German people. And it led to their unfortunate turn toward a blood and soil Nazi ideology that put all three nations through perhaps even worse experiences, all over again.

Or at least that is the standard story line we learned in high school, a simplified story line intended to help us make some sense of a strained period. But is it true? Scholars, of course, debate this as they debate everything. But if we had time it might be interesting to look at French goals (damaging Germany's war-making capacity and punishing the Germans, who had exacted reparations from France after the Franco-Prussian War), British interest in preserving Germany as a trading partner, and American idealism (the charter of the League of Nations was part of the treaty, as few people are aware). But this bad example has led to an exaggeration of the alleged good example of how World War II ended, with the Marshall Plan and the reconstruction of Western Europe. This, too, perhaps neglects other factors like the Soviet threat as a further spur to our idealism, and the main factor that made a different approach possible: clear military victory and occupation. It is useful to pose these questions early about what we think we know about right and wrong ways to end wars.

The title of this chapter is borrowed from T. S. Eliot's "East Coker."[1] It suggests a twofold view of *jus post bellum* action or ending wars well. The beginning of a war aims at a specific end, but the end of the military conflict can also be the beginning of an equally important *jus post bellum* process. Viewed from one angle, the whole point of just war reflection is, of course, to bring about a condition of greater justice by the end of a conflict than at the beginning and perhaps, where possible, even a morally good stability, a just and lasting peace. However, a just peace is easier to achieve than a lasting one.

This chapter will flesh out these linkages between war's endings and its beginnings, particularly those issues of security and ethics associated with just war theory's historic twin emphases: the morality of the decision to go to war (*jus ad bellum*) and the ethics of how war is conducted (*jus in bello*). With these in mind, the chapter will investigate some of the tensions between our ethical imperatives (such as intervening to stop the killing) and the consequences—intended and unintended—of our actions. I conclude with three principles regarding ethical action at war's end rooted in traditional just war concerns regarding moral responsibility, restraint, humility, and limits.

Looking Back: Just War Lessons from the Past

As demonstrated by World War I and World War II, which have literally become textbook cases, it takes more than a military victory for success in warfare. The larger reasons for going to war and the civilized control over its means, ends, and aftereffects play a large role in determining the long-term outcome. So not only is the end aimed at in beginning warfare; in another sense, the end of hostilities is the beginning of another type of work that needs to be done. After World War II, the Germans were if anything even more hated than after World War I, and Germany was divided between East and West. Partly because of the beginning Cold War, but also partly because of a conscious decision not to repeat the disaster following World War I, the Allies occupied and began to rebuild Germany immediately after V-E Day. This became, by 1947, the historic Marshall Plan and other measures to help restore a devastated aggressor on a scale unprecedented in history. Also—and this is little known—the Christian Democrats of Europe, notably Konrad Adenauer in Germany and Robert Schumann in France, held quiet talks when public ones were impossible, which played no small role in healing the historic tensions between Germany and France, and started the process toward forming the European Union.[2]

Although our era has its own perilous conflicts, these older examples provide some general lessons that we can scrutinize and debate without the passion of contemporary political currents. Just war deliberation has always included end-related categories like just cause, right intention, and reasonable chance or likelihood of success. Just cause and right intention have gotten a good deal of attention in the tradition; reasonable chance of success has been relatively less developed—and besides, what is reasonable when you have to undertake as wrenching and uncertain a course of action as attacking an aggressor or potential aggressor? It would be an exaggeration to say that success has been somewhat narrowly defined in military terms, but it would not be entirely mistaken. In many circumstances leading to war, immediate self-defense or elimination of an unjust and threatening regime may seem so great an imperative that detailed examination of what will follow the military victory is ignored or postponed until more urgent problems are resolved. And clearly, this is not in the least illegitimate—and may even be urgently called for—under the right conditions. In World War II, when the United States invaded Europe, what did it think of its probability of success? Did America really think it could reform an entire continent that seemed to have gone politically crazy?

So, our cause and intent for going to war are clearly linked to our ideas about war's settlement (success) and the postconflict phase, just as the decisions made after a war ends sow the seeds of future peace or war. At this point it is worth observing, as purportedly G. K. Chesterton and others have, "if a thing is worth doing, it is worth doing badly." What I want to say (which is not exactly what Chesterton was saying) is not that we should settle for mediocrity, but that in the nature of our fallen world sometimes we take up a task because it is necessary. In other words, we act because we must—as politically responsible moral agents—whether or not it is going to end with a full range of ultimately desirable outcomes. In this respect there may have been a kind of wisdom in the relative neglect of the just war criterion of likelihood of success that we noted earlier, in that war is so uncertain that we should not expect to be able to predict or even plan very well for its ultimate outcome. This is not to be contrarian about the whole notion of *jus post bellum*; I am merely pointing out that maybe one of the ways that we end wars well is by not trying to end them too well. As Charles Péguy once noted, there is something that has produced more wars than injustice, and that is the pursuit of justice.³ In other words, it is often the revolutionary zeal of those who want to impose their form of justice that extends conflict and can result in gross postwar violence by ideological regimes. This point will be clearer as the chapter progresses because I think it needs to be incorporated into the otherwise quite laudable efforts of several recent thinkers to make us reflect more fully on our potential responsibilities at the end of conflict.

Recent conflicts such as Afghanistan and Iraq, and perhaps the lingering histories of Korea and Vietnam—as well as asymmetric warfare and nonstate actors—have given our sense of *jus post bellum* consideration greater urgency. In warfare that is not all-encompassing such as we saw in World War II, there may be a need for much greater attention to how to bring a necessary but more limited military action to as good an end as possible, and consequently much more careful thought at the very beginning about what the shape of that end actually will be. Praiseworthy military efforts, such as throttling terrorists or responding to gross humanitarian emergency, however, run great risks of impossible mission creep—and in several directions. To put this in concrete terms that partly illuminate a whole series of problems, we can see that in Afghanistan as in World War II, it was a justifiable choice to invade the territory of dangerous forces. There has been broad, bipartisan, and even international agreement about that, even though anyone with an ounce of historical knowledge about that country knows that Afghanistan has been the graveyard of several empires. And that is why international forces, which succeeded in invading and overthrowing the Taliban relatively easily, have spent most of the past decade trying to bring about a tolerable condition within Afghanistan that will make the invasion and the inevitable withdrawal worth the effort. In historical perspective, it would be difficult to say what the end would look like that motivated the beginning, and we are now engaged in trying to discover one that we did not and could not have known entirely when we started.

By contrast, formal military success in Iraq was perhaps also rather easy, though there were overly optimistic assessments about what a post-Saddam Iraq would look like. For the sake of the present discussion, let's leave aside the original threat: the weapons of mass destruction (WMDs) that we forget everyone believed Saddam possessed (and Saddam himself pretended he had for multiple motives).[4] If they had been there as predicted, making the war perhaps quite justified, Iraq would still have proved difficult to pacify. Iraq seems now to be shaping up into a tolerable new regime that in fact does embody conditions of greater justice than prior to the war, though those goals were originally viewed as secondary to the WMD threat. Ironically, it was an inadequate military presence that increased the chaos over the past several years. Though Iraq and Afghanistan present different lessons, they warn us about how complicated and provisional specified ends to conflicts can easily become, and this is the nature of the conflicts we are likely to face for some time. We can try to develop some ethical postconflict criteria to guide us in these wars, but it is unlikely they will be anything more than general principles rather than a separate *jus post bellum* disconnected from the traditional categories of *jus ad bellum* and *jus in bello*.

It would be quite nice after a war to be able to leave behind a country organized like Switzerland (or, as a fallback position, Ireland) that would be highly unlikely to create future threats. But in the nature of things, the kinds of nations that call for invasion by world powers are going to be very troubled before and, in all likelihood, still quite troubled after, whatever the good intentions of the invading forces. We see this in Iraq and Afghanistan, of course, but even countries like Germany and Japan took a lot of tutelage after World War II to prepare them to rebuild political and social institutions and to get themselves into reasonably ordered conditions—tutelage largely carried out and financed by America. And it is not clear that we would have done this, when our own nation was in need of rebuilding after the war, without the Soviet threat.

Furthermore, in many discussions of *jus post bellum* today, it is asserted that it is better for international institutions, rather than the victor, to manage the postconflict phase of war. That removes to a large extent the possible claims that the victor nation is merely imposing a regime and set of values to its liking. In principle, this is a good idea. In practice, it is probably a recipe for ineffectiveness and political manipulation—witness Versailles and the League of Nations. To be candid, if some international body were responsible for, say, reconstructing Iraq and guiding it toward viable political institutions, would the Iraqis be better or worse off than they have been under largely American guidance? Do existing international institutions have the capacity, much less the political will, to handle this? Again, the near-abandonment of Baghdad by the UN in August 2003 is a case in point. Just as in the case of the failed League of Nations, the contemporary ideal of postconflict leadership by the international community—meaning the UN—will have to wait for much better developed international institutions with at present unimaginable safeguards to prevent them from becoming obstacles to rather than instruments of just, effective, and lasting arrangements.

Jus Post Bellum Following Different Types of Conflict

It is apropos to move on to other possible criteria to guide action in postconflict. There is a kind of gradient, so to speak, of things a military action may be intended to achieve: (1) the destruction of immediately threatening forces or weapons—a surgical strike, as seems conceivable in some circumstances; to (2) an increasingly ambitious set of goals, leading to the crippling to a greater or lesser degree of an entire regime's military capabilities or other modes of pressuring neighbors; and finally to (3) the removal and replacement of the regime with one more conducive to international peace. All of these definitions of what would constitute success in a military action of course presume that the entire set of other just war criteria (*ad bellum* and *in bello*) are also being applied. Can we begin to develop additional *jus post bellum* criteria for each of these kinds of military action in a systematic way? Could we say, for instance, that the military action should aim at the least invasive goal consonant with the overall desire for greater justice and peace?

This is not an easy question to answer in general terms. Before the First Gulf War, the administration of George H. W. Bush consulted with a number of people about just war criteria. Questions were raised about what would constitute success if the action undertaken were limited, as it later was, to merely removing Saddam Hussein's troops from Kuwait. Where an obviously aggressive regime remains in place, it also remains a perennial threat to its neighbors and others, which may necessitate further warfare or tie up troops and resources that may be needed for more urgent purposes. It may still be worth doing. On June 25, 2010, it will be sixty years since the first international forces went into action to defend South Korea. There are 30,000 American troops stationed along the demilitarized zone, seemingly in perpetuity, as a guarantee of the 1953 armistice. Whether it would have been possible to invade the north sixty years ago is clearly unclear. Whether it would have been a better idea to remove Saddam Hussein in 1991, when the situation might have been better managed, rather than in 2003 when it was bungled, is another complex question. But given the uncertainties about Saddam's possession of WMDs and his proven capacity to use them when it suited his goals, what was the minimum invasive use of force needed? It depended on the goal we wanted to achieve.

As Michael Walzer has rightly argued, most postconflict situations call for "restoration plus," which is to say a return to a more just or less immediately threatening circumstance with a recognition that something more is needed, since the previous condition was precisely what led to the need for military action in the first place.[5] Restoration plus points us in the right direction in a situation like Iraq in 1991—a sense that a country unjustly invaded, Kuwait, had to be freed from an aggressor and that something more needed to be done about the aggressor regime itself. But restoration plus could not clearly specify how large or small the plus side of the formula needed to be. The principle of restoration plus is a useful one, but is only the beginning of *jus post bellum* thinking and needs other criteria to make it meaningful.

What might those additional criteria be? In the new literature on this topic, several further principles are often suggested. All of them seek to specify the plus in specific terms that observe *proportionality* with respect to the original aggression: economic sanctions, elimination of the aggressor's WMDs, demilitarization or at least reduction in a renewed threat, political therapy or rehabilitation of aggressive regimes.[6] Many theorists wish to hold the ultimate threat—replacement of the offending regime with another—for only the most outrageous cases. This is prudent, at least in the first analysis, because total defeat of an enemy, assumption of governmental functions, and the nation building required are not only very difficult tasks, but especially so given the kinds of nations at present that are likely to present themselves as candidates for this severe political therapy. There is also much talk on this point about respecting national sovereignty, which is fine; it is difficult to see, however, how national conditions that led to bad outcomes before war will change much without a push from outside. The whole enterprise risks running afoul of domestic and foreign political factors, as we have seen in both Iraq and Afghanistan—to say nothing of the difficult Islamic fundamentalism in both countries, which makes the effort in even the most pressing cases fraught with difficulty.

The central question that may have to be asked more and more frequently in these cases, unfortunately, is this: What are our options, short of taking complete responsibility, for dealing with all of the places in the world that pose global threats? When an Iraq or Afghanistan, Pakistan or North Korea, were merely local actors creating local trouble, the international community could look at these conflicts and make prudential judgments about when they did or did not rise to a threat level that demanded outside intervention. The prudent judgment of legitimate authorities can never be done away with. But as we all know, the growing ease of obtaining WMDs, along with the capacity of radical terrorist groups to exploit troubled regimes as training grounds for murderous assaults on both military and civilian targets—assaults that can produce a high degree of political agitation and international tension—have magnified the importance of formerly local disorders to unprecedented proportions. North Korea and Iran appear to be resistant to all outside influence, and threaten international security both through their own WMDs and their potential to share these weapons with extremist groups.

Nonetheless, I think that where we have chosen the warpath, there are some *jus post bellum* criteria that can be applied with at least the same degree of consistency as other war criteria. Discrimination of combatants from innocent civilian populations, for example, seems fairly straightforward. Political and military leaders bear the brunt of responsibility for unjust aggressions. Whole peoples, who have often been victims of similar aggressions within their own nations by those same military and political leaders, should not be held responsible for what the truly guilty parties have done. Yet even here, the details start to become sticky. If just compensation or rebuilding needs to be paid for in a country unjustly attacked, should we expect to require only individuals themselves to be held accountable? In postwar conditions, there are usually many mouths to feed, distribution systems blocked, power grids destroyed, services of all kinds disrupted. Resources are always limited, so where should they go? As a general principle, innocent civilians are innocent. As a concrete practice, it might create certain injustices to treat peoples from aggressor and aggrieved nations in exactly the same way.

There is always a temptation for revenge after violent conflict, so another criterion that seems related to discrimination is postconflict right intention. To me, however, this would mean an extension of the discernment of right intention in *jus ad bellum* considerations. It is not exactly unheard of that we develop different notions of what a good end will be after the conflict has taken place. That can never mean a shift to a wrong intention: to colonize or exploit or engage in other goals that are always impermissible. I do not think, for example, that the United States tried to do any of these things in Iraq, though it was so accused. For the most part, it is relatively easy to sort out whether victors are ending wars well under the usual just war criteria.

Perhaps this is an overly pessimistic view of the current moment. But I have seen discussions that suggest there should be international penalties for those who violate emerging principles of *jus post bellum*, as there are for ignoring *jus ad bellum* and *jus in bello* criteria. Perhaps someday we will inhabit a world in which this is possible. I do not think we do now, and it is hard to imagine a world where, most of the time, warfare ends that neatly. And it is here perhaps that my third notion of ending well, by not trying to end too well, may apply. Just war thinking is moral thinking, and therefore all the morally desirable outcomes—not merely to avoid evil but to do good, as Aquinas put it famously—can and sometimes should come into play. But here is a list of moral precepts that a serious proponent of *jus post bellum* has put forward: "a healing mind-set, just restoration, safeguards for the innocent, respect for the environment, *post bellum* justice, the transition of warriors [to nonmilitary, peacetime actors], and the study of the lessons of war."[7]

This is a hopeful attitude, sort of like hoping that whenever a divorce takes place, the two parties can part amicably, like mature adults. Relations between nations that have gone to war are probably at least as complex and stormy as relations between two married people contemplating divorce. As von Moltke is alleged to have quipped, "No plan of battle ever survives contact with the enemy." End of war plans are even further down the road, and we do not want to compound the inevitable imperfections of everything to do with warfare by judging the cessation of hostilities by criteria that may lie beyond our human means. Some of the above principles should be relatively ironclad, such as safeguards for innocents, just restoration as possible, and justice postwarfare. Others, such as protection of the environment and transitioning war-fighters, and especially a healing mind-set, are more in the nature or desirables rather than strict criteria.

Indeed, it is easy to take all of this as desirable as long as we are not going to have national or international institutions trying to enforce them. But to me a more interesting case—or at least one more relevant to our contemporary situation—concerns the wars that must be undertaken and then terminated without meeting many basic (let alone desirable) *jus post bellum* criteria. In Iraq, we stayed and did the job, it now appears, and we have also put in place a better government, helped rebuild much of the nation's infrastructure, protected innocent noncombatants as well as we were able, and so forth. The results, despite the reservations anyone may reasonably have about the decision to go to war, are tolerable given the complexities.

But what of a case like Afghanistan, which was easy to take on initially but has become increasingly hard to maintain—or to see a way out of? At the time of this writing, people I respect make very different judgments about what we do now. I am most inclined to think that some working arrangement with the warlords and perhaps even some elements of the Taliban might result in conditions that we could live with for a while. Of course, one hears strong voices calling for withdrawal and other strong voices claiming that it may yet be possible to achieve something resembling the Iraqi results. I am skeptical of this last claim, since it would mean creating something in Afghanistan quite far from the historic norm and might involve our military forces in a protracted conflict with much loss of life and expenditures better devoted to less intractable cases. So if we withdraw without many of the *post bellum* criteria being met, does it reflect back on the decision to go to war in the first place? Does our end contradict our beginning?

I do not think that is necessarily the case in Afghanistan, nor do I think it would be the case as a general principle. In the uncertain days after September 11, 2001, it was thought that to disrupt al-Qaeda training camps in Afghanistan might deter other, even more horrific attacks. Perhaps that could have been carried out by more limited means, such as surgical strikes or an aggressive drone campaign like the one we employ in Pakistan and other terrorist training spots. But I am not persuaded that such an approach would have worked in Afghanistan, and there are even more difficult cases. It is difficult, for instance, to think how things could go any better in a Somalia or a Yemen than they have in Afghanistan if a more extensive military campaign were to become necessary, and yet we may have to invade and withdraw to defend ourselves and the world from the violence that quite easily spills out of places like that and many others.

Three *Post Bellum* Principles

In conclusion, here are three general postconflict principles that are consonant with the just war tradition and which emphasize principles of order, restraint, and humility. The first principle is this: Actions taken to disrupt a clear threat, even if they mean a complete invasion, can be terminated early if the conditions go back to something roughly like a restoration for the people without the reconstitution of the threat. I think we see that as a possible outcome in Afghanistan. Restoration plus is always better, but sometimes the plus may be minimal yet still worth the fight.

A second principle follows from the first: Even if so-called chaos occurs after withdrawal, something that might be called restoration minus may not be per se a line that should not be crossed. Many countries exist in a kind of chaos anyway, and while no one aims at that directly by going to war, if a benign chaos results perhaps it makes war justifiable. In a world with many loose WMDs, this is obviously an expedient to be used rarely and with great caution. Still, it might be necessary, and we do not want to deny ourselves any morally licit tools merely because they do not lead to all the outcomes we prefer.

Principle three: There is an almost technocratic perspective in some *jus post bellum* reflections of an assumption of mastery, as if human beings, and especially masses of people in the wake of social upheaval, can be engineered into one or another configuration or at least provided with the tools to do so for themselves. This has truth up to a point, but only a limited point. We do not even know how to solve many problems involving injustice and violence within our own country in peacetime. So even as we hold up before ourselves the highest standards, we do well to maintain a true humility—to proceed in fear and trembling, to use the biblical language—about what we or any other human actor can do as we plan and as we conclude armed conflict. We are imperfect human beings even when we set out in a just cause, and all along the way we should be mindful that "in my beginning is my end."

Notes

1. East Coker is the second of Eliot's *Four Quartets*.

2. See Roberto Papini, *The Christian Democrat International*, trans. by Robert Royal (Lanham, MD: Rowman & Littlefield, 1996).

3. Quoted in Jacob Peter Mayer, *Political Thought in France* (New York: Ayer Publishing, 1979), 119.

4. This was best documented by Kerry Woods et al. in *Foreign Affairs*. See "Saddam's Delusions: The View from the Inside" in the May/June 2006 issue. Available at www.foreign affairs.com/articles/61701/kevin-woods-james-lacey-and-williamson-murray/saddams-delusions-the-view-from-the-inside.

5. Michael Walzer, *Just and Unjust Wars* (New York: Basic Books, 2003), 119.

6. On these points, see Brian Orend, "Justice after War," *Ethics & International Affairs* 16, no. 1 (Spring 2002): 43–56.

7. Louis V. Iasiello, "*Jus Post Bellum*: The Moral Responsibilities of Victors in War," *Naval War College Review* 57 no. 3/4 (Summer/Autumn 2004): 40.

CHAPTER 5

A MORE PERFECT PEACE

Jus Post Bellum and the Quest for Stable Peace

ROBERT E. WILLIAMS JR.

JUST SOUTH OF THE Department of the Treasury near the Ellipse in Washington, DC, stands a monument to General William Tecumseh Sherman. Although Sherman is best known for his statement that "war is hell," a claim used to justify the scorched-earth policies he adopted on the march through Georgia, there is a different statement, dated February 23, 1882, featured prominently on the monument: "War's legitimate object is a more perfect peace." Unlike war is hell, which challenges the just war theory's basic premise that the conduct of war is subject to moral restraint, Sherman's statement regarding the object of war has deep roots in the just war tradition.[1] Like similar statements made by thinkers from Aristotle to British military analyst B. H. Liddell-Hart, it forces us to confront the paradoxical idea of fighting for peace. It also requires us to consider the concept of justice after war, or *jus post bellum*.

In fact, one of the most important lessons of the war-torn twentieth century is that it is not enough to win a war. The peace must be won as well. The difference between winning and losing the peace is the difference between the establishment of order and stability and the promotion of anarchy and instability. Woodrow Wilson took the United States to war in 1917 in the name of "a war to end all wars." American involvement secured victory for the Allies, but the peace was lost and a second great war involving many of the same states engulfed the world just two decades later. World War II provided the opportunity for a second effort to establish a Wilsonian world order, and, whether a consequence of better statesmanship, improved institutions, more propitious circumstances, or, more broadly, the benefits of hard-earned wisdom, it proved to be the war to end all wars, at least among the principal protagonists. For almost seven decades since the end of the war, the defeated Axis powers have been the linchpins of a stable peace in their regions of the world.

Ending wars well, like fighting them well, is a multifaceted endeavor. There is a strategic dimension of the problem in which the central concern is how to secure the material objectives of the war most efficiently, but there is also a moral dimension in which the central concern is how to secure peace with justice. Just as Sherman's war is hell doctrine suggests that the strategic objectives in war are paramount, even to the point that considerations of justice must be set aside, so there is an argument that strategy trumps morality in the conclusion of a war as well. If—so the argument goes—those responsible for crimes against peace must be eliminated without the niceties of war crimes trials, so be it. If the destruction of the loser's war-making potential requires economic measures that impoverish the citizens of the defeated state, so be it. This attitude, however, runs contrary to the belief that respect for moral obligations is compatible with, or even essential to, effective strategy. The seeds of the next war, after all, may be sown in the terms of an oppressive peace. This, at least, is a venerable counterargument.

Postconflict justice is not the only consideration policymakers must keep in mind when thinking about how to end a war well, but it is an important one. And while there are a number of principles that contribute to *jus post bellum*, those that relate to the objective of stable peace are paramount. After all, no peace that sows the seeds of the next war can be considered just or, in any meaningful sense, peace.

The argument presented here proceeds from General Sherman's observation that the rightful purpose of war is, fundamentally, a more perfect peace. After tracing the philosophical roots of this claim regarding the proper end of war and noting the difference between its limited and more expanded versions, we turn to the concept of a war to end all wars. Although most closely associated with Woodrow Wilson, there are others who have suggested that war might be the means by which universal and perpetual peace is created. While certainly an ambitious claim, I argue that this is not an altogether unreasonable extension of the view that the proper end of war is peace. In fact, while wars of a certain type continue to pose a serious problem for the international community, there is considerable evidence that the kinds of wars that Wilson hoped to end—interstate wars, and especially those involving the great powers—have, since 1945, become the rare exception rather than the rule in international relations. Not only is interstate war on the decline, it is on the decline for reasons that are generally understood and that can be applied to a variety of situations. On the other hand, intrastate wars—civil wars—are neither on the decline nor especially well understood, at least not in a way that promotes confidence in the prospects for their elimination. A particular characteristic of civil wars is the tendency of a significant percentage of them to return after a peace settlement has been reached (sometimes over and over again), and this makes them especially problematic from a perspective that takes seriously the argument that war's legitimate object is a more perfect peace. For this reason, we must ask what the emerging understanding of *jus post bellum* can offer to the quest for stable peace in the aftermath of intrastate wars. This is the question posed, with tentative answers, in the final section below.

Peace as the Purpose of War

War has long been regarded as the fundamental problem of international relations. In its interstate form, it has been considered analogous to the disorder characteristic of the state of nature, a consequence of anarchy. Intrastate war, on the other hand, seems more directly to replicate or to create the state of nature. But to view war solely as the central problem of international politics is to overlook the positive function it has been thought to play in the international system. Put simply, war is also an instrument by which order and justice may be established.[2]

As far back as Aristotle, there existed an understanding that the purpose of waging war is to create peace. In the *Nichomachean Ethics*, Aristotle stated that "we deny ourselves leisure so that we can be at leisure, and fight wars so that we may be at peace."[3] Augustine wrote in *The City of God* that "it is an established fact that peace is the desired end of war. For every man is in quest of peace, even in waging war."[4] Rather than articulating a paradox regarding the relationship between peace and war, Augustine was merely indicating what he took to be a truism. As a product of war, peace comes either in the form of a "profitable settlement" or in the form of "harmonious ordering" (*tranquillitas ordinis*, also rendered "ordered peace"). The former is a state of affairs that the victor regards as preferable to that which existed prior to the war; it is, in this perhaps self-interested way, a better peace. The latter, Augustine believed, is a natural inclination of human beings. Whatever causes, rooted in sin, may drive them to fight, humans desire to live in harmony with those around them. Thus, war may also lead to peace as a return to harmonious ordering.[5]

In the late medieval period, Thomas Aquinas addressed issues related to war in his *Summa Theologica*. Like Augustine before him, Aquinas focused on *jus ad bellum*, that is, the question of whether, or under what circumstances, it is morally permissible to go to war. "In order that a war may be just," he wrote, "three things are necessary." War being impermissible in situations in which an appeal for justice to a higher authority is possible, Aquinas listed as the first requirement "the authority of the prince, by whose order the war is undertaken." Sovereign authority is necessary because "it does not belong to a private individual to make war, because, in order to obtain justice he can have recourse to the judgment of his superior. . . . But, since the care of the State is confided to princes . . . it is to them that it belongs to bear the sword in combats for the defense of the State against external enemies." The second requirement, according to Aquinas, is "just cause," examples of which include defense against an attack, restoration of properly wrongly taken, and the punishment of evil. Finally, Aquinas stated that waging a just war required a right intention to promote good or to avoid evil: "Those who wage war justly have peace as the object of this intention."[6]

A concern for peace as the object of war carried over into more modern formulations of just war theory. Hugo Grotius approvingly quoted Aristotle's view that "the purpose of war is to remove the things that disturb peace."[7] In the twentieth century, and echoing General Sherman's statement of the principle, B. H. Liddell-Hart wrote, "The object in war is a better state of peace."[8]

The peace envisioned by Aristotle, Augustine, Grotius, and even Liddell-Hart was hardly perpetual peace. All would have grimly accepted the belief attributed to Plato that "only the dead have seen the end of war."⁹ Not only has no war yet succeeded in eliminating the resort to war for all time and under all circumstances, many wars have failed even to end the condition of enmity and the security dilemma affecting the parties to the conflict themselves.

This point is a reminder that there is a difference between conceiving the object of a particular war as the achievement of a better state of peace and conceiving it as the elimination of war. The two ends, arguably, are not just different in degree but different in kind. The former speaks to a limited and completely attainable goal of all who engage in war; the latter envisions something that never has been and, realists argue, never will be. It would be a mistake, however, to think there is a choice to be made between the immediate demands of peace between two combatants and peace on a broader scale. Peace by pieces may be the way progress occurs.¹⁰ But, in either case, the peace that is desired is what Sherman called a more perfect peace—that is, a peace that is more stable, more widespread, and more just than the peace that was interrupted by war.

Wars to End War

There is, of course, a more expansive notion of what is entailed in a more perfect peace. Although the idea that a war may be fought in order to put an end to war is generally associated with Woodrow Wilson, it has found expression in various societies in the modern world. The sixteen-year conflict over the control of Yorubaland (in modern-day Nigeria) that began in 1877 was called a war to end all wars by Balogun Latosisa of Ibadan.¹¹ Mao Zedong wrote that "the aim of war is to eliminate war . . . Mankind's era of wars will be brought to an end by our own efforts, and beyond doubt the war we wage is part of the final battle."¹²

In his war message to Congress on April 2, 1917, Woodrow Wilson spoke of the European conflict into which he was leading the United States as a war to end all wars. Where Wilson got the memorable phrase is unknown, but H. G. Wells, no doubt unaware of the Balogun Latosisa of Ibadan, claimed to have coined it.¹³ Within months of the outbreak of war in Europe, Wells had published a brief book titled *The War That Will End War* in which he argued that the war "is now a war for peace. . . . It aims at a settlement that shall stop this sort of thing for ever. . . . This, the greatest of all wars, is not just another war—it is the last war!"[14] Wells explained why, in spite of his "declared horror of war," he had parted company with those circulating petitions calling for an end to the fighting: By defeating Imperial Germany, "the way will be open at last for all these Western Powers to organise peace." Consequently, "Every sword that is drawn against Germany now is a sword drawn for peace."[15]

Wells had embraced the paradox that war may be necessary for the creation of stable peace. Wilson would do so as well. But they were not the only ones committed to the idea of waging war for peace. The Trustees of the Carnegie Endowment argued that "the most certain means of instituting a durable peace among the nations is to pursue the War against the Imperial German Government until the final victory of democracy."[16]

Wilson's commitment to the logic behind a war to end all wars elevated it to the level of policy in the United States. His use of the phrase, together with equally emphatic assertions concerning the spread of democracy and the reform of European balance-of-power politics, provided a uniquely American justification for a most un-American policy. It meant that he was taking the United States into a European war to promote American ideals.[17] But he promised what he could not deliver. As a consequence, his detractors have labeled his ideas utopian and his most idealistic utterances hollow, while his supporters have been forced to concede that he is a tragic figure.[18] In his defense, however, Wilson's idea of a war to end all wars borrowed not only from liberal ruminations about the war; it tapped into a long line of philosophical reflection about the very purpose of war. More importantly, it foreshadowed concrete efforts—some of them his own and some the efforts of later generations—to turn war into peace. As we will see, there is a substantial literature suggesting that Wilson, while he may have been visionary, was not a utopian.

The idea that what General Sherman called a more perfect peace is possible has both ancient roots and modern manifestations. The Hebrew prophets spoke of a day when nations "shall beat their swords into plowshares, and their spears into pruning-hooks; nation shall not lift up sword against nation, neither shall they learn war any more."[19] The Abbé de Saint-Pierre, writing in the early part of the eighteenth century, articulated in his *Project for Perpetual Peace* a plan for peace through the establishment of an international organization responsible for mediating conflicts among states. At the end of the same century, Immanuel Kant published his celebrated pamphlet *Perpetual Peace*, which argued for a free confederation of states with governments based on republican principles as the basis of peace. Adam Smith argued that commerce would make societies more peaceful. Richard Cobden, in the nineteenth century, took up the theme to emphasize the pacifying tendencies of free trade. Similar arguments were advanced by Norman Angell in *The Great Illusion*, published just five years before the start of World War I.[20]

But, in addition to the philosophical speculations regarding the possibility of peace, it is important to keep in mind the actual policies implemented, especially in the aftermath of major wars when significant reforms have been implemented. As claimed by Charles W. Kegley Jr. and Gregory A. Raymond in a recent study, "paradoxically, the horrors of war have often stimulated creative innovation and change."[21]

Attempting to create a lasting peace after a war that was so destructive that Catholics and Protestants would not sit down together to negotiate, a major reform of the international system was constructed in 1648 in a set of agreements that, collectively, is called the Peace of Westphalia.[22] In the aftermath of a century-long effort to establish religious universalism, peace was made on the basis of a novel concept—*cuius regio, eius religio*—that permitted each sovereign to determine the faith and the laws of his state. One of the foremost students of the Peace of Westphalia concludes that after 1648, religious warfare, which was so common and so destructive between 1517 and the end of the Thirty Years War, ceased to be a feature of European politics.[23]

Following the Napoleonic Wars, the map of Europe was redrawn and the balance of power restored by the Congress of Vienna. More importantly, the Concert of Europe was established, and in a series of congresses (Aix-la-Chappelle in 1818, Carlsbad in 1819, Verona in 1822, and London in 1830, 1832, and 1838–39) managed political affairs in Europe and prevented war among the major powers at least until the Crimean War of 1853–56. Following World War I, Woodrow Wilson carried a detailed plan for a more peaceful world with him to Paris. In important respects, he succeeded in remaking the international system in the image of his Fourteen Points. The United Nations Charter, drafted at the end of World War II, is in many respects a compendium of peace proposals.

Even more significant than the long list of well-articulated plans for perpetual peace or the record of diplomatic achievements—the declarations written, the treaties ratified, and the organizations established in the aftermath of great wars—is the historical record, the evidence that a more perfect peace is in fact possible. While the persistence of war—and especially wars that appear daily in the media—seems to belie any speculation that the dreams of a world without war are within reach, there is mounting evidence that some wars to end war have in fact been successful in achieving their lofty goals. Perhaps the most striking evidence of this is the fact that the globe is largely covered by zones of peace,—large geographical areas, including some that are continental in scope, in which war has become if not unthinkable at least highly unlikely. The remarkable debellicization of Western Europe in the years since World War II is the best-known example, but there are others.[24]

Since the 1950s, a substantial body of work has been produced by some of the leading scholars of international relations to demonstrate and explain the end of war and the beginning of peace. Although commonly treated together in the literature, two distinct approaches to the question of how stable peace evolves can be discerned. The first is, broadly speaking, empiricist. It is, in other words, an approach focused on the fact of stable peace and its causes. It focuses on the development of security communities, zones of peace, and peace among democracies. The second is constructivist in its general orientation. It emphasizes changes in thinking about the efficacy and the morality of war. What is important to note, however, is that both approaches view stable peace as an emerging reality rather than a distant dream. Unlike the work associated with the Abbé de Saint-Pierre, Kant, and even Wilson, the focus of this literature is on identifying and explaining peace that exists here and now, not on devising plans for a peace that exists only in dreams.

The seminal work associated with the empiricist approach is Karl Deutsch's *Political Community in the North Atlantic Area*, published in 1957. Noting the increasing irrelevance of war in the relations of the states of Western Europe and North America, Deutsch developed the concept of a security community in which there is a "real assurance that the members of that community will not fight each other physically."[25] Security communities, according to Deutsch, can be differentiated on the basis of the level of political integration each exhibits. The two categories Deutsch used were pluralistic and amalgamated security communities.

The idea of a security community is based on the observation that certain regions or, more generally, certain groupings of states have reached a state of stable peace. It notes the existence of an actual state of affairs and is aspirational only insofar as it considers the possibility of extending the benefits of a security community to additional states or other regions. It sees the world divided among zones of peace and zones of turmoil, but it accepts that an end to war is possible and that it has been achieved, although not universally.[26]

Perhaps most noteworthy of all the work on stable peace is that associated with democratic peace theory, which asserts that democracies do not wage war against other democracies.[27] So solidly grounded and widely accepted is the theory's basic proposition that it has been endorsed and made the basis of policy by Bill Clinton, George W. Bush, Tony Blair, and the European Union.

Constructivists have looked at the evidence from the words and deeds of states and have concluded that the idea of war has fallen out of favor. Or to be more precise, the idea that war is a prerogative of states for the promotion of the national interest as well as an effective and ethical means of settling disputes has become untenable. Scholars in this camp—admitting again that the distinction is not so sharp as to place most studies solely in one category or the other—have noted that a fundamental change has occurred in the normative framework within which issues of war and peace are debated.

John Mueller has argued that wars between great powers have become obsolete as a consequence of a growing consensus, centuries in the making but driven home by the world wars of the first half of the twentieth century that war in the developed world "is both abhorrent—repulsive, immoral, and uncivilized—and methodologically ineffective—futile."[28] The consensus has been bolstered by an increase in the emphasis states place on economic growth as an aspect of the national interest and a concomitant tendency to use economic indicators as the primary measure of state power. War, Mueller concludes, "like slavery or dueling . . . is merely a social institution, one people can live without."[29]

In a study that takes seriously the words that states use and the agreements they make with one another, Dorothy V. Jones has observed that since 1919, peace has been a clear and consistent objective of states. The seventy-nine major treaties and declarations between 1919 and 1989 that Jones examined for evidence of the ethical foundations of the international system suggest that the peaceful settlement of disputes, avoidance of the threat or use of force, and nonintervention in the internal affairs of other states are central elements in a well-developed and frequently reiterated "code of peace."[30]

The persistent elaboration of an ethical code for interstate relations is an element of what Michael Mandelbaum describes as "the invention of peace."[31] The "Wilsonian triad"—the ends of peace, freedom, and prosperity—once considered unimaginable became in the twentieth century the standard objects of political desire throughout the world, according to Mandelbaum.[32] Peace, in other words, although hardly universal in its realization, had become one of the "ideas that conquered the world."

All of these studies, from both empiricist and constructivist perspectives, take the ability of the international community to reduce the incidence of war as an established fact. In addition, most either explicitly or implicitly accept the idea that changes in the propensity of states to use war as an instrument of policy can come, and in fact has come, from the experience of war. That is, there actually have been wars that have played a role in ending conflict among certain states.

Wars That Engender War

Unfortunately, in spite of the fact that some wars have been successful at producing a more perfect peace, war, and the threat of war, persist. In an average year during the period 1989–2008, there were forty armed conflicts ongoing in the world, according to the Uppsala Conflict Data Program (UCPD).[33] Five (in Afghanistan, Iraq, Pakistan, Sri Lanka, and Somalia) produced over a thousand battle-related deaths in 2008. Thirty-one others (including conflicts in India, Myanmar, the Philippines, Georgia, Burundi, Ethiopia, and Sudan, among others) were considered to be minor, based on lower casualty rates. What is most striking about armed conflict since the end of the Cold War is the fact that the vast majority of conflicts have been intrastate in character. (Some, like the ongoing wars in Afghanistan and Iraq, are considered internationalized intrastate conflicts due to the role of external states in fighting that is essentially intrastate.) The only interstate armed conflict recorded in 2008 in the UCPD data set was a new conflict between Djibouti and Eritrea.[34] Thus, while interstate wars have declined significantly in number and severity since the end of World War II, civil wars have filled the gap, making it appear as if little progress has occurred in ending the scourge of war. The reality is that intrastate and interstate wars present two very different aspects. Virtually all that scholars have suggested about the invention of peace or the obsolescence of major war fails to apply to intrastate war.

Civil war is the dominant form of armed conflict. From 1945 to 1997, according to the Correlates of War Project, there were over four times as many civil wars (108) as interstate wars (23). The total number of battle deaths in civil wars (11.4 million) also dwarfed the number associated with interstate wars (3.3 million).[35]

While the rise of large zones of peace in the world and, more generally, the decline of interstate war is cause for hope that stable peace is not merely a utopian goal, the pervasiveness of civil war in several zones of turmoil is cause for deep concern. The end of the Cold War seems only to have exacerbated the trend in which civil wars dramatically outnumber other forms of armed conflict. In fact, all but seven of 121 wars since 1989 have been civil wars.[36]

The problem of civil war is complicated by the fact that as many as half of all civil wars have erupted following a peace settlement.[37] Over half of the states in the Correlates of War data set that experienced civil war (28 of 54) had more than one war. Put differently, 108 civil wars were spread among only 54 states. In another data set, 151 civil wars took place in 75 states. Far from a war to end all wars, the typical civil war in the post-1945 period has been a war to ensure more wars.[38]

There is, therefore, a need to think twice about the ability of war to end war. On the one hand, the Wilsonian vision of a world made peaceful by the spread of democracy, free trade, and common security policies has been largely realized if the incidence of interstate war, especially on a large scale, is accepted as the proper measure. On the other hand, within a very substantial portion of the world's states, particularly those whose populations Paul Collier numbers among "the bottom billion," a Hobbesian state of war—or what Collier calls "the conflict trap"—has become the norm.[39] For states caught in the conflict trap there seem to be great uncertainties about how to end wars well. Many wars end without either a vision or a plan for anything resembling a more perfect peace. While scholars are laboring to establish an empirical understanding of intrastate war—that is, to establish the "correlates of peace" for civil wars—little has been done to articulate principles of just peace in the aftermath of civil war. This points to a need to think systematically about how the emerging discourse of *jus post bellum* might take into consideration the problems associated with intrastate war. If just war theory continues to develop under the assumption that wars between sovereign states are the principal concern, its utility will be limited at best.

Jus Post Bellum Principles and the End of War

Every war has a cause: the desire for conquest (or to resist conquest), the settlement of a political conflict, the punishment of crimes, or the vindication of human rights, to name just a few of the many possibilities. Some wars have, in addition to a proximate cause, or a condition that makes war necessary, a *cause* in the sense of a purpose greater than that served by any particular war. While proximate causes are thrust upon the combatants, making the war necessary (or so they argue), causes are generally taken up only after the war has begun. The American Civil War offers a clear example of this pattern. Abraham Lincoln, confronted with a war of secession, had as his immediate aim the preservation of the Union. In a letter to Horace Greeley in August 1862, he stated, "My paramount object in this struggle is to save the Union, and is not either to save or to destroy slavery. If I could save the Union without freeing any slave I would do it, and if I could save it by freeing all the slaves I would do it; and if I could save it by freeing some and leaving others alone I would also do that."[40] In time and with a change in political circumstances, however, he endorsed the higher ambition—the Cause—of ending slavery throughout the United States.[41]

The higher ambition is not properly a part of the rationale for entering into war in the first place. As long as peace lasts, any notion of strengthening the conditions for stable peace or building institutions and norms to promote justice should be pursued through diplomacy. But the fact of war changes things. It provides opportunities to go beyond the limits imposed by the need to maintain amicable relations. Indeed, it sometimes provides those with ambitions, whether noble or base, with the chance to dictate rather than negotiate terms. Victory in war combined with both a desire and a plan for stable peace offers an unusual circumstance in which the political landscape can be changed by a single purposive will rather than through the clash of conflicting wills. As Clausewitz noted, "War is . . . an act of force to compel our enemy to do our will."[42] That will may be a will to promote stable peace. But whether the aim is the abolition of war in general or the prevention of a particular war, a just peace is a peace designed to last.[43]

No war can be said to have ended well that leaves in its wake conditions likely to engender the next war. David Lloyd George is said to have commented sardonically in 1916, "This war, like the next war, is a war to end war." While this witticism appears to have been placed in the British prime minister's mouth by the writer E. V. Lucas, its ironic message is nonetheless a reminder that even a war fought and concluded with the best intentions—the intentions to do justice and to establish the foundations of stable peace—may be, ultimately, no more than a link in the chain of causes of a future conflict.[44]

A just war is fought to remove the impediments to peace; a just peace ensures that impediments to peace are buried, never to rise again. For this reason, the creation of a just peace requires a clear understanding of what caused the war in the first place: *Jus ad bellum* and *jus post bellum* are thus closely connected.

Just peace requires that the causes of the recently concluded war be addressed; a just peace aims, at a minimum, to make the last war a war to end all wars between those particular parties over those particular issues. But a higher ambition may also be compatible with the pursuit of a just peace. The parties may seek to deal not only with the particular issues that caused the last war, but with any other problems that might be anticipated as a potential *casus belli*. If the minimum condition of just peace is a certain self-awareness (perhaps the ability to appraise honestly why a war is being fought), a broader conception of a just peace requires a more expansive understanding of the causes of war and the conditions of peace. Peacemakers after World War II were aided not only by the totality of the triumph over the Axis powers but by the insights of scholars such as John

Maynard Keynes, David Mitrany, and even one of Woodrow Wilson's harshest critics, E. H. Carr.[45]

The challenge, then, for those who think seriously about *jus post bellum* is to bring a wide array of empirical research on war termination, the conditions of stable peace, and the creation of security communities to bear on the still-evolving project to find or fashion moral norms applicable to the end of wars. And because the most common form of war in our time is intrastate war, those norms must be applicable to the particular conditions relevant to civil wars. Producing *jus post bellum* principles in light of research on the end of war is not a matter of trying to derive what ought to be from what is. Instead, it is a matter of trying to do what all good moral philosophers must do, which is to frame, in the felicitous phrasing of Russell Hardin, "morality within the limits of reason."[46]

Jus post bellum thinking is, if not still in its infancy, certainly not beyond adolescence. There is a growing consensus, stimulated by events in Iraq since 2003, that moral obligations in the aftermath of war deserve serious and systematic consideration. There is not, however, a consensus on specific *jus post bellum* principles to date. Much of the work on *jus post bellum* that has been done seeks either to adapt well-established principles associated with the just war tradition to postwar problems or to derive principles from what are thought to be best postwar practices. In this respect, *jus post bellum* theorists are doing what moral theorists have always done: conceptualizing the ideal while engaging the real. Different starting points along the spectrum between abstract principles and practical problems have, however, yielded very different lists of potential *jus post bellum* principles.

A consensus on foundations, if possible, would help to bridge the existing gap between those working to reapply such traditional just war concepts as proportionality and right intention to postwar settings and those working backwards from cases involving war crimes trials and economic reconstruction, for example, to the principles that might frame such practices. Finding a consensus on foundations, however, is bound to be difficult. Michael Walzer sidestepped the effort to articulate the foundations of his approach to just war theory in *Just and Unjust Wars*, but a commitment to human rights is evident throughout his analysis.[47] Thus, for those who take *Just and Unjust Wars* as a key statement in the modern framing of just war theory, as well as for those who see in the development of human rights an important resource for global moral discourse, a potential foundation for *jus post bellum* principles is readily available.[48]

One of the benefits of thinking about the requirements of just peace through the lens of human rights is that it carries the potential for helping to bring the principles of just peace and the law of postwar occupation into greater conformity with one another. International law scholars have been grappling for some time with the need to update the law of occupation. There is a body of thought, forcefully represented by one of the most widely respected scholars in the field, that a merger of the law of occupation and international human rights law is not only in the making, but to be welcomed.[49]

Making the fundamental principles of international human rights law the basis of just peace holds the additional promise of overcoming some of the challenges to the just war tradition posed by civil war. Intrastate war, which is now far and away the most prevalent form of warfare, has historically been treated as if it were generally outside the boundaries of just war theory. In fact, the *jus ad bellum* requirement of right authority is commonly construed as proscribing the use of violence by nonstate actors. Even in Walzer's modern formulation, just war theory maintains a fundamentally statist orientation.[50] Now, however, in a period in which intrastate wars are both more common and quite often more destructive than interstate wars, *jus post bellum* principles must be applicable to nonstate actors if they are to be considered relevant. Principles derived from basic human rights can be readily applied to all parties to a conflict regardless of their relationship to the state.

It is important to acknowledge, however, that there are problems from a legal standpoint in trying to make human rights the basis of a new regime for the end of wars, including civil wars. First, states assume obligations when ratifying human rights conventions; nonstate actors not only cannot become parties to human rights treaties, they generally are not bound directly by the agreements their state has made. Put differently, there is a statist orientation to international human rights law just as there is to traditional formulations of just war theory. Second, with a few noteworthy exceptions, such as the rights not to be tortured or deprived of life arbitrarily, human rights treaties generally allow derogation from specific obligations when the existence of the state is threatened. Civil war is the quintessential threat justifying such derogations. Third, while most of the major human rights treaties have been widely ratified (the Convention against Torture, for example, has 146 parties and the Genocide Convention has 141), there are holdouts against both entire treaties and, through international law's permissive system of treaty reservations, specific provisions of ratified agreements. If international law offers blanket coverage of the rights of individuals worldwide, it must be acknowledged that there are many gaping holes in the blanket. Finally, international human rights law generally is not as specific in the responsibilities it imposes and the remedies it proposes as it is concerning the law of armed conflict or the law of occupation.[51]

The creation of *jus post bellum* principles derived from a human rights foundation, however, does not require solving legal problems. What human rights norms do for just war theory is to supply a framework from which the principles of just peace can be drawn. In fact, from the standpoint of just war theory, it is best not to be drawn into the specifics of particular human rights treaties and debates over universality and relativity or the priority of some rights over others. For the most part, it is sufficient to focus on the rights that emanate from a thin morality that yields basic or foundational rights.[52]

A focus on human rights points toward one fundamental principle relevant to just war theory: Justice in war requires that the motives, means, and objectives of war be rooted in respect for the human rights of the parties to the conflict. A just war is one that seeks to protect or restore basic rights such as the rights to life, freedom, and (in some cases of intrastate war) equality or self-determination. A war motivated by concerns unrelated to human rights, such as a war to acquire power or wealth to benefit some narrow interest, cannot satisfy the requirements of *jus ad bellum*. Likewise, a just peace must be based on concern for the human rights of all, both winners and losers. Enslavement, arbitrary executions, the imposition of punishments unrelated to wrongs done, and the denial of subsistence are all incompatible with the requirements of *jus post bellum* because all deny basic human rights.[53]

This, of course, is a very general description of what just war theory looks like when articulated within a human rights framework. More specific principles deduced from a conception of basic rights are necessary to answer questions about power-sharing arrangements, war crimes trials, postwar reconstruction, the resettlement of refugees, the imposition of peacekeeping forces, and many additional issues that may arise in the aftermath of war. Although nonstate actors may not be legally bound by human rights treaties in the way that most states are, nothing prevents the application to them of just war principles grounded in respect for human rights. Rebel leaders and state authorities alike can be enjoined to respect the lives, liberty, and dignity of those involved in the war.

The development of *jus post bellum* principles that are applicable to intrastate conflict is especially important because civil wars, in far too many cases, have not ended well. The nature of the combatants, the dire poverty of many of the countries in which they occur, the role played in many cases by the desire to control natural resources or other sources of wealth, and a host of other factors complicate efforts to achieve a just peace in the aftermath of civil war. Given the frequency with which civil wars erupt again following negotiated agreements, there is a particular need to make stable peace the primary objective of *jus post bellum* principles. To this end, it may be that the next significant development will involve extending obligations to outsiders through the inclusion of peacekeeping among the requirements of a just peace.[54] If, however, there is a lesson to be gained from the initial failure and eventual triumph, however qualified, of Wilson's idea of a war to end all wars, it is this: A moral vision of peace refined by experience can, in fact, yield a more perfect peace.

Notes

1. Michael Walzer critiques Sherman's perspective on war (at least in its "war is hell" manifestation) in *Just and Unjust Wars: A Moral Argument with Historical Illustrations* (New York: Basic Books, 1977), 32–33.

2. Hedley Bull acknowledged that war is sometimes assigned "a positive role in the maintenance of international order" and even a role in promoting "just change." See *The Anarchical Society: A Study of Order in World Politics* (New York: Columbia University Press, 1977), 188–89.

3. Aristotle, *Nichomachean Ethics*, 2nd ed., trans. by Terence Irwin (Indianapolis: Hackett Publishing Company, 1999), 164 (Book 10, Chapter 7, §6).

4. St. Augustine, *Concerning the City of God against the Pagans*, trans. by Henry Bettenson (London: Penguin Books, 1984), 866.

5. William R. Stephenson Jr., *Christian Love and Just War: Moral Paradox and Political Life in St. Augustine and His Modern Interpreters* (Macon, GA: Mercer University Press, 1987), 39.

6. All quotations are from the *Summa Theologica* as quoted in Telford Taylor, "Just and Unjust Wars," in *War, Morality, and the Military Profession*, 2nd ed., rev. ed. Malham M. Wakin (Boulder, CO: Westview Press, 1986), 227–28.

7. *The Law of War and Peace (De Jure Belli ac Pacis)*, translated by Louise R. Loomis (Roslyn, NY: Walter J. Black, 1949), 375.

8. B. H. Liddell-Hart, *Strategy*, 2nd ed. (New York: Praeger, 1974), 339.

9. To my knowledge, this line is not found in any of Plato's dialogues. It was, however, attributed to Plato by Gen. Douglas MacArthur in his speech to the cadets at the United States Military Academy on May 12, 1962.

10. I first heard the phrase "peace by pieces" used by Inis L. Claude Jr. in a lecture on functionalism. I assume it to be one of the many memorable phrases he coined.

11. J. B. Webster and A. A. Boahen, *History of West Africa: The Revolutionary Years– 1815 to Independence* (New York: Praeger Publishers, 1970), 97. *Balogun* means "commander."

12. Quoted in Walzer, *Just and Unjust Wars*, 226–27.

13. Michael Howard, *War and the Liberal Conscience* (New Brunswick, NJ: Rutgers University Press, 1978), 74.

14. H. G. Wells, *The War That Will End War* (New York: Duffield & Company, 1914), 14.

15. Wells, *The War That Will End War*, 21–22.

16. Quoted in Howard, *War and the Liberal Conscience*, 81–82.

17. Robert A. Divine, *Perpetual War for Perpetual Peace* (College Station: Texas A&M University Press, 2000), 21–22.

18. For an early and important critique of Wilsonian liberalism in international politics, see Edward Hallett Carr, *The Twenty Years' Crisis, 1919–1939*, 2nd ed. (New York: St. Martin's, 1946), 73.

19. Isaiah 2:4. Cf. Micah 4:3.

20. Many of these writers and their theories are discussed in Michael W. Doyle, *Ways of War and Peace* (New York: W. W. Norton, 1997).

21. Charles W. Kegley Jr. and Gregory A. Raymond, *Exorcising the Ghost of Westphalia: Building World Order in the New Millennium* (Englewood Cliffs, NJ: Prentice Hall, 2001), 7.

22. Diarmaid MacCulloch, *The Reformation: A History* (New York: Viking, 2003), 469.

23. Daniel Philpott, "The Religious Roots of Modern International Relations," *World Politics* 52:1 (January 2000): 213.

24. See Max Singer and Aaron Wildavsky, *The Real World Order: Zones of Peace, Zones of Turmoil* (Chatham, NJ: Chatham House, 1993), 3–13.

25. Quoted in Charles A. Kupchan, *How Enemies Become Friends: The Sources of Stable Peace* (Princeton, NJ: Princeton University Press, 2010), 22.

26. The terms "zones of peace" and "zone of turmoil" are drawn from Singer and Wildavsky, *The Real World Order*.

27. The literature on democratic peace is voluminous. A brief and indiscriminate listing of books only might include Bruce Russett, *Grasping the Democratic Peace* (Princeton, NJ:

Princeton University Press, 1993); James Lee Ray, *Democracy and International Conflict* (Columbia: University of South Carolina Press, 1995); Spencer R. Weart, *Never at War* (New Haven, CT: Yale University Press, 1998); and Charles Lipson, *Reliable Partners: How Democracies Have Made a Separate Peace* (Princeton, NJ: Princeton University Press, 2003).

28. John Mueller, *Retreat from Doomsday: The Obsolescence of Major War* (New York: Basic Books, 1989), 217.

29. Mueller, *Retreat from Doomsday*, 264.

30. Dorothy V. Jones, *Code of Peace: Ethics and Security in the World of the Warlord States* (Chicago: University of Chicago Press, 1991).

31. Michael Mandelbaum, *The Ideas That Conquered the World: Peace, Democracy, and Free Markets in the Twenty-First Century* (New York: Public Affairs, 2002), 107. The phrase was previously used by Michael Howard as the title of a book: *The Invention of Peace: Reflections on War and International Order* (London: Profile, 2001).

32. Mandelbaum, *The Ideas That Conquered the World*, 26.

33. See Lotta Harborn and Peter Wallensteen, "Armed Conflicts, 1946–2008," *Journal of Peace Research* 46:1 (2009): 577–87.

34. Harborn and Wallensteen, "Armed Conflicts," 579.

35. T. David Mason, *Sustaining the Peace after Civil War* (Carlisle, PA: Strategic Studies Institute, December 2007), 1.

36. Mason, *Sustaining the Peace after Civil War*, 1.

37. Paul Collier, *War, Guns, and Votes: Democracy in Dangerous Places* (New York: HarperCollins, 2009), 75. Astri Suhrke and Ingrid Samset have taken issue with Collier's research on the recurrence of civil war. See "What's in a Figure? Estimating Recurrence of Civil War," *International Peacekeeping* 14, no. 2 (April 2007): 195–203.

38. Mason, *Sustaining the Peace after Civil War*, 2.

39. Paul Collier, *The Bottom Billion* (New York: Oxford University Press, 2007).

40. Quoted in Ronald C. White Jr., *A. Lincoln: A Biography* (New York: Random House, 2009), 504.

41. Walzer uses the phrase "higher ambition" to describe the tendency of those fighting against aggression to seek more than an escape from the immediate trials of war. He writes, "the experience of war as hell generates what might be called a higher ambition: one doesn't aim to settle with the enemy but to defeat and punish him and, if not to abolish the tyranny of war, at least to reduce the probability of future oppression" (*Just and Unjust Wars*, 31).

42. Carl von Clausewitz, *On War*, ed. and trans. by Michael Howard and Peter Paret (New York: Knopf, 1993), 83.

43. The distinction between "abolition" and "prevention" is raised in passing by Martin Ceadel in *Thinking about Peace and War* (New York: Oxford University Press, 1989), 5.

44. See E. V. Lucas, *Reading, Writing and Remembering: A Literary Record* (New York: Harper & Brothers Publishers, 1932), 294, 296, 302.

45. See John Maynard Keynes, *The Economic Consequences of the Peace* (New York: Harcourt, Brace and Howe, 1920); David Mitrany, *A Working Peace System* (London: The

Royal Institute of International Affairs, Oxford University Press, 1943); and Carr, *The Twenty Years' Crisis*. Michael Mandelbaum notes that Keynes influenced the post–World War II settlement in part because he participated in negotiations related to international economic relations, bringing with him experiences gleaned from his work in the Paris Peace Conference in 1919. See *The Ideas That Conquered the World*, 328–29.

46. Russell Hardin, *Morality within the Limits of Reason* (Chicago: University of Chicago Press, 1988).

47. Walzer, *Just and Unjust Wars*, xv–xvi.

48. See Robert E. Williams Jr. and Dan Caldwell, "*Jus Post Bellum*: Just War Theory and the Principles of Just Peace," *International Studies Perspectives* 7, no. 1 (2006): 313–15.

49. Adam Roberts, "Transformative Military Occupation: Applying the Laws of War and Human Rights," *American Journal of International Law* 100, no. 1 (July 2006): 618–22.

50. Michael Joseph Smith, "Growing Up with *Just and Unjust Wars*: An Appreciation," *Ethics & International Affairs* 11, no. 4 (1997): 8.

51. See Roberts, "Transformative Military Occupation," 599–600, for a brief discussion of some of these difficulties.

52. See Michael Walzer, *Thick and Thin: Moral Argument at Home and Abroad* (Notre Dame: University of Notre Dame Press, 1994); Henry Shue, *Basic Rights: Subsistence, Affluence, and US Foreign Policy*, 2nd ed. (Princeton, NJ: Princeton University Press, 1996), and *Human Rights: Concept and Context* (Peterborough, ON: Broadview Press, 2002), 62–65.

53. Williams and Caldwell, "*Jus Post Bellum*," 316–18. See also Brian Orend, "Justice after War," *Ethics & International Affairs* 16, no. 2 (2002): 46.

54. Paul Collier has estimated that an expenditure of $100 million per year on peacekeeping will reduce the chances that a civil war will be resumed from 38 percent to 17 percent over a ten-year period with economic benefits outweighing costs by a factor of roughly four to one. See Collier, *Wars, Guns, and Votes*, 96.

CHAPTER 6

ETHICS IN THE TIMES OF WAR

PAULETTA OTIS

THIS CHAPTER FOCUSES on ethical principles found in just war theory as they are practiced and applied during the different phases of war. The underlying assumption is that understanding the role ethics plays throughout a conflict will contribute to a more durable just peace. Focusing on how ethical principles are put into practice or ignored throughout the different phases of a war may make the invisible visible, even through the fog of war.

What happens at each phase of a war matters. It is not just the initial determination to go to war, or how to fight it, or how to end war that concerns just war theorists but all of the phases—planning, mobilization, conflict, demobilization, stability and support, nation building, and peacemaking. Ethical principles and practices influence each discrete phase and have cumulative effects on successive phases.

Wars have both long-term and short-term consequences not only because of their destructive power in terms of life and death, but because wars are justified and rationalized in terms of ethical principles and behaviors. Whether individuals or nations behave in relationship to their ethical ideals will be the standard by which they are judged at the end of a war. The justification for war will be evaluated as to truth insofar as the war was conducted in relationship to that justification. Too often, the ethical record of a war is ignored at the initiation of a peace process in an effort to end hostilities and make peace as quickly as possible. Failure to understand the justifications for war and the ethical conduct of the war inevitably leads to a frail and faulty peace.

If scholars and practitioners are to understand how to end wars, support just resolution, and ensure durable settlements, they need to know infinitely more than that the killing has stopped. It is incredibly naïve to think that men and women, even if of good will and faith, can simply appear near the end of a war and say "We are here to help; Let us conduct seminars and discussions on conflict resolution; We have a Peaceful God on our side." A clear vision is required to see how and why the war was fought, what the rules of the conflict were, and whether the rules and guidelines were followed.

It is assumed that just war theory is based on religious theologies and traditions that can be found in every religion and culture. In this chapter, religious ideologies and behaviors will be used as a surrogate measure of the more theoretical framework available in the study of ethics. Religion and religious actors frame the application of ethics in ways congruent with a specific culture and in relationship to threat perception. What religious actors do and say in the first days of war in reference to ethical traditions changes dramatically with the onslaught of hostilities, the killing and destruction of the enemy, war exhaustion, and the aftermath of war. Religion and the role it plays during warfare is the visible evidence of the practice of ethics by a people, and is the single most critical variable in the study of armed conflict because religion, like war, intrinsically and undeniably deals first and foremost with the issues of life and death.

At the beginning of conflict, ethics as based on religion becomes indistinguishable from culture in defense of the homeland, and the enemy is defined as the other. In the middle of war, ethics as based on religion contributes to the rules of warfare by defining who can and cannot be tortured, interrogated, or killed, and specifically wrestles with the rules of proportionality. At the end of war there is a dramatic change, and religious personages take the lead in peace movements by articulating ethical principles in relationship to their ideas of a just peace. Religion, and the roles it plays during warfare as the visible evidence of the practice of ethics by a people, is the single most critical variable in the study of armed conflict because, like war, it intrinsically and undeniably deals first and foremost with the issues of life and death. This is not to say that ethics and religions are the same thing. It is possible to behave ethically without reference to a religious tradition; it is possible to behave religiously without reference to a formalized ethical awareness. Nevertheless, religions are often the carriers of ethical standards insofar as many (if not most) writers on the ethics of war have come from specific religious leaders and traditions often bear the standard for ethics in local and world communities.[1]

This chapter will examine the ethical challenges that exist during each of the six major phases of warfare as defined in the academic literature and in the military planning process as variously used by the United Nations (UN), the North Atlantic Treaty Organization (NATO), the United States Department of Defense (DOD), and the United States Marine Corps (USMC).

The power of religious factors must be addressed at each of the phases of war in order to find power and changing circumstances that have lasting effects on the people who are both victims and perpetrators. Integral to the analysis is the role religion plays during the course of conflict in the dual roles of facilitating violence and supporting peace. It is the single most critical variable in the study of armed conflict.

Ethical Challenges in the Phases of War

This chapter posits six phases of warfare as suggested by academic literature and referenced in US foreign and defense policy.[2] The phases are specifically enumerated by the Department of Defense in an effort to provide a base for better understanding the different phases of warfare. This chapter takes those phases and discusses the religious factors relevant to ethical challenges pertinent at each phase.[3] Religion and ethics are handled as essentially value neutral, with potential for contributing to violence as well as peace. (In addition, observers of warfare note that what is a positive good for one side may be harmful or unethical for the other.)

The phases are: Phase 0: Shape; Phase 1: Deter; Phase 2: Seize Initiative; Phase 3: Dominate; Phase 4: Stabilize; Phase 5: Enable Civil Authority. These not only are the basis for military planning focusing on readiness and response, but provide a mind-set for military conceptualization about how war changes over time.[4] The phases have significant overlap and even some backwards movement.[5]

What seems surprising is that religious factors as they contribute to the ethical challenges of warfare in each of the phases are found neither in academic writing nor in military doctrine and policy. When religious

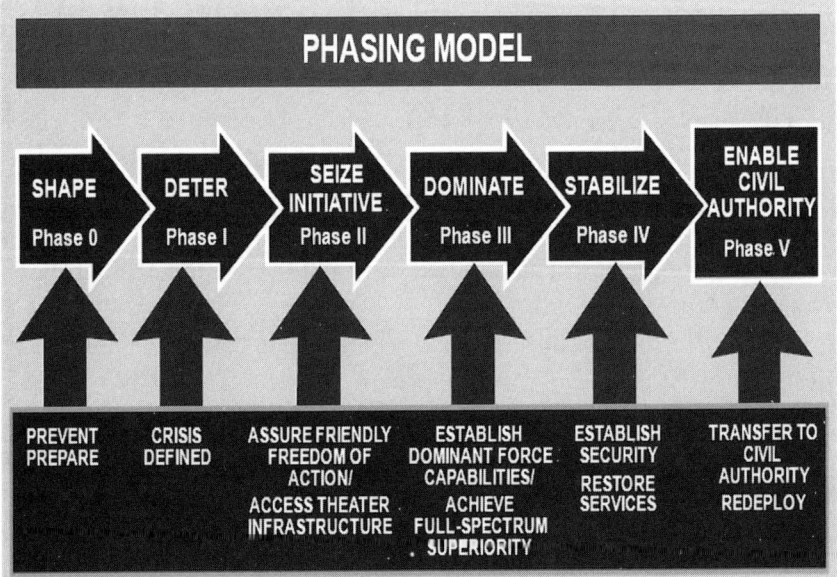

Source: Joint Publication 3-0, September 17, 2006, Incorporating Change 2, March 22, 2010.

factors are taken into consideration, they are generally and quietly subsumed under the rubric of culture. When there is discussion relative to religion it is most often in black-and-white terms—either religion is blamed for war and violence or there is the belief that religion is intrinsically peaceful and anyone that uses religion in the perpetuation of violence (terror, genocide, or war) has misused it. To assert that religion causes war is obviously an overstatement; "radical fundamentalism" is hardly a term devoid of negative implication. The phrase "they hijacked the religion" implies that something good was turned into evil. It is often quietly assumed that civilian and military personnel alike understand that religious factors are important, but they remain unarticulated because of the emotive content and political sensitivities. The idea of separation of church and state provides a handy blind behind which the topic can be hidden.

In this chapter I will discuss the phases of war used by the historians and military scholars and then add to that framework the religious inputs that correspond to each phase. The case studies used include Paul

Mojzes's work on Bosnia, S. J. Tambiah's understanding of ritual in Sri Lanka, Jean Hatzfeld's book on the Rwanda genocide, and the many case studies of the role of religion in Northern Ireland or South Africa.[6]

The question is: What role does religion play in each of the phases of warfare and how does that role highlight the ethical dilemmas at each phase?[7]

PHASE 0: The Religious Role in Times of Near Peace

If relationships within and between countries can be assessed as normal, then phase 0 is the normal stage. Normal does not mean that everything is completely stable in a country, but that social and governmental fractures are being handled or have not reached a critical stage. Ethical standards at this phase are studied, discussed, and applied in relatively peaceful conditions, implying that the some kind of ideal is codified. When conflict and war appear, these ideals are challenged by necessity, group survival, and the vagaries of war. The argument that war is inherently unethical is more intellectually palatable when there is relative peace and stability.

Reality tells us that the religious profile of any country can help indicate whether or not social and cultural fracture lines may occur, when they may occur, and how conflict may come about. The grievances of a religious group that go to the heart of justice are especially important because the religious community is often the voice of the dispossessed or those who believe they are unjustly treated. Grievances are often seen in such aspects as the freedom to educate children in the religion, the freedom to proselytize, or freedom to marry across religious communities. These indicators provide a baseline analysis as to the nature of competition and possible conflict. It also provides, to anyone paying close attention, definitions of self and other, and articulation of fears of a society that might be a basis for future conflict. Inherent in these are the scholarly, academic, and religious studies of war and discussions of *jus ad bellum* and *jus in bello*.[8]

Normal simply means that the state or society has the capacity to settle domestic quarrels with few coercive measures. It does not mean that there are no problems. Domestic issues are settled through stable governance—

political capabilities, legal responsibility, social acquiescence, and personal discipline lessen the potential for recourse to violence. When religious actors are actively involved in social justice through the use of systematic ethics in the political system, they lend an authoritative voice to the process.

In phase 0, names and definitions of actors, communities, leaders, and behaviors are studied and analyzed, including those from religious communities as they impact the overall picture with particular reference to issues of social justice. This information is neither dangerous nor threatening, and most major denominations keep track of their own people around the world; databases of missionary activities are not unusual. When religion plays a role in internal conflict, the bases for that conflict are better understood if the relationship between religion and the other factors of culture such as language, economics, territory, and power are also understood. The DOD Joint Publication 1–05, Religious Affairs in Joint Operations, indicates that phase 0 operations are those operations meant to provide a basis for interaction for those countries with which we are not at war. This includes (a) a general assessment of how the country is doing, and (b) whether there are indications of connections to global violence. It is important to note that this information is useful to nonkinetic efforts of the US government and DOD including military training, intergovernmental cooperation, humanitarian relief, crisis response, and even military sales.

Conversely, not having the information can lead to disaster (or at least mini-disasters). Recent lessons learned include the following: a Navy ship captain not knowing the religious dynamics in the Black Sea; the USMC landing in Tamil controlled territory when US forces provided humanitarian relief to Tamils without the express permission of the Sri Lankan government; and military personnel guidance concerning appropriate cultural and religious behavior in the Middle East. Not having good information about the religious dynamics of a country can inadvertently contribute to conflict. Intrusion into another country or culture (even humanitarian intervention) always changes the balance of social factors, which in turn change both perspectives and realities of social justice.

Phase 0 information is useful for anyone traveling abroad, but for government personnel traveling or working in another area it is critical. Cultural and religious awareness programs are now an integral component of teaching and training for all US military personnel. At a base level this may mean something as simple as staying out of trouble, showing respect to the citizens of the country, and trying not to complicate the operational environment

For scholars and those involved in predicting future conflicts or hot spots, the religious information and analysis is part of the challenge of prediction. It is certain that when religious voices are not effective in protecting and ensuring justice in a country, there will be ethical consequences if and when conflict ensues.

PHASE 1: The Road to War

In this phase, public discourse defines and frames national security by reacting to an incident or crisis, focusing national attention on a perceived threat, identifying competitors, and choosing among alternative responses. The facts are interpreted with an organizing theoretical framework of history and politics that help determine whether a specific incident is worthy of being called a threat. This process is led by politicians, public media, the military, governing officials, community leaders, and religious and human rights organizations. Religious leaders are assumed to have legitimacy based on their recourse to the divine, their previous influence in phase 0, and as spokesmen for endangered or threatened communities.[9]

The Department of Defense uses phase 1 operations to help shape the battlefield. This means that the military defines an enemy as a potential adversary and mobilizes its plans and preparations for possible contingencies. This requires a meeting of the minds—that is, members of the military and their academic colleagues generally agree that a potential threat is real and that it requires military preparation and planning—or that they believe that the civilian leadership sees a threat and that it will have to respond at a future time.

The calculation of short- and long-term threats that require a national military response is complex, and includes the discussion of just war criteria. This is the phase where ethicists, religious leaders, and academic debate and discuss whether the (possible) future war fits the criteria of just war. The ethical criteria available for just war theorists at phase 1 focus on whether going to war is *justifiable*. Although scholars may disagree about the wording, relative importance, and usefulness, most agree on the following:

- Last resort: A just war can only be waged as a last resort. All nonviolent options must be exhausted before the use of force can be justified.
- Legitimate authority: A war is just only if it is waged by a legitimate authority.
- Justifiable cause: A just war can only be fought to right a wrong.
- Right intent: A just war can only be fought with right intentions.
- Reasonable chance of success: A war can only be just if it is fought with a reasonable chance of success.

The discussion of whether a pending war is just is always contentious for several very good reasons. The individuals with ethical authority may not have had a vocal role in the community in phase 0. Their role may have been quiet, scholarly leadership; the prospect of war propels them into the spotlight whether they are ready or not. Each potential conflict is different; facts may not be available or agreed on, and there may be a number of differing perspectives among ethicists and religious leadership. Most importantly, public outcry may outweigh private considerations. The public, the press, and the politicians may simply ignore ethicists and religious authorities—to their future regret. Ethical leadership at this stage is crucial; without solid just war criteria, the future phases will be extremely problematic and world opinion at the end of the conflict will reflect the lack of adherence to ethical standards. The religious community may be blissfully unaware of the strategic context; during phase 0, they may have been concerned with general injustice in the world, humanitarian efforts, missionizing, and economic development instead. This benign neglect of the strategic atmosphere may leave religion and religious leaders in a catch-up situation once a threat is defined as real. The time given ethicists or religious leaders to thoughtfully evaluate the prospect of war in terms of just war standards is generally too short to make much of a difference. (This adds substance to the argument that ethical standards need to be thoroughly established during phase 0, before there is a requirement for a specific application.) The timing of the movement from phase 0 to phase 1 depends on whether a threat is determined to be significant enough to require an immediate response, and whether operations other than war are available or desirable. In the current decade, discussions of whether Iran, Mexico, China, or Palestine constitute threats of the possibility of future war have been discussed and debated, but war has not ensued. An attack such as September 11, 2001, generates an appropriate and timely response. Whether the threat is perceived, actual, or potential is important, but the other half of the coin is the public, political, and religious response. This equation can be influenced by religious leaders who encourage public awareness of the requirements and responsibilities of just war.

If the decision is to go to war, the society will embark on a program of mobilization, as discussed in the next section.

PHASE 2: Mobilizing for War

The ethical considerations so important during phase 1 often become muted or even ignored when the entire nation is mobilizing for war. There may be a split in the ethics and religious communities during this stage: those who support the war and have justified it in their own minds, and those who do not support war and largely fall into the background and are not heard by the public. The public discourse in ethics is often led by religious leaders, regardless of denomination or faith tradition.

Religion during this phase becomes increasingly visible and noisy. Religious leaders align themselves with the ethnic and national culture to resist a perceived threat to the continuation of the group. This is the period where national and religious symbols become indistinguishable. Religious rhetoric focuses on the nature of a country's citizens as God's righteous people who have been threatened by the outsider who is evil, misled, or simply bad. The stronger the identity between the culture and the religion, the more the leaders feel safe to lead both to war. Theology is either ignored or used selectively to propel the people to warfare. Mark Twain's *The War Prayer*, written in response to the Spanish American War, is a poignant example of just how a sermon can be used, how people react, and the irony of using churches to bring about death.[10]

During the mobilization phase, a threat is defined, clarified, and exaggerated by both political and religious entities. Referring specifically to the United States, John Mueller asserts that the United States's reaction to September 11, 2001, was part of a pattern of threat exaggeration. He goes back to 1941 when the United States underestimated Japan, suffered the consequences at Pearl Harbor, and resolved never to underestimate the enemy again. Mueller relates as evidence of this pattern the American reaction to atomic weaponry, North Korea, China, the Cold War, ethnic conflict, rogue states, Iraq's alleged weapons of mass destruction (WMDs), and the current so-called Islamic threat. The threats were communicated to the public in what he terms "theological boilerplate," but he also maintains that "after they have been recited millions of times in speeches, books, leaflets, brochures, letterhead, tracts, training manuals, banners, pamphlets, proclamations, announcements billboards, handbooks, bumper stickers, and T-shirts, one might begin to suspect that the sentiments could just possibly actually reflect true thought processes."[11] This pattern is seen in every culture that sees itself as facing a destructive enemy. What is different in the case of September 11, 2001, is that the threat was magnified because it was also defined as religious by both politicians and church leaders.

The official alarmism, often using religious terminology, was promoted by no less than the American president, members of Congress, religious leaders, academics, the press, and military officers. This implicates the entire official leadership of the United States. Peter Singer's book *President of Good and Evil* points out that President Bush, knowingly or unknowingly, referred to the eschatology of Presbyterian doctrine using phrases such as "city on the hill," "points of light," "heaven," and "good and evil," thereby politicizing "evil."[12] The immediate response was duct tape and color-coded warnings that signaled the fear and anger of the American public.

Christopher Coker eloquently explains in his recent book *Religion and Ethics* how the word "evil" puts war and death on another plain. Wars are not political, territorial, colonial, or personal—they are existential heavenly fights.[13] The God factor is involved and that encapsulates life and death issues on the eternal metaphysical plane. Public statements of military leaders initially mirrored the civilian lead: General Richard Myers, chairman of the Joint Chiefs of Staff, assured a television audience in

2003 that if terrorists were to engineer a catastrophic event that killed 10,000 people they would successfully "do away with our way of life."[14] Nevertheless, the military itself was planning and preparing for what was expected to be war. No matter how patriotic they were or how much they believed in the cause, the attitude tended to be sober, diligent, committed, and focused. Anyone in uniform knew what war would cost them, their families, and their country. As professional military, they prepared for war using a systematic threat assessment and a detailed planning process that tamped down hysteria and focused on operational planning. The dilemma of the military was the definition of the enemy: Was it Islam, Saddam Hussein, the Taliban, or simply a small group of evil people?

In the reaction to September 11, 2001, the intelligence community had a particularly difficult time.[15] It was not accustomed to dealing with religion. Several patterns emerged: The first was simply to ignore the religious and ethical dimension and assume that the basic cause of terrorism was political or economic. The second was to make religion the *only* factor that explained the violence, which led to the default position that Islam was inherently a terrorist religion.[16] Third, there was a mishmash of factors—petroleum, Arab elite maintenance, historical antagonisms, and culture—that could be used to distract attention from political complications, economic inequality, and religious theology. The problem morphed into one of defining the enemy: were they a religious group, a religiously motivated group, a culture, a criminal terrorist group, or something else? If the enemy was somehow also religious, the intelligence community had no systematic way of discussing that without implicating a religion as a factor in violence. The language was muddied and muddled. A system to integrate religion, ethics, and warfare was simply missing.

Several religious voices were heard at this time, providing theological reasoning, leadership, and church power to the production of fear. Tim LeHaye's bestselling book *Left Behind*, a fictional saga of the end times, sold 7 million copies by 2004 and 43 million copies of the sequels by 2007.[17] Religious leaders made strong statements that defined the enemy as anti-God or at least anti-Christian; one Christian leader stated that Islam was a "very evil and wicked religion"; another said that Muhammad was "an absolute wild-eyed fanatic"; and a well-known pastor stated that the Prophet was "a demon-possessed pedophile." It is clear that the religious leaders supported war against Islam as an evil, whether or not they fully realized the political consequences of their statements.[18] These were not statements based on theology, but on religious beliefs and practices; seldom was scripture and verse quoted and when it was, it tended to be very selective, from the prophesies in the books of Daniel and Revelation (liberally adapted), and focused on eschatology. Catholics and Quakers tended to remain quiet, trying to maintain a theological perspective and international outlook—but did not, in general, publicly address the voices of hate and fear until later.

The voices of reason that advocated perspective, risk assessment, careful analysis, and even systematic targeting were often drowned out by the noise. Most military professionals, regardless of their personal faith, took an even more measured perspective in full acknowledgment of the potential for the creation of an enemy that had the potential power of 1.3 billion Muslims in at least 37 countries if not carefully handled. In later stages (2006–9) the hysteria had died down a bit and cooler voices were finally heard. In fact, many of those who were loudest in the initial stages changed their tone (if not their words) over the next few years. By 2010, many were claiming to have been duped by faulty intelligence or led astray by political and religious leaders.

Many scholars ignore phase 2; it is noisy, inchoate, and unreasonable. Public reactions, leaders' statements, and both official and unofficial reaction seem overly emotional and irrational. However, this is where the ethical platforms of phases 0 and 1 are in clear evidence. Statements made at this stage are often used by both friend and enemy to polarize and project hatred.

The conduct of war as evidenced in phases 3 and 4 will be, at least in part, determined by the activities of phase 2.

PHASE 3: Full Spectrum War

Movies are made about this stage of war: The civilian and the soldier alike are heroic, tragic, and memorable. The role of religion seems simple: bury the dead, memorialize the fallen. The role of ethics seems equally simple: Hold the line. Neither could be further from the truth.

The conduct of war will give clear evidence of the ethical foundations built in phases 0 and 1. Ethicists speak of the laws of war and rightly so;

the actual conduct of a war will be a reflection of the concerns of basic social justice in phase 0, the threat perceptions, definition of enemy and calculations of just war in phase 1, and the emotions and behaviors evidenced in phase 2. These predispose a people to levels and types of violence that differ across wars. In this phase, concerns of the laws of war are the paramount concern of practitioners and scholars alike.

The ethical concerns at this phase of warfare, well known and oft-repeated, form the basis for the rules of armed conflict. These rules are taught to regular military forces and monitored by appropriate authority. However, there are two major concerns: First, they are also often obeyed in the breech, meaning that tactical operations are obscured by the passions of war; and, second, they do not address counterinsurgency as clearly as formalized warfare. The just war criteria at phases 2 and 3 are generally referred to as the rules of:

- Proportionality: The violence used in the war must be proportional to the injury suffered.
- Weapons: The weapons used in war must discriminate between combatants and noncombatants.
- Civilian status: Civilians are never permissible targets of war, and every effort must be taken to avoid killing civilians. The deaths of civilians are justified only if they are unavoidable victims of a deliberate attack on a military target.

Religious leaders, the believing public, and civilian leadership state that they are committed to winning the war, often adding the stipulation that winning might come at any cost and even if the definition of win is not clear. Certainly defeating the enemy and having the enemy admit wrongdoing is paramount in the minds of most people. In churches, synagogues, and mosques, there are prayers for the men and women in uniform; there are also prayers for peace, and the advocacy for winning against the forces of evil by defeating the enemy.

Religious leaders may contribute to warfare in this phase if they (1) justify different kinds of violence (ethnic, terrorism, insurgency, criminal, genocide, interstate war); (2) provide rationale for escalation of lethality (severity, intensity, scope, duration, and protractedness); (3) support invention of new weaponry and tactics designed to inflict maximum suffering (aerial bombing, daisy cutters, chemical or biological weapons); (4) justify injustice (ignoring short term vs. long term consequences); (5) dehumanize the enemy (justifying activities such as torture and harsh interrogation); and (6) provide the patriotic, sacrificial language and symbolism that mixes religious motivation with political motivation, to provide hope and inspiration for individuals facing death and destruction.[19] All of these reference just war principles, especially those related to proportionality and the targeting of civilians.

Religious leaders often publically state that a current war is a just war and that justice in war is something that one side has that the other doesn't. Statements to the contrary are deemed unpatriotic, and any questioning of the war effort is seen as not supporting the troops. The return of bodies to the family and subsequent burial are rituals meant as much for public consumption as for the families. Former Defense Secretary Cheney decided in 1991 that no pictures could be taken of the flag-draped caskets at Dover Air Force Base. It was reported that he believed the pictures to be demoralizing of the war effort, but the official reason given was that it was out of respect for the families. There were two major responses: Pictures were smuggled out in great quantity, and families felt deprived of the public and private honor due their fallen son or daughter.

Many people in the United States and around the world were shocked by the pictures of Abu Ghraib and Guantanamo. There was a short public outcry, and then torture became reinterpreted as interrogation with acceptable limits if used on an unrighteous enemy. Unbelievably, US churches and church leaders said very little publicly. The voices were silent, forgetting that the First and Fifth Amendment to the US Constitution were written precisely because torture based on religious identity and belief had been a common complaint leveled against the English and French. In 2004, some clergy even took positions such as "sometimes torture is necessary in the course of a war"; "war is war and there is nothing you can do about it"; "trust the government—we have responsible men of faith in this Christian government"; and "we will take care of the victims."[20] Only later, when scholars and intelligence professionals provided materials indicating that good intelligence was not related to pain and that torture itself might be counterproductive to national security, did religious leaders admit that it just might not be a good idea. The movement toward more professional treatment of enemy combatants, terrorists, or suspects was a long time coming—and was always subject to reversal when threat was perceived as immediate and costly. Revenge was escalated to the idea of justice.[21] Certainly the decisions made throughout this period were not based in ethical concerns, but in pragmatic terms of winning. The idea that many of the interrogation victims were technically noncombatants seemed to escape most observers, as were the principles of proportionality, since one group had ultimate power where the other was powerless. Ethical behavior and legal behavior related to the laws of armed conflict often seemed to be suspended.

However, men and women of faith were often truth-tellers, adhering to standards of personal and professional ethics. As only one of many examples, it has been reported that the army reservist who blew the whistle on Abu Ghraib was a man who simply believed that it was morally wrong.[22] In many cases, an individual stood up to what he believed were actions inimicable to his faith. What is notable is that institutions were not as courageous as individuals.

During phase 3 the operational forces—soldier, sailor, marine or airman—maintain what might be called an adrenaline high. Energy, focus, commitment, and devotion to duty are mobilized in support of the war effort. It is reminiscent of Jean V. de Bueil's writing in 1466:

> What a joyous thing is war . . . When one sees that one's quarrel is just and one's blood is fighting well, a tear comes to the eye. There comes to the heart a sweet feeling of loyalty and pity to see one's friend, who so valiantly exposes his body in order to do and accomplish the command of our Creator. And then one is disposed to go and live or die with him, and for love not at all abandon him. From that comes such a delectation, that he who has not tried it is a man who cannot say what a delight is. Do you think that a man who does that fears death? Not at all: for he is so comforted, he is so elated that he does not know where he is. Truly he fears nothing.[23]

Books such as *The Faith of the American Soldier* by Stephen Mansfield speak of the American soldier as the new crusader and encourage soldiers to keep the knight's vigil: the ceremony of cleansing, meditation, and sacrifice. "He should then consider the sacred words: Bless this sword, so that it may be a defense for churches, widows, and orphans and for all servants of God against the fury of the heathen," Mansfield writes. "He is to be a knight, chosen, destined, anointed by his God. It is a sacred thing. 'Lord make me worthy,' he prays and then, in the concluding silence, *Deus vult*. God wills it."[24]

The US military chaplaincy has been remarkable in its commitment to both God and country during the Iraqi and Afghanistan conflicts. Chaplain service is a unique part of the secular state in that US military chaplains are the only official service component with dual loyalty (not equal loyalty) to God and country. Although their duty is simple in its focus— serve the men and women on the battlefield—the underlying concept is a bit more complicated. According to the Joint Publication 1–05, Religious Affairs in Joint Operations, military chaplains must serve to protect freedom of religion and provide religious services to all service personnel. This directive adds the requirement that chaplains be qualified and able to give commanders advice on religious matters in the area of operations. This basically means that the joint staff recognizes the role of religion in the current conflicts, understands that neither the intelligence community nor the operational forces have sufficient understanding of religious factors, and asks their resident religious experts to become trained and proficient in world religions.[25] In many cases chaplains, through both specific reporting requirements and a ministry of presence, have been visible actors in supporting the rules of armed conflict and have spoken openly of *jus in bello*.

The average length of a war is approximately four to five years.[26] After going through phases 0–3, the protagonists are spent, the public has either become weary or lost its focus, the costs of the war have accumulated, and everyone wants peace. The wounds of war are in the bodies of the men and women and children. But equally important is the cost of the war in terms of its original justification and the ethical conduct of the war. Can hope be restored? Did people behave as human beings responsible to a higher authority? Was violence minimized? How was the war fought? The importance of these questions is simply whether life can be restored. That requires hope. But hope is not a course of action. In sum, these are the problems that are taken into phase 4.

PHASE 4: Stability and Support, Demobilization

This phase (building on previous phases) is a critical juncture for evaluating whether the ultimate goal of a just war is to establish a peace that is preferable to the peace that would have prevailed if the war had not been fought. However, more things can go wrong at this phase than perhaps any of the others. All of the good intentions of phases 0–3 can be undermined if the actions at this time are uninformed or simply clumsy. Stabilization is a process, not an end state, and comes at the diminishment rather than the cessation of hostilities. As stated in Joint Publication 3–0, these operations typically begin with significant "military involvement to include some combat, then move increasingly toward enabling civil authority . . . [and] increase the focus on supporting the efforts of host nation authorities, OGAs, IGOs, and/or NGOs." National Security Presidential Directive 44 assigns the US State Department the responsibility to plan and coordinate US government efforts in stabilization and reconstruction. These activities are to be interagency, and include elimination of root causes or deficiencies that created the problems by strengthening civil authority, rebuilding government institutions, fostering a sense of confidence and well-being, and supporting conditions for economic reconstruction. This also implies an initial realignment of military forces relative to the new mission, often referred to as stability and support operations. Near the end of this period, military forces leave—generally before stabilization results in true security.

Stabilization efforts by both military and civilians are hindered by complexity, attitude (the military breaks things and then civilians have to fix them), the human consequences of warfare, a requirement to rebuild and restructure the economy, and the difficulties involved with reinstituting or inventing a new system of governance.

The civilians working in stabilization and reconstruction are generally considered to be good people with fine motivation, as well as sophisticated skills. Many are religiously motivated, have strong faith traditions, and want to use the power of religion to transform the battlefield. What they have not systematically studied is how each phase of the war transformed the people in differing ways. The military is not very good at teaching them the realities of warfare—nor is that their job. There are serious consequences of going into a complex war zone without a good understanding of the nature of the conflict. The participants need to know about the uses and abuses of just war principles from phase 0–3 in order to react with sensitivity and intelligence. In other words, the activities of the first three phases will help determine what needs to be done, how long it will take, and whether there is a chance for a peaceful outcome.

Phase 4 often sees a breakdown in public morality and orderliness to the extent that the justification of the war and the conduct of war were in accordance with ethical principles. This phase is actually one of the most dangerous for civilian populations. Criminal activities may proliferate along with a black market, gangs, money laundering, prostitution, price gouging, and drug-related activities. The result is that security forces move between force and persuasion in response to civilian violence. Violence may escalate, encouraging police repression. All of this is occurring at the same time a government is emerging that must gain legitimacy over coercive force in relationship to the rule of law and the realities of justice. This creates an even more insecure environment for the people of the country at a time when the war supposed to be over.

It is generally acknowledged that religious organizations are useful on the battlefield when they deliver food and relief supplies, and subsequently play a significant role in peace and reconciliation. When religious groups and other nongovernmental organizations (NGOs) appear in the battle zone during phases 3 and 4, they are often considered distractions and made to feel less than welcome. At phase 5, NGOs are welcomed with open arms as the transfer of military to civilian responsibilities occurs.[27]

The cast of religious characters has changed: At phases 0 and 1, religious leaders contribute to the framing and mobilization of war. At the height of kinetic activities (phases 2 and 3) they are intrinsically involved in supporting the war effort. By war's end, religious leaders (either new people or those who have changed their minds during the course of the war) jump in, roll up their sleeves, and help work toward peaceful settlement and resolution. This is generally at a micro level, person to person, and includes mainly humanitarian efforts such as work with refugees, medical facilities, feeding stations, water and sanitation works, and management of resources. Activities move from crisis response to working with the human factor—that is, trying to find the sources of conflict, identify protagonists, support negotiation of differences, and generally root out the causes of violence and fix them.

Typical suggestions about how to do this are found in many publications, institutions, organizations, and classrooms. For example, Scott Appleby articulately proposes three modes of conflict transformation (overlapping phases 3, 4, and 5): the crisis mobilization mode, saturation mode, and interventionist mode.[28] What is important is that religious leaders, institutions, and academics are aware of the potential power of peace actors—people and processes with a religious base that work toward a more stable, peaceful environment from the ground up. These efforts, if coordinated and complementary to the efforts led by the government and military, could and should lead to a more durable peace. What often happens is that the government, military, and host government, along with indigenous groups, religious institutions, intergovernmental organizations (IGOs), and NGOs, all want the same thing—but have different ways of reaching the desired end state. The confusion can be debilitating and discouraging, and the results may not be commensurate with the effort. The number of outsiders in the battle space or area of operations tends to annoy military commanders, but in the long run may be beneficial in that the more outsiders observe, the less likely random violence can occur.

Interestingly enough, on the home front, religious actors (often in association with peace activists) choose this time to conduct peace protests. The cost of war is put in front of the people in the form of dramatized symbols. The causes of the war are either forgotten or revised. People who supported going to war in the first phase now march in protest of the seemingly wanton killing. Politicians ask for accountability. The churches and clergy pray for peace, lasting peace, and durable peace. Sympathy for veterans replaces honor for the soldiers. These activities continue into phase 5.

PHASE 5: Peace and Conflict Resolution

The ultimate goal of a just war is to reestablish peace. More specifically, the peace established after the war must be preferable to the peace that would have prevailed if the war had not been fought. Phase 5 is when joint operations are terminated, and when the stated military strategic and operational objectives have been met and the joint forces have been redeployed. This should mean that a legitimate civil authority has been enabled to manage the situation without further military assistance. It cannot be a return to phase 0, but it must nevertheless be socially transformative. There are two reasons: Phase 0 may not have been a just system for the society to begin with, and war changes things.

There are several military options: leave without much ado, transfer power officially to civil authority, support truce negotiations, or arrange a transfer to civil authority. The peacebuilding effort is believed to work if the civilian authorities can assert proper control and develop appropriate actions that build transparency and legitimacy in the reinstitution of legitimate governance. It is important at this stage for military forces to exercise restraint, obey rules of engagement, to persevere, and work to sustain civilian authority. The optimal situation is for civilian, government, and military forces to work as a team.

At this point, the winning side has several challenges. For instance, how to treat the population—the former enemy—that now looks human, and may have even been created by the same supreme being? Furthermore, how is the winning side to reconcile the costs, both human and financial, to the folks back home? How should wounded veterans be treated when they return—as patriots and heroes, or sacrificial lambs? Is it easier to build a monument to the dead rather than continue the cost of the war by having to support injured veterans? Religious leaders and institutions play a role in these discussions and in the decisions that follow.

There are many conflict resolution organizations that come into the operational area at this time, including individual practitioners, church organizations, universities, and the United States government. The US government supports the US Institute of Peace. Each of the military services teaches and trains for conflict negotiation and management in the civil affairs organizations or cultural studies groups. NGOs and IGOs are financially supported by the US government. Religious groups seem to be particularly self-righteous at this stage, but are effective to the extent that they work with religious leaders in the war zone.[29]

Phase 5 brings harsh realization on the home front: The costs in terms of lives and national wealth is at the forefront of public consciousness. Body bags, caskets, worn instruments of death, and pictures of devastated cities are played in the press as the toll of war. Then the "I told you so," "I never knew," and "I was mislead" statements come fast and furious. It is hard to find anyone who was for the war—ever—who will admit it.

Two things happen in quick succession: (1) the spending of lives is stopped, with soldiers demobilized and troops shipped home; and (2) spending of national wealth becomes an issue. For example, the following statement was made in April 2010:

> This week, conservative Sen. Tom Coburn, R-Okla., encouraged the president's fiscal responsibility commission to freeze defense spending and institute other reforms aimed at eventually cutting the military budget. Total Pentagon spending is higher today in inflation-adjusted dollars than at any time during the last 60 years . . . [t]his spending item that takes up 56 percent of our discretionary spending—defense. Conservatives, in their much-needed attacks on federal overspending, too often give the Pentagon a pass. For the budget of fiscal 2011, taxpayers are spending $708 billion on defense. Maybe it seems unpatriotic to criticize our military spending. Maybe it seems like you're not supporting the troops to look for defense cuts. But as a tribute to our soldiers, sailors and airmen this Memorial Day weekend, let's start dismantling the military-industrial complex that saps our wealth without helping our troops.[30]

Of significant concern are those ethical concerns that carry over from earlier phases: Was the war justified? Were there alternatives to war that were not considered? Was the war fought in regard to proportionality? Were the laws of war followed? And what are—or should be, or could be—the penalty for the countries, leaders, and individuals, who did not behave in accordance with ethical principles? This is a period where the terms justice, retribution, reconciliation, restoration, and forgiveness become important parts of the conversation. It is a time of sad reckoning when the war's costs, in human terms, are assessed in relationship to possible futures and we must ask whether it was worth it.

Something little noted and discussed is the effect that this entire conversation about ethics, just war, codes of conduct, and public perceptions has on individual service personnel. There is some evidence that if there is dissonance between an individual's ideals and what they expect from themselves and their actual behavior in war—if they participated in cruelty, ignored the laws of armed conflict, or otherwise did not live up to their own ideals—they may be more susceptible to posttraumatic stress disorder as they try to reconcile their beliefs with their behavior.[31] This is yet another good reason for a society to be stubbornly involved with the ethical principles and practices of war and to clearly state to those who fight their wars how going to war is consistent with the ideals that society values.

Conclusion

The ethical foundation for how war is conducted is built long before the first airplane flies, the first ship sails, or the first bullet is fired. In all of the phases of warfare, ethics is evidenced in religious beliefs and behaviors, which play an integral role in the actions and behaviors of the participants, whether military or civilian. It can be a force for killing or a force for peace—or both. It is never simply neutral.

The religious community cannot see itself as distant and divorced from war, as if war was not their business except to bind up the wounds after the damage has been done or to present themselves as self-righteous peace builders that come late into the war. They cannot behave as if they were the only ethical, moral, and spiritual leaders with truth on their side—an attitude clearly resented by the military leaders who must bear the very personal burden of the decisions they make on behalf of the society they protect.

The evaluation of whether or not a war was just or fought justly cannot be left to historians to write about years later. Conscious and continuous evaluation by clear-headed and clear-eyed ethical leaders is required at each phase—from the time a war is contemplated to the time of its end. Course corrections are only possible in the present tense. It is the responsibility of every citizen, civilian and military, to constantly question the rightness of the cause and the rightness of the actions in any time of war. The reason is simple: Human beings can get carried away individually or in groups and lose sight of who they are and who they want to be as individuals, friends, neighbors, citizens, and before God. Mistakes of omission and commission are costly in terms of life and death of both body and soul.

Just war traditions help, but they do not guarantee righteousness. The blame or honor—if there is any—for war itself and for how war is conducted must be laid at the feet of every individual.

Notes

1. This is clearly an anthropological approach to the issue; I do not mean to imply that religion and ethics are the same, only that the study of one can be used to approach the study of the other.

2. This may be a little confusing because phase 0 is counted as a phase; see the illustration on page 100.

3. The content of the phases roughly corresponds to the military historian's practice of focusing on before, during, and after (with so-called shoulders of mobilization and demobilization.)

4. Joint Publication 3–0 and other reference materials can be easily accessed at www.archives.gov/publications/lists/topic-military.html.

5. Change during a war has been addressed by most of the major theorists including Sun Tzu and Clausewitz, and acknowledged by every military planner.

6. Paul Mojzes, ed., *Religion and War in Bosnia* (Atlanta, GA: Scholars Press, 1998); S. J. Tambiah, *A Performative Approach to Ritual* (Oxford: Oxford University Press, 1979); and Jean Hatzfeld, *The Machete Season: The Killers in Rwanda Speak* (New York: Farrar, Straus and Giroux, 2003).

7. Most of the examples used in this chapter are related to the contemporary experiences of the United States; however, as in any comparative approach, it is assumed that useful examples could be drawn from any other country's war history.

8. In the military community these factors are studied as indications and warnings of possible violence.

9. John D. Carlson, John D. Owens, and Erik C. Owens, eds., *The Sacred and the Sovereign* (Washington, DC: Georgetown University Press, 2003).

10. Twain believed that humanism and Christianity's preaching of love were incompatible with the conduct of war. *The War Prayer* was submitted to *Harper's Bazaar* for publication, but on March 22, 1905, the magazine rejected the story as "not quite suited to a woman's magazine." Twain said, "I don't think the prayer will be published in my time. None but the dead are permitted to tell the truth." The prayer and tale can be found at Jim Zwick, ed., *Mark Twain's Weapons of Satire: Anti-Imperialist Writings on the Philippine-American War* (Syracuse: Syracuse University Press, 1992), 162.

11. John Mueller, "Simplicity and Spook: Terrorism and the Dynamics of Threat Exaggeration," *International Studies Perspectives* 6, no. 2 (2005): 209.

12. Peter Singer, *The President of Good and Evil: Questioning the Ethics of George W. Bush* (New York: Penguin Books, 2004).

13. Christopher Coker, *Religion and Ethics* (New York: Routledge, 2007).
14. *Fox News Sunday,* June 15, 2003.
15. There are seventeen major US intelligence organizations with as many as 30,000 employees in Washington, DC, alone. The intelligence community is important to this argument because it helps provide information that the national leadership uses to define the enemy and assess capabilities. Both are integral to just war requirements.
16. Note Pentagon publications such as *Radical Islamist Ideologies and the Long War: Implications for U.S. Strategic Planning.* Defense Threat Reduction Agency, 2007. Pub: HDTRA1–06-F-0054. These publications clearly identified Islam as the enemy in written materials, pictures, and associated PowerPoint presentations. Later documents were more tempered in their approach.
17. Tim LeHaye, *Left Behind: A Novel of the Earth's Last Days* (Colorado Springs: Alive Publications, 1995).
18. Hector Avalo, *Fighting Words: The Origins of Religious Violence* (New York: Prometheus Books, 2005).
19. For the purposes of this chapter, *severity* is the number of killed and injured, *intensity* is the number killed in a specific period of time, *scope* refers to the area, *duration* refers to the period of fighting or conflict resulting in death and injury, and *protractedness* refers to the increase in the difficulty of resolving problems associated with the underlying causality of conflict.
20. These statements were made by religious authorities, found in public media, and related in personal discussions to the author using an informal interview technique between 2004 and 2006.
21. For more on this subject, see *Educing Information*, a publication sponsored by the Intelligence Science Board and published by the National Defense Intelligence College. It is not classified and is available on line at www.fas.org/irp/dni/educing.pdf (December 2006), last accessed November 2011.
22. As widely reported in December 2006.
23. Jean V. de Beueil, *Le Jouvencel* [The Youth] (Paris: Librairie Renouard, H. Laurens 1871, [1466]). The complete text is freely available online at www.archive.org/details/lejouvencelparj00clergoog. Accessed November 16, 2011.
24. Stephen Mansfield, *The Faith of the American Soldier* (New York: Penguin, 2005), preface.
25. Pauletta Otis, "More than a War of Ideas: Ideology, Theology and Religion," in *Ideas as Weapons: Influence and Perception in Modern Warfare,* eds. G. J. David Jr. and T. McKeldin III (Arlington, VA: Potomac Press, 2008).
26. Ann Hironaka, *Neverending Wars: The International Community, Weak States, and the Perpetuation of Civil War* (Cambridge, MA: Harvard University Press, 2005), 3.
27. The Department of Defense has a certification process that NGOs use in order to legitimately work with the US Government. See www.Interaction.Org for more information on this topic.
28. Scott R. Appleby, *Ambivalence of the Sacred: Religion, Violence, and Reconciliation* (Lanham, MD: Rowman & Littlefield, 2000).

29. Bruce Wilshire, *Get 'Em All! Kill 'Em!: Genocide, Terrorism and Righteous Communities* (Lanham, MD: Rowman & Littlefield, 2006).

30. Timothy P. Carney, "War on the Military Industrial Complex," *The Washington Examiner* (June 9, 2010), page A7.

31. Jonathan Shay, *Achilles in Vietnam: Combat Trauma and the Undoing of Character* (New York: Scribners, 1994).

CHAPTER 7

JUST WAR AND AN ETHICS OF RESPONSIBILITY

JEAN BETHKE ELSHTAIN

JUST WAR IS NOT JUST ABOUT WAR. It is about a way of thinking about political life more generally, especially where the use of coercive force is contemplated and, sometimes, activated. The political vision or framework that just war is nestled within and helps to constitute is best called an ethic of responsibility. The just war position carves out territory that puts it at odds with hard-core realpolitik of the sort embodied in the infamous Melian dialogue in Thucydides's classic *The Peloponnesian War*, where the Athenian generals declare high-handedly to the hapless Melians that "the mighty do what they will and the weak suffer what they must."[1] Just war is also at odds with the claims embodied in pacifism as a possible stance for statecraft, understanding Martin Luther's musings that if the lion lies down with the lamb, the lamb must be replaced frequently.[2]

For this chapter my focus is twofold. First, I consider an ethic of responsibility rooted in the just war tradition, applied to late- and postconflict questions: an ethics of exit. I will specifically consider applicable just war principles such as order, justice, and restraint for postconflict consideration, and how they work in conditions of occupation and political rehabilitation as in the cases of Germany, Japan, and Iraq. Second, I will examine whether there are forms of authentic political forgiveness—not aloofness, detachment, or the contrition chic of television talk shows—but rather acknowledging the past and moving into a changed future. I argue that such is possible, that the postconflict order can be buttressed by a knowing-forgetting that releases present-day agents from the full burden of the past so that they are not weighed down by it entirely.

An Ethic of Responsibility

Many questions immediately arise when one speaks of an ethic of responsibility: responsibility to whom? And over what? If our responsibilities are infinite—ideas of universal justice—we can never get a handle on ideas and events. We drift into the universal ether in which everyone is somehow responsible for everything. The just war tradition concretizes one area of responsibility: the responsibility of statesmen and stateswomen for their polities; the responsibility of one polity for another; the shared responsibility of all states to a system that helps to sustain a world of diverse bodies politic.

Post–World War II, this ethics of responsibility got built up on the ground of the universality of human rights, shared revulsion of genocide, and the cry of "never again" where certain horrors were concerned. This resulted in a series of legal and moral commitments such as the UN Charter, the Universal Declaration of Human Rights, the Geneva Conventions, and the Convention on Torture. With the Cold War's end, we should not be surprised, therefore, that a new period of disorder ensued as characterized by the killing fields of Bosnia and Rwanda. This resulted in the return of that theme of responsibility once again, articulated as the Responsibility to Protect (R2P) under the aegis of the United Nations. This ethic holds that should a nation or group of nations be the victims of systematic, egregious, and continuing violence, the international community has a responsibility to do something about that situation. If the UN refuses to act, it follows that a member state or states, if there is a widely shared consensus on the horrors being perpetrated, may act legitimately to interdict the violence and to contain the horror.[3]

Because it is always a good bet that the UN will be paralyzed, and because the European powers often talk a good game but are prepared to do very little by way of humanitarian intervention, as it is now called, even in situations where one could make a strong case that they are historically implicated (Rwanda would be a powerful case in point), it follows that it is often the United States, as the state with more power to project its power than any other, may be called upon or call upon itself to act. Be that as it may, this underlying norm of responsibility, with the Universal Declaration of Human Rights and the Genocide Convention as backdrop, is one feature of an overall ethics of responsibility.

To these statements of political responsibility one must add the just war tradition. What does just war theory tell us about the goals or ends of war? How are these related to an ethics of responsibility, including an ethics of exit if one has intervened in a given situation? The end of war must be related intrinsically to the argument for the deployment of armed force in the first place, namely to repair or remedy a major injustice or act of aggression and punish aggressors. Another just cause might be to prevent nigh-certain and massive harm from occurring before it has occurred—although this is a controversial claim, with just war thinkers divided on the preemptive and preventive use of force. But all agree that the goal of the justified use of force is a more just situation than the one that pertained before armed conflict.

In the classical theological accounts that inaugurated the just war tradition in the West, this more ideal state of things is referred to as a tranquility of order—a decent civic peace.[4] Rooted in Greco-Roman thinking about the rightly ordered society, Christian thinkers like Ambrose of Milan and Augustine of Hippo argued that the political system of this world could be an approximation of the City of God, and that the latter judged the failings of the former. This approximation was limited at best, but a decent civic peace did make possible essential human security and attendant public goods such as safe roads, science, the arts, and commerce. Even a modest version of this order would be vastly preferable to the lot of many in war-ravaged places like Darfur and eastern Congo.

With political order—defined in part by the leadership of legitimate authority—a desired end state in the just war tradition, a determining criterion for making a decision for the use of armed force is a prudential one: Do you stand a good chance of success? And how will this affect the existing order? One is never permitted to make a bad situation worse or, perhaps better put, one is obliged to do everything one can to prevent that sort of unhappy outcome. Given this rough and ready framework of evaluation, what does an ethic of responsibility to protect call us to do, particularly in situations where an intervening power is preparing to exit the country within which it has been functioning? In other words, my focus for the considerations that follow is an ethics of exit. If one adheres to just war norms and the responsibility to protect, what does one commit to? One might call this the ethics of a just intervention and occupation with eventual withdrawal of combat forces.

Before one begins to articulate the criteria for an ethics of exit consistent with just war thinking and an ethics of responsibility, one must have available a comprehensive and accurate description for the situation on the ground. This is notoriously tricky, as competing sides to a disputed war will characterize the situation in ways that best serve their own already stated conclusions concerning what is to be done. Within a tradition of moral reasoning known as realism (not to be confused with classical *raison d'etat*), the ethicist obliges himself and herself to details, to amassing as much knowledge as possible in any given situation.[5]

For example: At certain points in the Iraq War, we were told that Iraq was in the throes of a civil war and that, therefore, the United States was mired—and here the Vietnam analogy kicked in—in the midst of that civil war. The conclusion was reached that our presence only made matters worse and therefore we should peremptorily depart, forcing the Iraqis to come to terms even if many thousands died before that moment was reached. Obviously that scenario did not triumph. Described in a different way, the conclusion was that more rather than fewer US troops were needed; that there was no civil war but, rather, an insurrection trying to foment one; and, finally, that a precipitous withdrawal of American troops would, in fact, lead to an exponential leap in violence and that there would be no happy ending further down the line.

How we take account of real-world details is so often excised from consideration if one treats the just war tradition as simply a set of abstract propositions that one can, rather mechanically, tick off as one assays any given situation.[6] Instead, just war thinking is thicker than that; it is imbued within situations rather than being a thin layer painted over events. One must reason within the categories rather than applying them as a kind of abstract test. Given the eventual outcome in Iraq, it appears that those who determined that a buildup of US forces was needed in order to stabilize the situation and to prevent the horror of a full-scale civil war were right—that they more accurately and more concretely described the situation at hand.

What does just war theory tell us about the goals of war? I have already insisted that the goals or ends of war must be intrinsically related to the initial argument for conflict as couched in just war criteria—namely, to repair or to remedy a massive injustice and to punish aggressors. The goal, remember, is a more just situation than one that pertained before the resort to armed force. Given this rough and ready framework of evaluation, what does an ethics of exit require if one adheres to just war norms?

Here in schematic form are the criteria, consistent with just war, of an ethics of just occupation and exit as central features of an overall ethic of responsibility. The first is this: The country that has committed to military operations must assess its degree of responsibility for the postwar situation. If its role was major, its responsibility is significant. If, on the other hand, its role was minor, its responsibility is correlatively diminished. Certainly a major power should bring as many partners on board as possible when it commits to war, particularly given what we know of UN stalling and ineptitude where the brutalities of dictatorial regimes and the endemic horrors of failed states are concerned. Waiting for the UN in many of these circumstances may actually exacerbate the scenario, as in the case of Kosovo.

Second, the country engaged in major military operations also bears a major burden in repairing the infrastructural and environmental harm that is the direct result of military operations. For example: Civilian teams should concentrate on the basic necessities of life first—water and electricity. Then attention can be paid to schools, hospitals, and the other basic institutions of society. These are the first steps toward the tranquility of order, the roots of any decent civic order.

Third, repair of the political infrastructure is necessary if the point of a just war is a just peace. This means leaving the people in the country that was the site of conflict in better shape than before the intervention. This country in question should be rehabilitated to return as a full member of the international community, adhering to certain minimal norms as such. I call this an ideal of minimally decent states. Of course, there are many states that are far from minimally decent, but one aim of intervention and exiting ethically should be to do what one can to position a new regime as belonging in the camp of the minimally decent.

Minimal decency is far too modest a goal for many, and far too idealistic a goal for others. That should not surprise us given that just war thinking weaves its complex way in between various utopians, on the one hand,

and hard-core political realists, on the other. There is a delicate balancing act involved here as one labors to restore authority—only this time *legitimate* authority. The worst possible outcome of an intervention is a scenario reminiscent of Chapter XIII of Hobbes's great classic *Leviathan*, a world within which human life is "nasty, brutish, and short."[7] The international community has a huge stake in the outcome and should play a helpful—not a blocking or undermining—role. Failed states pose as much of a threat to international peace as rogue states.

Fourth, continued provision must be made for defense and security. If a country has been disarmed, the occupying power has taken on responsibility for its security and protection from external and internal enemies. How long this provision will be, and how extensive, will depend on threat assessment and the rapidity with which the country occupied rebuilds its own defense and internal security capability.

Fifth, a major interest and responsibility should be to deter the reemergence—to stay with the example of Iraq—of yet another Saddam Hussein–type republic of fear. The complexity is that deterrence necessarily bears both an internal as well as an external aspect as one reflects on *jus post bellum*. The way that the United States protected Western Europe (including a new German democratic state) throughout the Cold War and the decades of bipolarity, from both internal revanchism as well as external threats, is a case in point. So, too, today, the United States, as one feature of having exited ethically, must remain tied to a new Iraq in ways that are thick. In other words, just as the Allies would never have permitted a Nazi state to reemerge in Germany, so we have a responsibility, should internal forces of stability and decency falter and collapse, to do the same in Iraq—and, by extension, in any analogous situation in the future, lest the Iraqi (or some other) people be victimized many times over. Of course, this particular example of Iraq yields a more general conclusion along these lines. I suspect that if such *jus post bellum* criteria are debated and considered explicitly as part of the overall set of issues attendant upon a decision to deploy armed force (*jus ad bellum*), it would add much to the gravamen of the situation. That is entirely appropriate from an ethical point of view.

If the Bush administration was correct—and I think it was—that the September 11, 2001, attacks and the terrorist attacks of the 1990s underscored the fact that we were in a new strategic environment, it followed and follows that our thinking about war and peace must take account of that new environment. Throughout the years of the Cold War there were many just causes that could not be addressed, could not be pursued militarily—for example, open intervention in behalf of the Hungarian freedom fighters in 1956—because of the terrible dangers of a nuclear exchange between the superpowers.

But today many of the old constraints of the bipolar world no longer exist. We are in the process of building new constraints and considering new responsibilities, and considering what those might be in this new situation. Many of these constraints will be self-imposed because we do not face, at this point, a major foe who threatens us directly and explicitly. It follows that it is altogether a good thing that we have available to us a tradition of restraint when the cause is just, and that the *jus post bellum* we are talking about is a continuation of that tradition of ethical reflection and restraint. At the same time, reflection and restraint do not mean paralysis, they do not mean inaction, and they do not mean moral condemnation only. There is an active dimension that must be considered. In short, an ethics of responsibility calls for action; condemnation alone does not suffice in some situations.[8]

There are many who, in the aftermath of the Cold War, have lamented that the insecurity that ensued in some regions meant that traditional restraints on the use of armed force had been abandoned. But that is not the case. Certainly so long as our discussions of these matters take place in and through categories of the just war tradition, then embedded restraints are undeniable—they are there. We must continue to think through them and with them.

Where further elaboration is necessary is in the *jus post bellum* phase of the conflict, in part because so many of our images of postwar and postoccupation situations are somewhat archaic. The past provides two primary angles of vision regarding the goals of postconflict and an ethics of exit.

There is, first, the argument that the purpose of war is restoration of the status quo *ante bellum*. The model is a familiar one: State A has invaded state B. State B mobilizes and fights back. State A is deterred and sues for peace. State B calls for a restoration of violated borders, namely, status quo *ante bellum*. There is a variation, too. State B, claiming it is the victim of unjust aggression, insists that State A must be punished.

The treaty settling the conflict punishes State A by annexing part of its territory to State B, or insisting that State A pay reparations, and so on. This is commonplace. But status quo *ante bellum* is not, for the most part, what contemporary *jus post bellum* is about if a conflict was one aimed at overthrowing a dangerous and oppressive tyranny. Perhaps state borders will remain the same, but little else.[9]

The second model, one with which we are most familiar in these circumstances, has a historic lineage—namely, the occupations of Germany and Japan after World War II. The German occupation was marred by the fact that a tyranny responsible for the deaths of even more people than Hitler's Germany, Stalin's Soviet Union, was one of the occupiers. It is a bit difficult to speak of just occupation in such circumstances.

Be that as it may, on the Western side of the alliance, the aim was a stable, democratic German regime and state: a minimally decent state plus, one might say. That aim was achieved in Germany. In Japan something occurred that would nowadays be unthinkable: one powerful Western country writing a constitution for a conquered state. This would look too much like hubris to us now, and we might even question the legitimacy of such a regime. But in the case of Japan, the outcome was a stable, constitutional democracy. There is no enthusiasm in Japan, and there has not been such since the conclusion of World War II, for restoration of a highly militarist and autocratic society.

Neither the status quo nor the transformation models discussed above quite cover our current situation. We need a third model, one that looks to the creation of minimally decent, stable states and that relies to a great extent on certain processes of democracy to achieve the end of minimal decency. I refer to such things as elections, representative assemblies, consultative coalitions, and constitution writing. This path is fraught with difficulties; it is cumbersome, and it virtually guarantees a period of uncertainty and instability. But the outcome, if things work out, is the vesting of a new government with the legitimacy it would otherwise lack, particularly in conflicts involving countries with distinct and striking cultural histories and differences.

Political Forgiveness: "Knowing Forgetting"

When the political theorist Hannah Arendt called forgiveness the greatest contribution of Jesus of Nazareth to politics, she surely did not have in mind an individual figure crying: "Can you forgive me?"[10] And, obviously, the spectacle that unfolds on daytime television in America every day was far from her mind, a spectacle she would have denounced as vulgar and beneath contempt. Rather, she was gesturing toward a way for repetitive cycles of vengeance to be broken; for the often deadly playing-out of horrible deeds done and equally horrible vengeance or payback sought to be disrupted by an unexpected act that opens up space for something new to begin that alters the horizon of expectations in some way, introducing the possibility that bloody deeds will not haunt generation upon generation, dooming sons and daughters to repeat the sins of fathers and mothers.[11]

Although individual acts of forgiveness—one human being to another—most often take place outside the full glare of publicity, there are others that are noteworthy. One thinks here of Pope John Paul II who, having barely survived an assassin's bullets, uttered his first public words from his hospital bed to his violent assailant, addressing him as "my brother, whom I have sincerely forgiven," words that were later followed by the pope's extraordinary visit to his brother and would-be killer in jail. Of course, the pope did not draw from this act of forgiveness an argument that his attacker be released from prison, for the civil authorities also have their job to do. But the point is that there is a gravitas manifest in this narrative that is altogether lacking in American quasi-therapeutic, talk show–type confessions that are most often blatantly self-exculpatory rather than expressive of a demanding faith, Christianity in this instance, the faith of which forgiveness is a constitutive dimension.[12] Pope John Paul was practicing what Greg L. Jones calls the "craft of forgiveness," and in so doing, displayed to the world the ways in which forgiveness is not primarily about a singular confessional moment, but about an enactment within a particular way of life: a way of life shaped not by a foggy sentimentalism, but by certain hard-won and difficult truths.[13]

Despite the power of the pope's example, it seems odd to think of it as a political intervention. Moreover, I doubt that this is quite what Hannah Arendt had in mind when speaking of political forgiveness. She was more concerned with interrupting a flow of events that seems to be on autopilot when mass murder, acts of retribution, and then more acts of killing become just the business as usual, so to speak.

Within the frame of such broad-based events, often driven by political purpose, individuals who are shaped by the practice of forgiveness should try to practice what they believe or preach. But only exceedingly rarely can an individual by himself or herself stem the rushing tide of violence. Are there, then, forms of authentic *political* forgiveness? Who forgives whom and for what? Remember that forgiveness is not a one-way street; it implies a relationship or some transitive dimension. Forgiveness in general is not primarily about self-exculpation in any case, as per pop culture distortion, but about the creation of a new relationship or order of things, the restoration of an order of things, or the healing of a relationship that has been broken or torn by violence, cruelty, or indifference. That is why forgiveness primarily takes place between persons, or perhaps small communities.

Forgiveness is also something quite different from aloofness or detachment—just not giving a damn—which is also mistakenly presented nowadays as a form of forgiveness. What is at stake, then, is a tougher discipline by far than public acts of easy repentance, and forgiveness proffered as a kind of willed amnesia. How does one sift such matters? Political forgiveness must have a public dimension, for politics itself is public speech of a certain kind. Further, when people sincerely try to make amends it would be churlish to withhold from them any possibility that what they say or do might make any difference in the future. Perhaps one key to our discussion lies here. The public repentance of a political figure—an act related to forgiveness, certainly—cannot simply be a matter of words. Words and deeds cannot be disentangled: "by their deeds ye shall know them."[14] Again, this is far easier to conjure with and even to see on the level of individual transformation than anything like forgiveness between nation-states or warring political parties or factions. Here the sheer weight and density of history seems at times intractable: How can one get past a particularly horrible series of events? Doesn't one have to punish people before one can move on? Forgiveness of a strongly political or public sort presumes communities, places, and histories of a tangible, concrete sort. Real issues are involved and the stakes are often high, up to and including entire peoples who are crying to heaven against specific injustices and horrors. Justice is often the issue and justice should be served.

When Arendt lamented the ways in which events take on a cyclical and repetitive quality, it was history or a particular version of it she surely had in her sights. People are very fond of citing the philosopher George Santayana's claim that those who don't know their history are doomed to repeat it. But perhaps the reverse is more likely: namely, that it is those who know their history too well who are doomed to repetition. Perhaps a certain amount of knowing-forgetting is necessary in order to elude the rut of repetition.[15] If a people's collective horizon is limited to the re-encoding of past glories or horrors, the past eviscerates any possibility of future transformation. By knowing-forgetting, then, I have in mind a way to release present-day agents from the full burden of the past, in order that they not be weighed down by it utterly.[16]

Forgetting, in this case, does not mean that one falls into radical present-mindedness and the delusion that the past counts for nothing; rather, one assesses and judges just what the past does count for in the present—how much it should frame, shape, and even determine present events. As Lawrence Cahoone has pointed out, too much past overwhelms the future. But too little past empties the future, or the selves we carry into the future: "Beings without memory would have no need for retribution, but no identity either."[17]

Too often these days when forgiveness is mentioned, as I have already suggested, it gets translated into a kind of bland nonjudgmental sentiment: "There but for the grace of God go I," translated erroneously as "I can't say anything at all about anybody else's behavior and words." But if this is the tack one takes, forgiveness is altogether unnecessary. There can never be anything to forgive if no real wrong has been suffered, no real sin committed, no evil deed perpetrated, no record of historic injustices mounted. There are certain tendencies in modern liberal culture that push us along the route of cheap grace in these matters. We are all invited to validate one another incessantly, but never to offer correction and reproof—on the level of individual relationships and in the wider social and political arena, alike. One thinks here, for example, of the whole self-esteem movement dedicated, as it is, to the principle that any criticism and any insistence upon the maintenance of certain norms or standards be rejected as a form of harsh judgmentalism. Only bland affirmations that help us to put everything negative behind us will do. But those practicing the craft of forgiveness recognize in such affirmations a flight from the hard work of forgiveness rather than stirring examples of it. Moreover, forgiveness in public or political life also involves the painful recognition of the limits to forgiveness, if what one seeks is full expiation, a full accounting, total justice, or a kind of annihilation of the past. There are wrongs suffered that can never be put right. Indeed, this recognition is itself a central feature of an overall structure of political forgiveness, or so I want to suggest, for it opens up space for a person or a people to partially unburden themselves from the hold the past has on them.

Here is a concrete, if hypothetical, example of what I have in mind, beginning with what might be called the individual political level and then moving to tougher cases. Suppose that a young woman first becomes aware of the history of female inequality with all the many affronts and structures of encoded inequities to which women have been subjected in the past, including the history of her own culture. A feminist consciousness dawns. How does this past weigh upon her? If the past is read as nothing but a story of women's oppression, she will too easily take on the identity of a present-day victim, as if no forces have been involved in shaping her other than the concatenated effects of male dominance and perfidy. She will see the world solely through the lens of victimhood, a particular temptation in a culture that specializes in creating stock victims and in which claims to victimization carry special rhetorical resonance.[18] This invites, in turn, a politics of resentment and grievance-seeking, even retribution for past wrongs, that often gets called justice.

But there is another possibility. Aware of these past wrongs, the young woman in question becomes a champion of fairness and equity, understanding, as she does, that politically there are things that can be done to forestall future repetition of wrongs from which women have suffered in the past. But she also refuses to read the past as a doleful tale of nothing but—as if no women were villains, and no men anything other than villains. The past is not forgotten but is kept alive as a tradition that must be continuously engaged. She understands that her twenty-year-old male contemporary is not responsible for bringing the previous structure of dominance and power into being. But she is also alert to the need to assess and to judge his actions from the standpoint of current standards of fairness. This imposes a burden on her, too: the burden of accountability incumbent upon all free agents. Is forgiveness involved in this latter scenario? Forgiveness of a sort is involved, in the sense that the young woman relinquishes part of the burden of the past, or a highly skewed version of that past, not allowing it to define her within the vortex of fear, loathing, resentment, and victim identity. This, then, is a form of knowing-forgetting.

There are many examples one could turn to. How does a culture fully expiate for the Shoah? For slavery? Wrongs that cannot be wholly righted must, nonetheless, be acknowledged, and part of that acknowledgment will consist in a knowing and explicit articulation of the terrible fact that full expiation is impossible.[19] This is not forgetting as a type of collective amnesia; rather, it is an acknowledgment of the full scope of a given horror and the inability of a subsequent generation or generations, not themselves directly responsible for that horror, to put things right. The events stand. Acknowledgment of these events is required both by those directly implicated and by those who merely stood by and did nothing.

Remembrance of violent deeds goes forward in all its fullness and detail. A recounting of events serves as an ongoing judgment upon those most responsible, which is tied at the same time to a tragic recognition that some wrongs cannot be righted. This must have been what Arendt had in mind, at least in part. In her controversial book *Eichmann in Jerusalem*, she justified the hanging of Adolph Eichmann because he had perpetrated terrible crimes against humanity "on the body of the Jewish people"; but she did so in full recognition of the fact that no scale of justice had thereby been put right and that hanging every known Nazi war criminal could not do that.[20] Reversion to a strict *lex talionis* in cases of genocide, if one interprets that requirement as a strict tit-for-tat, would be hideous, implicating victims in perpetrating precisely the sorts of deeds that caused them so much suffering. Ironically, then, knowing-forgetting as one feature of a form of political forgiveness may be most apt, not only philosophically but politically, where truly horrific abuses are concerned. Thus, Arendt knew that young Germans, infants in the Hitler years or born subsequently, could not be held accountable in any direct way for what had occurred during their lifetimes. But they were obliged to remember in order that they could be free to act in other ways. This is knowing-forgetting: recollecting the past, yes, but not being so wholly defined by it that one's only option is either to be executioner or victim (in Albert Camus's memorable phrase), rather than an accountable human agent.

Here are a few recent concrete examples of the dynamic I have in mind. They take place in the most difficult of all arenas for the dynamic of forgiveness and knowing-forgetting to play out: namely, the realm of relations between peoples and states. But if forgiveness is to have real political weight as one feature of what it means to try to attain both justice and decent order and peace, it must be tested in many arenas. My first example is drawn from the bloody ground of Northern Ireland and its centuries-old troubled relationship with Great Britain. As everyone surely knows, Irish Catholics in Northern Ireland have long been a tormented people, relegated to second-class citizenship in what they perceive to be part of their land. But Irish Catholics, relatively powerless in the overall balance of what international relations thinkers refer to as strategic forces, have also been tormentors, as the history of IRA terrorism and death-dealing to British soldiers and to Northern Ireland Protestants attests.

It is, therefore, significant that one clear feature presaging the peace accord voted on in 1998 was the exchange of requests for forgiveness made by church leaders, both Anglican and Catholic, but most famously by Cardinal Cahal Daly of Armagh, Northern Ireland. On January 22, 1995, Cardinal Daly publicly asked forgiveness from the people of Britain in a homily delivered in Canterbury Cathedral, England, the seat of the primate of the Church of England, the Archbishop of Canterbury. Cardinal Daly's words on that occasion are worth pondering, especially with an eye to the vision of a horizon of justice and decent reciprocity embedded therein:

> We Irish are sometimes said to be obsessively concerned with memories of the past. It is salutary, however, to recall that the faults we attribute to others can be a projection of faults within ourselves which we have not had the courage to confront. . . . What is certainly true is that we all need a *healing of memories* [emphasis mine]. Healing of memories demands recognition of our own need for forgiveness; it requires repentance. The original biblical term for repentance, *metanoia*, is a strong word indicating the need for radical conversion, change of attitude, change of outlook, change of stance; and all this is costing and can be painful. The old word contrition expresses it well. . . . This healing, this conversion, this reciprocal giving and accepting of forgiveness are essential elements in the healing of relationships between our two islands and between our divided communities in Northern Ireland. . . . On this occasion . . . I wish to ask forgiveness

from the people of this land for the wrongs and hurts inflicted by Irish people upon the people of this country on many occasions during that shared history, and particularly in the past twenty-five years. I believe that this reciprocal recognition of the need to forgive and to be forgiven is a necessary condition for proper Christian, and human, and indeed *political relationships* [emphasis mine] between our two islands in the future.[21]

The Cardinal continued with words about starting "something new" and about how frightful it would be to "slide back into violence," an always present possibility. What he was saying and doing, Daly added, was avowedly political in the sense of drawing out of the Gospel "conclusions which are relevant to our daily living as individuals and as a society." Forgiveness was then also offered and in turn sought by the Anglican primate of Ireland.[22] And in July 2002, the IRA apologized for over thirty years of violence against civilians. A question arises here: Is this form of forgiveness, to the extent that it is accessible and enactable, available only to communicants of the Christian faith? The Cardinal suggests not, when he addresses human and political relationships more generally. For some, this is a hopelessly idealist stance, out of touch with tough realities. But the riposte would surely be that it is precisely tough realities that invite this stance; indeed, such realities suggest this stance as a necessary part of a process of negotiation, reconciliation, starting something new, and moving away from strictly retributive notions of justice and toward more hopeful possibilities.

Here is a second story. During World War II, thousands of ethnic Germans were expelled from Czechoslovakia. Their property was seized. Many were murdered. All were turned into refugees. This is the story of the famous (and infamous) Sudetenland, once home to nearly three million Germans, as well as 65,000 Jews and 800,000 Czechs. The German population was by far the largest. First, the Germans, when they annexed the Sudetenland, sent the Jewish population into exile. Next, according to a report in *The Wall Street Journal*, "Czechs eliminated Germans. Eduard Beneš, the pre-Communist postwar president, decreed their expulsion in 1945. At Potsdam, the Allies approved. As Germans fled toward Bavaria, Czechs took revenge: they murdered 40,000 Germans; many died at the end of a rope."

This episode was long buried in the Communist deep freeze; but since 1989, "the expulsion has become a national nettle . . . Czechs know that every Sudeten German wasn't guilty of Hitler's crimes."[23] Although President Vaclav Havel condemned the expulsion, then–Prime Minister Vaclav Klaus (in 1994) wanted to keep the episode closed. In the meantime, Jewish and German victims of expulsion began seeking the return of their family homes on a case-by-case basis, especially those who resided in or near the belle epoque spa area of Karlovy Vary (Karlsbad). The policy agreed to by the Czechs permitted Jewish families with claims to regain their houses, but not German families. The German descendants, of course, do not understand why their troubles count for nothing; for them a primordial feature of justice was violated and has yet to be put right. One is quoted as saying that "my only crime was that for eight hundred years my ancestors lived in that place." German descendants want repeal of the 1945 expulsion decree, and many say they want to return to their homeland and to villages long emptied—ethnically cleansed—of their kind.

But this won't happen, and it isn't clear that it should happen. Why? Because recognition of a wrong does not carry along with it a clear-cut remedy and does not mean that the old wrongs can, at present, be righted to any significant extent, if what is sought is compensatory justice or restoration of the status quo ante. Perhaps, then, there is nothing left for the expropriated people of German descent to do but to go on with their lives, knowing that what happened to them has at long last been recognized—for President Havel admitted that they had suffered a great injustice. Under such circumstances, where retributive justice is entirely out of place and compensatory justice is prudentially impossible and philosophically murky (given the entire story of World War II), acceptance of the gesture of recognition Havel proffered becomes a form of forgiveness that makes possible other instances of soul-searching and recognition as time goes on. This is hard to take, of course, but it may be the only way to forestall the quaffing of the bitter brew of injustice suffered and recompense sought by future generations. The Havelian gesture seems right: We Czechs, he is saying, although we were victims, also knew sin.

There is a follow-up to this story about the Sudetenland that details the ways in which Germany agreed to apologize for its invasion of the former Czechoslovakia, and the Czechs, in turn, expressed regret for the postwar expulsion of millions of Sudeten Germans. The Germans apologized for Nazi "policies of violence" and the Czechs expressed regret that their expulsions had "caused suffering and injustice to innocent people." But, of course, things are not thereby made right in the eyes of those who suffered most, and an organization of Sudeten Germans took strong exception to the agreement, because it provided them "with neither a claim to compensation nor a right to return to expropriated properties." As well, according to press reports, many ordinary Czechs were incensed because, given the story of the Nazi occupation, they opposed any apology to any groups of Germans.[24]

One appreciates why the mutual gestures involved here are either too little or too much, depending on the angle of vision from which one is viewing them. Nevertheless, these small steps, each of which acknowledges the violation of elementary, humanitarian principles, should not be sneezed at altogether. As I have already noted, full reparation and compensation are not in the cards, either in this case or in the vast majority of similar cases. But acknowledgment and recognition of injustice are possible, and this rudimentary requirement of justice may become a constitutive feature of a larger pattern of political forgiveness. Maybe what this tells us is that there is a political version of forgiveness that must step back, most of the time, from expectations of full reconciliation and certainly from absolution. There are no sacraments, no blessings, and no benedictions in politics. Thinking politically, one might ask what sorts of deeds warrant the solemn drama of forgiveness of this sort related to, yet different from, those acts that constitute a personal redemption narrative.

Nothing I have said thus far should be taken as a permit to refrain from action where action is possible to prevent an egregious collective wrong from being committed, or to punish an act of horrible, life-destroying aggression. We charge statesmen and stateswomen with the daunting task of protecting us, after all. As well, in life with those we love, the process of forgiveness is an enactment that is part of the very dailiness of our existence: It makes the quotidian livable. In the affairs of what used to be called men and states, however, these enactments are not and cannot be so ordinary and so direct. But that does not altogether forestall knowing-forgetting, with its complex interplay of justice and forgiveness—official recognition of mutual wrongs, some form of reparation, perhaps, and even state-level apologies. The scales may be somewhat righted. A quest for such fragile achievements within our imperfect earthly state is what the politics of forgiveness is all about.

This brings us directly to one of the most dramatic cases before our eyes over the past several years, namely the South African Truth and Reconciliation Commission (TRC). Created by an act of the postapartheid democratic parliament in 1995, the objectives of the commission were nothing less than to help set in motion and to secure a new political culture in South Africa. The work of the Commission was divided into three distinct but related parts: (1) a full accounting of gross violations of human rights (defined as the killing, abduction, torture, or severe ill treatment of any person), or any attempt, conspiracy, incitement, instigation, command, or procurement to commit an act by any person acting with a political motive; (2) consideration of amnesty appeals; and (3) possible reparative measures. Nearly all of these activities took place in full view of the public.

The purpose of this process was not, as some mistakenly or cynically suggest, to pat perpetrators on the head and send them on their way. Rather, those who violated human rights in a gross way were denied the status of martyrs to the old order. Nor will they be maintained in prison as a symbol of the past and a burden on taxpayers. Instead, they must face a very new community that has full knowledge of what they did—when, where, and how. As Charles Villa-Vicencio told me, "an authentic historical record of human rights abuse" is vital because it serves "as a basis for assisting future generations to defend democracy and the rule of law in the face of any future attempt at authoritarian rule."[25] The political aim is to create the conditions for domestic peace rather than for the new South Africa to be tormented by a virtually endless round of trials and punishments that would preoccupy it for years to come. This is a terribly complex business that takes certain theological steps toward political ends and purposes: acknowledgment, contrition, preparedness to make restitution, and the extending and receiving of forgiveness as a form of ongoing reconciliation.[26]

The TRC was not without its critics, mainly because in so many cases retributive justice was not done. However, the South Africans counter that they are employing a politically restorative justice, a form of political forgiveness concerned with justice. This means it is neither cheap forgiveness nor the dominant mode of retributive or punitive justice. Restorative justice aims for a future that generates no new victims of the sorts of systematic misdeeds and criminality that blighted the South African past.

Politically restorative justice, they argue, addresses the legitimate concerns of victims and survivors while seeking to reintegrate perpetrators into the community. This, they insist, is an alternative both to contrition chic, with its sentimentalized gloss that masks a huge indifference, and to the horror of wrongs suffered and vengeance sought generation after generation, a *lex talionis* shorn of mercy.[27]

Determining how the concept of political restorative justice would fare if put to the test between nations is, to say the least, a daunting task: An internal domestic order is one thing; the international arena another. That said, as a way to stabilize a fragile, new democracy and to do so in a manner that speaks both to justice and to mercy, it is a major contribution. Supporters of the TRC are quite prepared to admit that its creative view of justice is in part a compromise, but not of a sordid sort; rather, of a sort that makes politics itself possible. In a sense, certain quite legitimate demands of justice, including forms of just punishment, are foresworn in order that they might be reinstated in an order grounded in justice rather than in injustice. Ironically, the moral rehabilitation of the political world requires, at the outset, that certain features of just punishment be evacuated temporarily in the interest of a restorative project.[28] Full reparation, compensation, and just punishment are never possible when one confronts large-scale horrors. This point about full reparation was made to me by Renee de Epelbaum of Argentina's Mothers of the Disappeared. "That is utopian," Renee de Epelbaum told me, "and we are not utopians. We are political realists who seek justice."

Conclusion

The ghastliness of contemporary warfare—from Hitler's killing fields to those in Bosnia and Rwanda—may tempt us to simply get it over, to end the bloodshed and to move on. However, in case after case the seeds of the next conflict are sown in the denouement of the last, and thus we need to pay careful attention to the ethics of war's end. One critical aspect of this is what I have called the ethics of exit, specifically the trade-offs between order, justice, and restraint in the process of political rehabilitation. There are unique cases where this has been successful, most notably in postwar Germany and Japan; there are other cases where the end result is less clear, such as coalition efforts in Iraq following the fall of Saddam Hussein. One of the things that makes exit so difficult is that the unresolved business of war, from personal to national grievance, has a hold on the survivors—particularly those who have suffered loss. Of course, in the real world the idea of forgive and forget is not a helpful truism, but it is possible to both know and forget: to acknowledge the past without allowing it to dictate all of one's future, a release from the full weight and burden of the past. If wars are to truly end with a substantive peace, then the political independence that exit entails, in tandem with the spiritual independence connoted by knowing-forgetting, are necessary ingredients.

Notes

1. Thucydides, "The Melian Dialogue," in *The Peloponnesian War*, book 5, chapter 17, 2.
2. Attributed to Martin Luther.
3. Gareth Evans and Mohamed Sahnoun, "The Responsibility to Protect," *Foreign Affairs* 81 no. 6 (November-December 2002): 99–110.
4. *Tranquillitas ordinis* (tranquility of order) was first discussed by Augustine in his book *The City of God*.
5. Moral realism defends the idea that moral claims do purport to report facts and if the facts are indeed correct, the claim is true. To learn more see Russ Shafer-Landau, *Moral Realism: A Defence* (Oxford: Oxford University Press, 2003).
6. Eric Patterson describes the immaturity of such an approach in his *Just War Thinking: Pragmatism and Morality in the Struggle against Contemporary Threat* (Lanham, MD: Lexington Books, 2007).
7. Thomas Hobbes, *Leviathan*, ed. Richard Tuck (Cambridge: Cambridge University Press, 2006), 89.
8. Jean Bethke Elshtain, *Just War against Terror* (New York: Basic Books, 2003).
9. Michael Walzer, "War's End, and the Importance of Winning," in *Just and Unjust Wars*, 3rd ed. (New York: Basic Books, 2000), 109–26.
10. I first published this material on "knowing forgetting" as a chapter in Nigel Biggar's *Burying the Past: Making Peace and Doing Justice after Civil Conflict* (Washington, DC: Georgetown University Press, 2003). I thank Dr. Biggar and Georgetown University Press for allowing me to reuse some of that content for this work.
11. See her discussion in Hannah Arendt, *The Human Condition* (Chicago: The University of Chicago Press, 1958). Whether this is the only way to halt violence, or repetitive violence, in any case, is, of course, subject to strenuous debate.
12. L. Gregory Jones, *Embodying Forgiveness: A Theological Analysis* (Grand Rapids, MI: Eerdmans, 1995).

13. See Gerhard Forde, "On Being a Theologian of the Cross," *Christian Century*, October 22, 1997, 947–49, for a discussion of why a theology of the cross is not about sentimentalism, but rather about sin, redemption, punishment, reconciliation, God's justice, and so on. Forde worries that much contemporary language spoken from the pulpit has taken on all the coloration of the wider, sentimentalized surround—the "I'm okay, you're okay, everybody gets a pass" mentality. This turns the church into a support group, Forde asserts, "rather than the gathering of the body of Christ where the word of the cross and resurrection is proclaimed and heard."

14. An allusion to the Gospel of Matthew 7:16, 20.

15. As will become clear in the following discussion, knowing-forgetting is also a type of remembering. I thank Lawrence Cahoone of Boston University for his emphasis on this point.

16. Patricia Cook, in *The Philosophy of Forgetting: An Inquiry through Plato's Dialogue*s, notes that the Greeks conceived of forgetting in at least twelve different ways. These included passing by, disregarding, blotting out of one's mind, and not remembering. But the list also included forgiveness of a wrong, a kind of amnesty. These many different meanings are usually translated into English without differentiation as, simply, forgetting. Dietrich Bonhoeffer, in his *Letters and Papers from Prison* (New York: Macmillan, 1967), speaks of the capacity to forget as a gift of grace-again, not to be dominated by the past by musing on what should have been.

17. Lawrence Cahoone, "Commentary on Jean Bethke Elshtain" (paper delivered at Boston University, November 5, 1997), 3.

18. A friend told me recently of an experiment in which a group of American teenagers was told to separate themselves according to whether they thought they were powerless or had some power. The result? Everybody wanted to be powerless. That, clearly, is the preferred identity these days, and it is a terrible problem because it blunts our ability to see real victims when they stand before us with their concrete—not abstract or ideological—claims.

19. See the French Bishops' Declaration of Repentance issued on September 30, 1997, near a former Jewish deportation camp in a Paris suburb. The bishops declared that their predecessors in the Vichy era had been too "caught up in a loyalism and docility" toward civil authorities and had thus done far too little to spare French Jews from deportation and death. The declaration does acknowledge those who spoke out and acted courageously but concludes that there was insufficient indignation, insisting: "The time has come for the church to submit her own history, especially that of this period, to critical examination and to recognize without hesitation the sins committed by members of the church, and to beg forgiveness." The full text of the declaration appears in *Origins* 27, no. 18 (October 16, 1997): 301–5. See also L. Gregory Jones, "True Confessions," in *Christian Century*, November 19–26, 1997, 1090.

20. Hannah Arendt, *Eichmann in Jerusalem* (New York: Penguin Books, 1964).

21. Cardinal Daly's homily was not published, but it did receive extensive coverage in the Irish press (see, for example, *The Irish Times*, January 23, 1995).

22. Cardinal Daly's homily was itself a response to a prior expression of the English need to ask for Irish forgiveness, made by George Carey, the Archbishop of Canterbury, at Christ Church Cathedral, Dublin, on November 18, 1994.

23. All quotations here are drawn from "Czech Republic Fields Demands of Germans, Jews, for Lost Homes," *The Wall Street Journal*, July 15, 1995, I6.

24. All quotations here are drawn from Alan Crowell, "Germans and Czechs Agree to Part on Wartime Abuses," *The New York Times*, December 12, 1996, A12.

25. Author interview with Charles Villa-Vicencio, 2005.

26. Crowell, "Germans and Czechs Agree to Part," 4.

27. The fullest elaboration of political restorative justice is to be found in Charles Villa-Vicencio, *Walk With Us and Listen: Political Reconciliation in Africa* (Washington, DC: Georgetown University Press, 2009).

28. For this insight I thank Lawrence Cahoone.

CHAPTER 8

ENDING THE US CIVIL WAR WELL

Reconciliation and Transitional Justice

DAVID A. CROCKER

IN HIS WIDELY ACCLAIMED STUDY of the ending of the US Civil War, historian Jay Winik dramatically narrates the war's last month and argues that Northern and Southern leaders ended this deadly conflict well.[1] During a mere but momentous thirty days, these political and military men—especially President Abraham Lincoln and generals U. S. Grant, Robert E. Lee, William T. Sherman, Joe Johnston, and Nathan Bedford Forrest—avoided the bad endings of most civil wars and internecine conflicts when they decided and acted to reconcile adversaries and create one nation where before there had been only loosely allied states.

Winik asserts that most civil wars "end quite badly, and history is rife with lessons that how wars end is every bit as crucial as why they start and how they are waged."[2] In this chapter I analyze and evaluate Winik's account through the lens of what has come to be called transitional justice.[3] Policymakers and scholars of transitional justice critically consider how countries or regions—following conflict between or within states—do and should reckon with past wrongs and make (or fail to make) transitions to a better future. Argentina and Chile, South Africa and Uganda, Cambodia and East Asia are only a few of the nations or regions that have taken up transitional justice challenges. I distinguish the transitional justice perspective from two others. First, the just war tradition normatively evaluates the starting and conducting of war. Usually the conflicts treated are those between states, but the South African Truth and Reconciliation Commission is one example of a country's employing the just war tradition to assess a conflict internal to a country. As many chapters in this volume show, scholars working within or in relation to this tradition are considering to what extent, if any, the just war tradition can be extended to illuminate *jus post bellum* as well as *jus ad bellum* and *jus in bello*.

A second policy and—at least implicitly—normative framework is Amnesty, Reintegration, and Reconciliation, or AR2. The aim of AR2 to improve the long-term peace building potential of the military doctrine known as Disarmament, Demobilization, and Reintegration, or DDR. In DDR, security forces demobilize combatants by putting the latter in secure locations and disarming them. In AR2, which complements rather than competes with the just war tradition, the emphasis is on armed reconcilers building long-term peaceful relations among former adversaries.[4] Transitional justice is also concerned with reconciling former enemies and long-term development, but it depends less on military and more on government and civil society actors. Moreover, although the goal of reconciliation is important in transitional justice, those who work in this framework (a) evaluate various ideals of reconciliation and (b) balance reconciliation with other goals such as truth and justice. In this chapter, I will leave open the question of whether these three traditions might complement or overlap each other.

The chapter proceeds in two steps. First, it summarizes Winik's account of those Civil War leaders—especially Lincoln, Grant, Lee, Sherman, Johnston, and Forrest—whose decisions and actions, Winik argues, reconciled Northern and Southern combatants (and noncombatants) and importantly contributed to forging a new and unified nation. Second, although there is much that is appealing in Winik's account, the second section argues that his focus on April 1865 (a) distorts our understanding of the war by overemphasizing the goal of North-South thick reconciliation among combatants and underemphasizing the black (and white) goals of racial justice and interracial democracy. Winik's account, I argue, does not break sufficiently with the view that postconflict Reconstruction, in contrast to reconciling events of April 1865, was an unmitigated failure imposed by radical Republicans, Northern "carpetbaggers," and Southern "scalawags." Drawing on Winik's work in conjunction with that of Eric Foner, Benjamin G. Cloyd, David Blight, and other Civil War historians, I assert an alternative interpretation of April 1865. Rather than seeing Appomattox and what followed as a bright shining moment that mitigated the alleged evils of Reconstruction, it is better to see April 1865 (and its reconciling leaders) as part of a larger, slower, more protean transition from slavery to racial justice and from states' rights and self-determination to enhanced national power in the service of racial justice and interracial democracy. Furthermore, these tensions are illustrative of similar challenges faced in contemporary civil wars, from Central Asia to Africa's Great Lakes region.

April 1865 and Reconciliation

Winik eloquently formulates his main claim as follows:

> These men of battle [Confederacy's military leaders] knew that war most often engenders hatred. But by their collective actions in ending the war, they, along with Lincoln, helped constitute a country. In mid-April, as the cataclysmic events rushed together . . . they were asking something quite remarkable of the people whom they had just lead through four years of bloody battle: to become good citizens of the United States that had thwarted their bid for independence and stymied their urge for self-determination. And above all, Lincoln, and men like Grant and Sherman, would call on the North to be equally remarkable, appealing to reconciliation, not vengeance, to common ground, not revenge, to mutual citizenship, not difference.[5]

Before examining Winik's detailed evidence to support this claim, let us ask what Winik means by reconciliation. On the one hand, he certainly means more than a minimalist conception, in which reconciliation is nothing more nor less than nonlethal coexistence in the sense that former enemies—whether groups or individuals—cease tyrannizing and killing each other.[6] Whatever else they achieved, Lincoln and the Northern and Southern military leaders ended a carnage that claimed more than 620,000 lives (one-fifth of the South and one-twelfth of the North). Winik, however, correctly argues that the sort of reconciliation that issued from these leaders' actions was much more robust than the mere cessation of killing. The reconciliation that Winik finds and affirms comes very close to South African Bishop Desmond Tutu's definition of *ubuntu*, a person-to-person relation characterized by forgiveness, mercy (rather than justice), a shared moral vision, mutual healing, and social harmony.[7] Arguably, forgiveness was less obvious in post-Appomattox reconciliation than in Tutu's ideal of *ubuntu*. Moreover, *re*integration of North and South into one polity is central for Winik but not in postapartheid Africa, where Afrikaners and blacks were antecedently part of one polity in only the most minimal sense. Winik, like Tutu, however, clearly stresses healing and the integration of former enemies as well as a shared moral vision of citizenship in a nation in the making.[8]

Abraham Lincoln

Let us turn now to each of the leaders that Winik puts forward as key agents of reconciliation. The first is and must be Abraham Lincoln. With his almost exclusive focus on April 1865, Winik neglects what would seem to be the best evidence for Lincoln as reconciler—the last lines of his second inaugural address (delivered March 4, 1865):

> With malice toward none; with charity for all; with firmness in the right, as God gives us to see the right, let us strive on to finish the work we are in; to bind up the nation's wounds; to care for him who shall have borne the battle, and for his widow, and his orphan—to do all which may achieve and cherish a just and lasting peace, among ourselves, and with all nations.[9]

I shall have occasion subsequently to call attention to the way in which Lincoln's qualifying the peace that he seeks with the word "just," as well as the word "lasting," suggests a more complex interpretation of Lincoln than that which Winik offers. Nevertheless, this concluding peroration in March 4, 1865, does support much of Winik's view of Lincoln as reconciler. And later in March and throughout April, additional evidence of Lincoln's leniency in reckoning with the Confederates is abundant.

On the James River at City Point, in close proximity to an anticipated, perhaps final, but certainly bloody battle between Union forces and Lee's Army of Northern Virginia, Lincoln meets on the boat *The River Queen* with his top lieutenants: generals U.S. Grant and William Sherman, and Admiral David Porter. The four discuss how to corner Lee and whether great bloodshed might be avoided. The military men also hear Lincoln articulate what Winik calls the River Queen Doctrine: the lenient terms for ending the war that Lincoln wanted to have offered to the South:

> To get the deluded men of the rebel armies disarmed and back to their homes . . . Let them once surrender and reach their homes, [and] they won't take up arms again . . . Let them all go, officers and all, I want submission, and no more bloodshed . . . I want no one punished; treat them liberally all around. We want those people to return to their allegiance to the Union and submit to the laws.[10]

Winik's comments on the River Queen Doctrine drive home his interpretation of Lincoln as reconciler:

> If the United States were truly to be reunited as one nation, Lincoln believed deeply that the war must not conclude with wholesale slaughter, nor could it slowly dwindle into barbarism or inquisition or mindless retaliation. All, he felt, would bode ill. To unite the country anew, it must be marked by reconciliation, by the lubricants of civil order, by a rejuvenated sense of what Lincoln termed on the *River Queen*, the "rights as citizens of a common country." For this reason, as Admiral Porter would later observe, Lincoln now "wanted peace on almost any terms."[11]

After Grant's April 1 breakthrough of Lee's lines near Petersburg and the ensuing Confederate evacuation of Richmond, Virginia, the capitol city of the Confederacy, Lincoln pays a short visit to the city on April 4—still smoldering from fires set by fleeing Confederates. Three events stand out in Winik's account of this extraordinary visit, each of which he submits to make his case for Lincoln's lenient policy toward Confederate political leaders and military. First, after viewing recently captured Confederate prisoners, Union commander Maj. Gen. Godfrey Weitzel asks Lincoln how the prisoners should be treated. Winik reports one version of Lincoln's response to Weitzel's: "If I were in your place, I'd let 'em up easy, let 'em up easy."[12] This suggestion stands in stark contrast to shouts of "Hang him! Hang him!" that Lincoln heard minutes before meeting

Weitzel. Who did the crowd want to be hung? Not Lincoln, but Confederate president Jefferson Davis, who had fled the city only forty hours earlier and was rumored to be captured and in the process of being hauled back to the city.[13]

Winik immediately follows the Weitzel episode with what he calls Lincoln's private (and unannounced) stop at the home of an old Richmond friend and Confederate general, George Pickett, the man who led the infamous Gettysburg charge. Lincoln cradles Pickett's baby and whispers to it in earshot of Pickett's wife, "Tell your father I will grant him a special amnesty—if he wants it—for the sake of your mother's bright eyes and your good manners."[14]

In both his book and TV documentary, Winik fails to recount a third episode in Lincoln's Richmond visit, and I suspect it is because it does not so neatly fit his theme of Lincoln as reconciler of North and South. Before and after meeting Weitzel, a throng of black Richmondites, both slaves and freeman, greeted Lincoln jubilantly. Many sought to touch him, and several fell to their knees. According to historian Doris Kearns Goodwin, Lincoln responded emotionally: "Don't kneel to me . . . that is not right. You must kneel to God only, and thank him for the liberty you will hereafter enjoy."[15]

Less than a year and a half earlier, Lincoln's Emancipation Proclamation had announced partial emancipation of the slaves, and on January 31, 1865, the House of Representatives passed the 13th Amendment to the Constitution ending slavery forever. With these historic events as a backdrop, in front of George Washington's statue in Richmond's Capitol Square, Lincoln addresses the largely black crowd that had followed him through Richmond's streets. As remembered by Admiral Porter, Lincoln told his black listeners to "cast off the name of slave and trample upon it . . . Liberty is your birthright. God gave it to you as he gave it to others, and it is a sin that you have been deprived of it for so many years."[16] For Lincoln, the aim of ending the bloody war well was not only to reconcile the white South and the white North but also to reckon with the past wrong of slavery and enable blacks to make the transition from slavery to citizenship. Although Lincoln urged "charity for all," William Lee Miller perceptively argues that "an undue or overdone or inappropriate 'charity' to the defeated white South might, in effect, deny elementary justice, let alone charity, to the former slaves."[17] The work to be finished is not only to heal North and South (as I shall argue in more detail in the next section), but also to continue the long walk toward black freedom and citizenship.

Less than a week after Lincoln's trip to Richmond, Lee surrenders to Grant at the Appomattox courthouse. On April 11 in his last public speech, Lincoln—rather than triumphantly celebrating the Northern victory—expresses the "hope for a righteous and speedy peace."[18] He also pedantically explains steps in which Union-occupied areas in Louisiana and other states are securing civil order as well as black civil and political rights. Three days later, April 14, Lincoln meets with his cabinet to take up questions it had addressed before but which now are even more pressing—given that the surrender of other Confederate forces seemed imminent.

Winik skillfully uses records and memoirs of Lincoln's final cabinet meeting to drive home his view of Lincoln as postconflict reconciler and nation builder:

> It has been simmering beneath the surface for months, and now Lincoln will confront perhaps his greatest challenge yet: to subdue the Confederate forces once and for all, while at the same time laying groundwork for the peace to follow. In short, the complex and demanding matter of a postwar America, of reintegrating the South into the Union and forging the nation anew. He calls it Reconstruction. A word that more adequately captures his spirit, however, is "reconciliation."[19]

First, consistent with the River Queen Doctrine and his advice to Weitzel, Lincoln categorically rejects Union punishment of Confederate leaders and combatants: There must be "'no persecutions,' 'no bloody work after the war was over,' no expectation that he would 'take part in hanging or killing these men, even the worst of them.'"[20] Even Confederate political leaders such as Jefferson Davis should be scared out of the country rather than tried and punished. Lincoln rightly feared that penal sanctions would drive unrepentant rebels into guerilla action. Second, instead of punishment, as usually happens after civil wars, the rebels must return home and accept citizenship in the nation, forsake the temptation of engaging in guerrilla warfare, and benefit from a reestablishment of civil order and government. Third, although he prohibits slavery and assigns the Union army to ensure law and order in the Southern states, Lincoln insists that former rebels have an important role in reorganizing their governments. Fourth, as soon as the war is over everywhere, the federal government should encourage normal commercial relations, collect taxes, do land surveying, and reestablish mail routes.

Knowing that radical Republicans in Congress are bent on immediate black suffrage and at least partial disenfranchisement of former rebels, Lincoln is relieved that Congress does not convene for eight months and that the executive branch will have a relatively free hand. Lincoln does not and cannot share in these largely Northern politicians' "feelings of hate and vindictiveness."[21] Goodwin adds one of Lincoln's points surprisingly absent from Winik's account: "Enough lives have been sacrificed. We must extinguish our resentments if we expect harmony and union."[22] And Goodwin adds Secretary of State Stanton's recollection of Lincoln's demeanor at the meeting. According to Stanton, not only did Lincoln speak kindly of General Lee and other Confederates but he also "exhibited in marked degree the kindness and humanity of his disposition, and the tender and forgiving spirit that so eminently distinguished him."[23]

In Winik's narrative, Lincoln played the major role in the reconciliation of North and South that in April 1865 allegedly saved the nation. Yet both sides' highest military leaders also were important reconcilers—Union generals U. S. Grant and William Sherman and Confederate generals Robert E. Lee, Joe Johnston, and Nathan Bedford Forrest. In the *River Queen* meeting at City Point, President Lincoln, also Commander in Chief of the Union military, made it very clear that, while "pressing" for victory, he wanted to avoid a final bloody battle and a punitive treatment of rebels. All this in the interest of peace and a reintegration of rebels as US citizens. First, Grant and Sherman and, then, Sherman and Johnston, followed Lincoln's lead.

Ulysses S. Grant and Robert E. Lee

Winik is at his narrative best in his moving account of the vicious fighting leading up to Appomattox, Grant's encircling of Lee's forces, and especially the ensuing surrender ceremony in the Appomattox courthouse on April 9, 1865. He emphasizes that in the interest of ending the awful war well, each general rose to the occasion and freely contributed to peace and reconciliation in small as well as big ways:

Appomattox was not preordained. There were no established rules or well-worn script. If anything, retribution had been the larger and longer precedent. So, if these moments teemed with hope—and they did—it was largely due to two men who rose to the occasion, to Grant's and Lee's respective actions: one general magnanimous in victory, the other, gracious and equally dignified in defeat, the two of them, for their own reasons and in their own ways, fervently interested in beginning the process to bind up the wounds of the last four years. And yes, if paradoxically, these were among Lee's finest hours, and they were, so, too, were they Grant's greatest moments.[24]

Within the framework of Lincoln's River Queen Doctrine, what reconciling actions did Grant autonomously take? First, Grant let Lee—who was going against President Davis's injunction to fight on—choose the site of the surrender.[25] Then, at the meeting itself, after verbally stating what he had written the day before as the terms of surrender and before committing them to writing, Grant added that he hoped the meeting's action "may lead to a general suspension of hostilities and be the means of preventing any further loss of life."[26] Second, Grant wrote out terms: that Confederate soldiers were to agree to cease fighting and the Confederate officers were to be exempted from handing over their side arms, private horses, and baggage so that "each officer and man will be allowed to return to their [sic] homes, not to be disturbed by the United States Authority so long as they observe their parole and the laws in force where they may reside."[27] Expecting much less generous terms, Lee responded, "this will have a very happy effect upon my army." Winik adds that these terms mean that Lee's men "would not be penned as prisoners of war; they would not be paraded ignominiously through Northern streets; and, most importantly, they would not be prosecuted for treason."[28] When Lee questioned whether nonofficers would also be able to keep their own horses, Grant answers, in what Winik judges to be "one of his [Grant's] boldest strokes":[29]

> Well the subject is quite new to me. Of course I did not know that any private soldiers owned their animals; but I think we have fought the last battle of the war—I sincerely hope so . . . I will arrange it this way. I will not change the terms as now written, but I will instruct the officers I shall

appoint to receive the paroles to let all the men who claim to own a horse or a mule take the animals home with them to their little farms.[30]

Responding to Grant's generosity, Lee (as Winik describes it) says that "this will have the best possible effect upon the men. It will do much toward conciliating our people."[31] And upon hearing that Lee needed food for his federal prisoners, numbering a thousand, and for his own troops, Grant proposed providing rations for 25,000 soldiers and Lee agreed that would be "an abundance."[32] The surrender ritual concluded, Lee departs the McLean House at Appomattox and as Lee rides past Grant "each silently lifted his hat to the other."[33] For Winik, "in no small measure, this one poignant moment captured the spirit of Appomattox more than the words ever written about that day."[34] Economic determinists and political realists might scoff at such acts as at best insignificant and at worst as camouflaging or prettifying the impersonal realities of dominance and submission. Winik's counterclaim opens up a role for small but symbolic actions of great leaders: "The ultimate fate of nations is often measured and swayed not by large events, but by tiny ones, small, symbolic gestures that shape men's passions, assuage or incite their fears, and quell or inflame lingering hostilities for years to come."[35]

Grant's small but momentous acts were not yet finished. When Union troops started riotously celebrating upon hearing of the surrender, Grant ordered them to stop their jubilation because, he said later, "we did not want to exult over their downfall."[36] Grant knew that bad winners, like sour losers, incite later hostility. Two months later Grant interceded to save Lee from a treason indictment; Grant believed not only that the surrender agreement ruled out treason trials but also, like Lincoln, that the lenient agreement likely would dissuade rebel forces from taking to the hills in dispersed guerilla action.

Following the surrender ritual, Robert E. Lee also was conciliatory in acts big and small. According to Winik, Lee now devoted himself not to winning the war but ending it well. Not only did he tell some rebel soldiers outside his tent "I have done the best I could for you," but after entering the tent he told them to "go home now, and if you make as good citizens as you have soldiers, you will do well, and I shall always be proud of you."[37] The next day, in his final order to his troops, Lee officially declared that "by the terms of the agreement officers and men can return to their homes;" and, as Winik notes, Lee says absolutely nothing to challenge the authority of the Union government or encourage his men to fight on as guerillas.[38] And while Lee turned down Grant's request that Lee go to Washington and confer with Lincoln, Lee does pledge to give "his whole efforts to pacifying the country and bringing the people back to the Union."[39]

Realizing (but not sufficiently emphasizing) that leaders are ineffective without active followers, Winik argues that the two leaders' reconciling acts set the tone for their soldiers' role in the formal surrender on April 12. Winik does not mention that accounts differ with respect to the formal surrender of the two armies. Drawing on the famous account of Bowdoin professor and decorated Union general Joshua Chamberlain, Winik states that "without having planned it—and without any official sanction—Chamberlain gave the order for Union soldiers to 'carry arms' as a sign of the deepest mark of military respect. A bugle call instantly rang out. All along the road, Union soldiers raised their muskets to their shoulders, the salute of honor."[40]

The account continues that Confederate General John B. Gordon in turn "ordered his men to answer in kind, 'honor answering honor.'" And that reciprocal act was followed by the "stillness" at Appomattox, from which Bruce Catton derived the title of his famous book.[41]

Yet Chamberlain and Winik may have spun the event in ways that suited a victor's surrender if not victor's justice. In the Museum of the Confederacy in Richmond, we read the following in the exhibit on Appomattox:

> The classic description of the surrender parade on April 12, 1865 by Brig. General Joshua Chamberlain told more about the spirit of national reconciliation that reigned when he wrote it [decades after Appomattox] than it did the mood at approximately 50 years before. White Southern and Northern men and officers fraternized in the days following April 9 with mutual respect mingled with mutual hostility. Most Confederate soldiers had already stacked their arms and battle flags on April 10 and 11 and participated in a formal parade only when Federal army officers ordered it. Contrary to Chamberlain's inspiring story of victors saluting their vanquished foes, the Federal soldiers did not 'present' arms (a salute) but merely shouldered their arms (signaling silence in the ranks).[42]

Winik offers three additional events during the days following Appomattox to support his portrait of Lee as reconciler. First, the day after hearing of Lincoln's April 14 assassination, Lee in a newspaper interview not only condemned Booth's act as one "that must be deprecated by every American."[43] He also refrained—once again—from urging rebel guerilla action against the federal government, accepted that slavery was abolished, and renewed his pledge to Grant to pursue peace.[44] Moreover, Winik makes the important point that in this interview Lee uses the term "the country" to refer not—as he had done for the past four years—to the Confederacy but to the United States of America.[45] Second, concerned to get him to abandon his intransigent commitment to further struggle, Lee on April 20 wrote Confederate President Jefferson Davis and urged him to end hostilities (including guerilla action) and accept peace. Davis, still heading a government on wheels (train and horse-drawn buggy) and in search of a haven safe from Union occupation, ignored the plea. Winik, however, suggests that Lee had realized that the letter would leak to the press and—due to his revered stature—be influential in causing the surrender of other rebel armies, such as those headed by Joe Johnston and Nathan Bedford Forrest. With respect to both Lee's interview and his letter to Davis, Winik remarks that Lee "may no longer have had an army, but he had his voice, which could set the tone of reconciliation in the tense days to come."[46]

A third episode involving Lee does not so unambiguously fit Winik's portrait of Lee as reconciler. Late in the spring of 1865, the story goes, in Richmond's elite St. Paul's Episcopal Church, a well-dressed black man came and knelt at the communion table as the priest was about to administer communion. In Winik's telling, the rest of the congregation "froze," and the priest hesitated for blacks had always received communion after white congregants.[47] From out of the congregation a "white man arose, his gait erect, head up and eyes proud, and walked quietly up the aisle to the chancel rail . . .[and] knelt down to partake of the communion, along the same rail with the black man."[48] The white man, promptly followed by other white communicants, was of course General Robert E. Lee. In the History Channel's documentary based on Winik's book, this act of Lee and the congregation at the communion rail is offered as April 1865's culminating event of reconciliation.

One would love to believe that this episode happened! When I described it at the conclusion of my presentation to the conference from which the present paper is derived, more than one person present remarked that the communion scene brought tears to their eyes. If the event did happen as Winik tells it, it would be evidence not so much for his argument that Lee played a crucial role in healing North and South, but even more for my contention that Winik puts insufficient emphasis on the additional and urgent tasks of promoting racial justice.[49]

William T. Sherman, Joe Johnston, and Nathan Bedford Forrest

Winik's treatment of the reconciling roles of both Union General Sherman and Confederate General Johnston follows the lead of their military superiors, respectively. Sherman imitates Grant's magnanimous surrender terms and food rations; Johnston respectfully accepts. The two depart, however, from the Grant-Lee model in a couple of ways. Sherman, after destroying Atlanta and laying waste to the countryside in his march to Savannah and his infamous pronouncement "war is hell," might seem an unlikely agent of healing. Yet Winik reveals a romantic side of Sherman, and, as we shall see, there is good evidence that Sherman took to heart Lincoln's River Queen Doctrine and Grant's example. Johnston, like Lee, had had enough of war and killing and urged his men to abide by surrender terms, "discharge the obligations of good and peaceful citizens, . . . and [thereby] . . . restore tranquility to our country." Like Lee, Johnston violated Davis's express order to fight on, prompting Winik to exclaim: "In the larger flow of history what ultimately must stand out is not Johnston's military ability or his daring in battle, but this one decisive act in which he brazenly violated the chain of command—and in doing so, helped heal a country."[50]

Over the next two months the other confederate military leaders followed Lee's (and Johnston's) example rather than Davis's order. Among them were those who for years had been engaged in the very sort of bloody guerilla warfare against the North that Lee and Johnston wanted to avoid. Yale, Harvard, and Edinburgh-educated Richard Taylor surrendered to Major General Edward Canby on May 4 and the two generals and their lieutenants celebrated together with food, drink, and each side's martial tunes. However, most interesting was the dramatic turnabout of the fierce guerilla and (arguably) terrorist Nathan Bedford Forrest. Rejecting calls to head for the hills, Mexico, or the Trans-Mississippi theatre, he announced to his troops that they should surrender. Winik finds abundant evidence for this interpretation and reproduces much of Forrest's surprisingly conciliatory farewell speech, in which the influence of Lee is manifest, to his troops:

> Civil war, such as you have just passed through naturally engenders feelings of animosity, hatred, and revenge. It is our duty to divest ourselves of all such feelings; and as far as it is in our power to do so, to cultivate friendly feelings towards those with whom we have so long contested, and heretofore so widely, but honestly, differed. . . . The attempt made to establish a separate and independent Confederation has failed; but the consciousness of having done your duty faithfully, and to the end, will, in some measure, repay for the hardships you have undergone. . . . I have never, on the field of battle, sent you where I was unwilling to go myself; nor would I now advise you to a course which I felt myself unwilling to pursue. You have been good soldiers, you can be good citizens. Obey the laws, preserve your honor, and the Government to which you have surrendered can afford to be, and will be, magnanimous.[51]

Although Winik does not mention it, one other facet of Forrest's career tarnishes this call for friendly feelings,—one that requires us to set Winik's overall interpretation in a larger context. To Winik's credit, he does remark that prior to the Civil War Forrest was a slave trader and that during the war he led rebel troops in an assault on Union-held Fort Pillow, an infamous incident known as the Fort Pillow massacre in which both white and black soldiers, trying to surrender, were slaughtered. Moreover, Winik denounces Forrest for never adequately justifying or expressing remorse for the killings. What Winik does not do is to indicate that in late 1866 or early 1867, Forrest joined and perhaps helped found the Ku Klux Klan. Although it is questionable that he ever became the Klan's grand wizard, and although he likely distanced himself from the organization when its strategy to curtail black progress turned from pranks to violence, it is troubling that Winik fails to mention Forrest's career after the spring of 1865. The friendly feelings that Forrest recommends to his men are to be for Union combatants and not for the blacks for whom those troops were fighting. We begin to doubt whether Forrest's farewell speech was part of what Winik refers to repeatedly as a bright, shining conciliatory moment that would mitigate later racial and political conflict. Forrest's turn to the Klan may have been an effort to make it clear to all that the reconciliation that he had advocated less than two years earlier did *not* include blacks.

Ending the War, Reconstructing the Society

The first section of this chapter analyzed and raised some questions about Winik's claim that in April 1865, a few leaders in both North and South performed actions big and small that reconciled the combatants and built a new and unified nation. To evaluate further this claim and Winik's arguments for it, we must ask five related but different questions: Did these leaders perform actions intended to be reconciling and, if so, was reconciliation their only aim? What were the immediate consequences of these actions? To the extent that there was some harmony between North and South in the immediate aftermath of the war, were the leaders' reconciling actions of April 1865 the only causes of this harmony? Did these putative reconciling actions help to avoid even worse fracturing and violence than would have occurred without them during and after Reconstruction? Did these actions save America and build one nation?

With respect to the first question, let us assume that Winik is correct in ascribing reconciling intent to the actions of Lincoln, Grant, Lee, Sherman, Johnston, and even Forrest. Although there is some question about knowing each agent's motivation, the documentary evidence fits well with the ascription of a reconciling intent and even is compatible with Lee's church episode. In each of the decisions and actions—large and small—canvassed in our first section, Winik seems justified in saying that these leaders were trying to end the war's carnage, bring about nonlethal coexistence and some sort of harmony among former enemies, and heal the war's wounds. Were other motives involved as well? Due to limitations in space, I mostly consider Lincoln's aims and actions.

To do justice to Lincoln's aims in April 1865, we must go back to his aims and preparations during the war for the postwar period, what he would call Reconstruction and not reconciliation. From 1863 on, Lincoln was not only trying to win the war but to lay the groundwork for a reconstructed nation. He aimed to bring former rebel states back into the

Union as quickly as possible and recommended that only 10 percent of those voting in the 1860 presidential election would have to pledge loyalty to the Union—whether or not they had previously supported the Confederacy. And Lincoln did believe that local self-determination was important and that Washington should not impose specific institutional arrangements on any state. However, Lincoln did not believe in conciliation between North and South at any price. Willing to be flexible and experimental on the details of the new state governments, he was adamant on two points: (a) each returning state must constitutionally abolish slavery, and (b) each state must cooperate with the Union forces and administrators in helping both freemen and former slaves (freedmen) make a transition to a nonslave society. Winik fails to recognize that a certain kind of reconciliation—on the slave-owning and racist South's terms—could have been accomplished by making emancipation or Negro welfare a matter of home rule (which, after Reconstruction became, as Foner remarks, a euphemism for white supremacy).[52] He refused, however, to do so. Before the war's end Lincoln was willing to consider compensating slave owners for the emancipation of their slaves and to go slow on the question of black suffrage. He was not willing to compromise on the question of slavery itself or even on the importance of equality before the law.

For Lincoln, racial justice as well as white-white reconciliation was important, and the former could not be sacrificed to the latter. One source of Lincoln's commitment, as Eric Foner shows, is Frederick Douglass, for Douglass saw clearly that a morally unacceptable basis for the reuniting of North and South would be to abandon the commitment to emancipation and equal rights for former slaves and freemen. Quoting Douglass, Foner refers to such reconciliation as "'peace among whites'. . . . paved with the shards of African Americans' broken dreams of genuine equality and full citizenship."[53] In this connection it is important to place Lincoln's famous second inaugural's phrase "with malice toward none; with charity for all," discussed briefly in the first section, in the context of the whole speech, which social ethicist and Lincoln biographer William Lee Miller calls "the most profound of all condemnations of American slavery."[54] Miller insists that we do justice to the speech's paragraph immediately preceding the final peroration about malice and charity:

Fondly do we hope—fervently do we pray—that this mighty scourge of war may speedily pass away. Yet, if God will that it continue, until all the wealth piled by the bond-man's two hundred and fifty years of unrequited toil shall be sunk, and until every drop of blood drawn with the lash, shall be paid by another drawn with the sword, as was said three thousand years ago, so still it must be said "the judgments of the Lord are true and righteous altogether."[55]

Miller sees this "horrendous vision" of divine retribution on both sides of the conflict as not only a stinging denunciation of the "abomination of slavery and a revulsion against the war but also the most somber determination to finish that war and end the great evil."[56] The charity that must be for all, including Northern charity for the South, must not be a substitute for or at odds with racial justice. As Miller says, with echoes of Reinhold Niebuhr's nuanced views on the relation of love and justice, "'charity' extended to one party to a political dispute may, if it affects the disposition of policy itself, be uncharitable and even unjust, to another party:"

> The possible role of the virtue of charity in this collective case [the seceding states treason against the United States government] was more complicated than in the instances of forgiveness to individuals, because it would have an effect, for good or ill, on the reshaping of an entire society—the new South—and because in that reshaping there was alongside the soon-to-be-defeated Confederates, another claimant, asking for justice at least if not charity, the soon to be freedmen. An undue or overdone or inappropriate 'charity' to the defeated South might, in effect, deny elementary justice, let alone charity, to the former slaves.[57]

On this compelling and evidence-based view, Lincoln's conception of "the work we are in," whose task it is for the nation to "finish," is not merely "reconciliation," as important as that is, but "a *just* and lasting peace."[58]

Lincoln's complex Reconstruction and postwar aims do raise some important questions beyond the scope of this chapter. If Lincoln had lived and been able to complete his second term, could and should he (and other leaders) have done more than what actually transpired to require former slave owners to redistribute a portion of their land to freedmen or reconstructed state governments to provide freedmen with public or abandoned land? Could and should Lincoln have distinguished between slavery as such and flagrant slave-owner abuse of slaves—even though Southern laws permitted the latter as well as the former? Could and should Lincoln have distinguished between treason, on the one hand, for which he wanted no Confederate charged or punished, and barbaric military conduct—by North as well as South—on the other? Although he did personally pardon many deserters and those in dereliction of duty, Lincoln agreed to punishment and even execution of those Union soldiers who committed the most serious offenses. As Miller remarks:

> Lincoln did not pardon every accused person for whom an appeal came to his desk. His mercy, although generous, was discriminating. He did not pardon any soldier found guilty of rape. He did not pardon a soldier, however tearful his wife's pleas, who deserted three times and was incorrigible. Writing to [John J.] Nicolay about the long July 18, 1863, session with a hundred cases, in which Lincoln seized on any excuse for mercy, [John] Hay added: "He was only merciless in cases where meanness or cruelty were shown."[59]

Moreover, Miller observes that on December 8, 1863, with respect to the South, Lincoln issued the Proclamation of Amnesty and Reconstruction whose generous terms were coupled with the one exception that "the amnesty did not extend to 'all who engaged in any way in treating colored persons or white persons, in charge of such, otherwise than lawfully as prisoners of war.'"[60] Lincoln was very much aware that governments should not be vengeful and that "blood cannot restore blood."[61] Yet during and after the war, perhaps, he could and should have established fair judicial processes and punishment for those convicted of violating the laws of war (as they existed at that time). In the interest of deterrence in the future if not retribution for the past, could and should Lincoln (and others) have let up somewhat less easily not only on Confederate military and prison commanders, but also Union personnel who committed heinous crimes?[62]

Although he approves of what he mistakenly takes to be Lincoln's policy of complete amnesty, Winik is not completely unaware of the theme of racial justice in his narrative of April 1865 and in his remarks about Lincoln's lenient plans for postwar America. Winik does say that the new nation's task was "making flesh of emancipation."[63] And he does say that

Lincoln's long-term goal was the Houdini-type task of "rebuilding and restoring the conquered South while maintaining the loyalty of white Unionists, protecting black freedoms and controlling a rebellious white majority."[64] But then Winik summarizes this more nuanced formulation by saying that Lincoln's "longer-term goal nonetheless remained fixed as a rock: end the war and revive the Union."[65] This way of putting it, however, misses that for Lincoln (a) abolishing slavery—at first a means to ending the war—became fused with or in tandem with the goal of saving the union and (b) the "revival" of the Union was also to be a "new birth of freedom" in which slavery would be abolished and government would be "of the people, by the people, and for the people."[66]

At another point Winik recognizes that Lincoln struggled to balance two potentially irreconcilable goals: slave emancipation and suffrage, on the one hand, and "the urgent practicality of quickly healing the nation" on the other.[67] This formulation does put nicely the problem as well as the risk that Lincoln would only be able to achieve one of these goals without the other. Yet, Winik does not acknowledge that Lincoln in fact was forging a postwar policy in which reintegration of the South had to be in terms of slavery's demise as well as progress toward black equality before the law and political participation. Instead, Winik changes the subject and construes Lincoln's conundrum as choosing between punishment of rebels for treason versus letting them up easy. In transitional justice discussions, the trade-off is often seen as between punitive justice and reconciliation. What we learn from Lincoln's efforts to end the civil war well is not only that punishment sometimes should be foregone, but also that ending a war well includes a *just* peace. And, among other things, a just peace integrates the nation on the basis of racial justice and interracial democracy.

It might be accepted that only Lincoln had this aim for racial justice in the postwar South, but that Winik's other chosen leaders saw the task in ending the war as solely one of thick reconciliation. With respect to Lee and Johnston, if not Forrest, there surely was the additional aim to stop the carnage and rebuild the devastated Southern economy. For how else to interpret the request the soldiers' private horses and mules be included in the surrender terms? On the Union side, Sherman's motives were more complex in his contribution to the war's ending. Winik's portrait of Sherman is persuasive: "an inveterate racist by today's standards" and a proponent of "hard" if not total war whose destruction of Atlanta, march to

Savannah, and destruction of Columbia, South Carolina, were informed by the aim of avenging the North as well as showing the South that the game was up.

Yet, there was another and surprising side to Sherman, one that Winik altogether neglects. In Foner's words, "William T. Sherman and his 60,000-man army . . . dealt slavery its death blow in the heart of Georgia and added a new dimension to the already perplexing land question."[68] Not only did Sherman destroy slave-worked plantations, but he met "in a dignified, almost solemn manner" in what became known as the Savannah Colloquy with twenty black leaders, learned of their passion for their own land and their rights as citizens, and issued Special Field Order No. 15.[69] This order set aside South Carolina's Sea Islands and substantial land south of Charleston for black settlement and gave forty acres and a mule to each black family.[70] Foner is quick to make it clear that "Sherman was neither a humanitarian reformer nor a man with any particular concern for blacks" and that his intent with Field Order 15 was mainly to relieve pressure on his army caused by the large number of poor blacks following it.[71] Yet many acts have mixed motives, and Sherman could have found less humane ways of reducing the numbers of expectant and even joyous blacks trailing his army. It is likely that Sherman was coming to appreciate if not embrace "the goals—the right to the fruits of one's labor, access to land, equal rights as citizens—that would animate black politics during and after Reconstruction."[72]

The second and third questions—about the *actual* impact and role of leaders' reconciling actions—are much more difficult to answer with any assurance. Winik certainly is aware that deep hatred existed between the former enemies, whether combatants or noncombatants, both during and in the immediate aftermath of the war.[73] He assumes without much evidence, however, that this enmity dissipates; and he asserts, without any argument, that what significantly causes the alleged reduction of animosity was the leaders' reconciling actions. Winik concedes that feelings of hatred on both sides, and the motive of vengeance on the part of the North, present monumental challenges to reconciliation. He does not give us, however, reason to believe that these feelings weakened in the war's immediate aftermath or that the decline, if it did occur, was importantly due to his selected leaders' actions.

With most white citizens of Richmond, the animosity toward the North (and affection for the Confederacy) seemed just as strong a year after their city burned as when they lived with pride in the Confederacy's vibrant capitol. In 1866, Confederate veterans in Tennessee, including one of Winik's reconcilers, Nathan Bedford Forrest, founded the Ku Klux Klan. The loose organization soon turned to terrorism—against blacks and pro-Reconstruction whites—and spread throughout the South. With respect to both Southerners and Northerners, news of the treatments of their respective soldiers in the other side's prison camps resulted in deep and abiding hatred. Benjamin G. Cloyd, historian of Civil War prisons in both North and South, quotes the following remarks by noted Civil War Scholar David Blight: "No wartime experience . . . caused deeper emotions, recriminations, and lasting invective than that of prisons."[74] The Northern version of these attitudes, coupled with the motive of vengeance, was among the factors resulting in the May 1865 trial and hanging in Washington, DC, of John Wenz, the commander of the notorious Andersonville Prison in Georgia. It is likely that Lincoln would have faulted the trial as unfair and would have pardoned Wenz or at least reduced his sentence. The point here, however, is not to single out the North's treatment of Wenz or the South's denial of atrocities at Andersonville but to substantiate that mutual recriminations occurred not only in the war's aftermath but throughout Reconstruction.[75]

One dimension absent from Winik's characterization of the ending of the Civil War is the struggle of blacks—slaves, freemen, and then freedmen—to destroy the Confederacy and its slavery by successively resisting their masters' rule, escaping slavery, fighting with the North, and celebrating emancipation not reconciliation: "Rather than passive victims of the actions of others, a 'problem' confronting white society, or an obstacle to reunion, blacks were active agents in overthrowing slavery, winning the Civil War, and shaping Reconstruction."[76]

The Civil War was not only a fight between brothers in a white family for and against local self-determination. It was also—and arguably more basically—a struggle between those defending and those wanting to end slavery and, subsequently, racial inequality. As we saw in examining Lincoln's visit to Richmond on April 4 (a scene, recall, omitted from both Winik's book and the History Channel's documentary), the blacks who flocked to Lincoln were jubilant at the fall of Richmond and joyously anticipated the end of the military conflict because their chains were being broken.[77] White Richmondites were appalled to see that many of the Union soldiers who occupied their city were black. In the days following Lee's and Johnston's surrender, some blacks retaliated against their former masters by taking white possessions, taking over mansions, or even whipping their former whippers. Blacks, aspiring for equal treatment and citizenship, would be for many Southern (and Northern) whites, in Foner's words, an "obstacle to reunion" rather than a party to the so-called bright moment of reconciliation. Even the relation of the white Union soldiers to their black colleagues was one of grudging appreciation rather than harmony.

Our third question concerns the possible causes of postconflict reconciliation. To the extent that some (thicker or thinner) harmony between former foes did take place at war's end, could it be attributed to something other than the small and large acts of the political and military leaders? Other candidates, which Winik does not examine, would be prior relationships among soldiers and ordinary people, physical and emotional exhaustion, relief at the war's termination, and entrepreneurial cooperation between Northern capital and Southern agriculture intent on building a New South.

I turn now to Winik's ambitious claims about the long-term significance of his select leaders' putative reconciling actions. Was April 1865 a brief shining moment before the bitter taste of Reconstruction? Winik's boldest claim is that the leaders' actions saved America or made it one nation, perhaps for the first time. His weaker claim is that while April 1865 failed to reconcile the nation during the "painful, slow, and flawed nightmare" of Reconstruction, things would have been much worse without the reconcilers of April 1865:

[April 1865 is] an essentially magic moment when a handful of leaders, inspired by Lincoln's vision in the North and Lee's dignity in the South, rose to the occasion to prevent a far greater, more raucous, more bloody, and even more civil war-ridden era, which would have made the Reconstruction period seem like a picnic.[78]

For Winik, the wonderful harmony (friendly feelings) that did take place at war's end was indeed submerged by contention and bloody civil strife. He contends, however, that matters could have been much worse without the initial reconciliation. It was only after Reconstruction ended in 1877 that the reconciling legacy—betrayed by Reconstruction—finally reasserted itself.

Let us examine critically each claim. I have already questioned whether the war and its aftermath was one of overall reconciliation and whether the reconciliation that did exist was a product of leaders' decisions and actions. With respect to Reconstruction itself, Winik comes all too close to the now discredited view that Reconstruction was an unmitigated disaster. Although scholars of the period see Reconstruction beginning in 1863 with (and before) the Emancipation proclamation, the black Freedmen's Bureau, and US Army–organized cities in occupied areas, Winik reduces Lincoln's postwar strategy to reconciliation and largely neglects black protagonism, the varied and contradictory phases of Reconstruction, and—in spite of its flaws—the many achievements of Reconstruction. The Reconstruction historian Eric Foner concisely and movingly formulates these points:

> Rather than passive victims of the actions of others or simply a "problem" confronting white society, blacks were active agents in the making of Reconstruction. During the Civil War their actions helped force the nation down the road to emancipation, and in the aftermath of that conflict their quest for individual and community autonomy did much to establish Reconstruction's political and economic agenda. Although thwarted in their bid for land, blacks seized the opportunity created by the end of slavery to establish as much independence as possible in their working lives, consolidate their families and communities, and stake a claim to equal citizenship. Black participation in Southern public life after 1867 was the most radical development of the Reconstruction years, a massive experiment in interracial democracy without precedent in the history of this or any country that abolished slavery in the nineteenth century.
>
> The transformation of slaves into free laborers and equal citizens was the most dramatic example of the social and political changes unleashed by the Civil War and emancipation.[79]

The struggle of blacks and their white allies—whether the Federal Army, pro-Union Southerners ("scalawags"), or Northerners who came to help or exploit the South's economic situation ("carpetbaggers")—

made for contentious debate, political struggle, and finally violence. Although blacks engaged in some defensive violence, Foner lays most of the blame on the Ku Klux Klan and those white Southerners who acquiesced to its maintenance of white supremacy. This black struggle for racial justice and democracy continued through the phases of Reconstruction: the rehearsals for Reconstruction (1863–66), which empowered blacks and their communities; Andrew Johnson's presidential reconstruction (1867–70), which returned power to former slave-owning planters; and Radical Congressional Reconstruction (1870–77), in which the federal government reasserted itself, and, passing the 14th and 15th Amendments, established black suffrage and curtailed white violence. Although in 1877 the white Redeemers finally weakened if not destroyed Reconstruction, the civil rights movement of the 1950s and 1960s revived that legacy, and mid-60s Civil Rights legislation made strides to institutionalize it.

Instead of judging Reconstruction's achievement as due to the struggle of the black individuals and groups and their white allies, including federal and state officials before and after Johnson's presidential reconstruction, amazingly, Winik attributes whatever positive effects it had—preventing an even more conflictual period—to his bright moment's reconciling acts. Not only does Winik fail to acknowledge (let alone celebrate) many of Reconstruction's most important achievements, he also fails to give us a reason to believe that there is any causal link to the reconcilers of April 1865.

What about Winik's most robust claim, that April 1865 saved America? He does not go into any detail about the sort of unified America that he believes is the legacy of April 1865. It certainly is not Reconstruction. Nor is Winik's moment the same as Foner's: "For a brief moment, the country experimented with genuine interracial democracy. Then Reconstruction was overturned by a violent racist reaction. This book [*Forever Free*] tells the story of that turbulent era, its successes and failures, and it long-term consequences up until this very day."[80]

Rather, for Winik, the America that the essentially magical moment saved was one in which Americans became a more unified nation after the bloody conflict was put behind them. It is also an America in which everyone is swept up and reintegrated by new inventions, new economic opportunities, and the game of baseball.[81] What is terribly deficient in this vision of reunion is that it leaves out blacks (and many others). Just as the back-slapping and embracing civil war soldiers—both blue and grey—had Gettysburg reunions replete with Forrest's friendly feelings in 1913 and 1938, so Winik's vision of a unified America largely excludes blacks. Winik's book is guilty of the same narrow vision as Ken Burns's TV documentary "The Civil War." The criticism that Foner makes of Burns applies just as well to Winik: "Reunion represented a substantial retreat from the Reconstruction ideal of a color-blind citizenship. The road to reunion was paved with the broken dreams of black Americans, and the betrayal of those dreams was indispensable to the process of reunion as it actually took place."[82]

To be reconciled to the America that Winik celebrates is to be reconciled to an America that fails to see that its Civil War did not end as well as it could have, and whose Reconstruction is still unfinished. For a war to end well, there must be more than an end of conflict and the onset of friendly feelings. There must also be a coming to grips with and the start of efforts to eliminate the causes of that war. What Winik neglects is what the tradition of transitional justice has emphasized: to move forward after great evil, a country must also look backward. It does so by confronting, resisting, and combating the causes of the evil and the conflict. It also does so by revealing the truth about the past. And just as Reconstruction is America's unfinished revolution, so proponents of transitional justice know that just and effective reckoning with past wrongs often takes many generations. In these processes truth about the past—obtained by truth and reconciliation commissions or historians—has an important role to play. Historian Winik has given us many neglected facts of April 1865 and the US Civil War's ending well. Historian Foner corrects the distortion in Winik's picture and sets before Americans the unfinished task of ending the war well by forging a more inclusive and just society. Rather than giving us Winik's happy ending of reconciliation in 1865, Foner inspires us to take up the unfinished task to achieve both healing and justice:

> One reason, perhaps, why Reconstruction was for so long shunted to an obscure backwater of national memory is that Americans, like other people, prefer historical narratives with happy endings. Certainly, Reconstruction was in many ways a failure. In part, the story of Reconstruction history

reveals in vivid hues aspects of our national history—especially our long experience with racial violence—that are hardly pleasant to contemplate. Yet properly understood, Reconstruction was also an era of noble dreams, of inspiring efforts by ordinary men and women to create a more just society for themselves and their countrymen. As South Africans demonstrated in the 1990's by establishing a Truth and Reconciliation Commission to uncover and publicize the history of apartheid, the search for historical truth can be simultaneously empowering and healing. In this country as well, "the facts of Reconstruction"—the era's true history—can serve as an inspiration for the unfinished task of forging from the ashes of slavery a society of interracial democracy and social justice.[83]

Notes

I am grateful to my student and research assistant John David Evans for assistance in the research and editing of this paper. I also benefited from the comments and suggestions of John Coski, Eddie Crocker, Larry Crocker, and Karie Cross.

1. See also the History Channel documentary "April 1865" (A&E Television Networks, 2003).

2. Jay Winik, *April 1865: The Month That Saved America* (New York: Harper 2001), 181.

3. David A. Crocker, "Reckoning with Past Wrongs: A Normative Framework," *Ethics & International Affairs* 13 (1999): 43–64; "Punishment, Reconciliation, and Democratic Deliberation," *Buffalo Criminal Law Journal* 57, no. 2 (2002): 509–49; "Reckoning with Past Wrongs in East Asia," in Mike Mochizuki and Charles Burress, eds., *Memory, Reconciliation, and Security in East Asia* (Stanford, CA: Stanford University Press, 2012).

4. Michael Moser, "The 'Armed Reconciler': The Military Role in the Amnesty, Reconciliation, and Reintegration Process, *Military Review*, 87, no. 4 (November/December 2007): 13–19. See also Maj. John J. McDermott, "Reconstruction as a Case Study in Flawed Conflict Transformation" (Fort Leavenworth, Kansas: School of Advanced Military Studies, United States Army and General Staff College, 2008); and "Reconstruction and Post-Civil War Reconciliation," in *Military Review* (January-February 2009): 67–76.

5. Winik, *April 1865*, 375–76. See also 354 and 387.

6. Crocker, "Punishment, Reconciliation, and Democratic Deliberation," 528.

7. Desmond Tutu, *No Future without Forgiveness* (London: Image, 2002), 23, 31, 54–55.

8. See, especially, Winik, *April* 1865, xiv, 207, and 351. See John Carlin, *Playing the Enemy: Nelson Mandela and the Game That Made a Nation* (New York: Penguin, 2008) for a riveting account of how Nelson Mandela contributed to this sort of national reconciliation through the South African rugby team's unexpected victory in the rugby World Cup of 1995.

9. Abraham Lincoln, Second Inaugural Address, March 4, 1865.

10. Winik, *April 1865*, 68. Winik is drawing on the following accounts: David Herbert Donald, *Lincoln* (New York: Simon and Schuster, 571–74); Shelby Foote, *The Civil War*, Vol. 3: *Red River to Appomattox* (New York: Random House, 854–57); and Burke Davis, *To Appomattox: Nine April Days* (Durham, NC: Eastern Acorn Press, 1992), 24–28. See also Doris Kearns Goodwin, *Team of Rivals: The Political Genius of Abraham Lincoln* (New York: Simon and Schuster, 2005), 713.

11. Winik, *April 1865*, 68.

12. Winik, *April 1865*, 208. Cf. Historian Nelson Lankford describing two other accounts of the Lincoln/Weitzel conversation, in one of which Lincoln says "let them down easy." *Richmond Burning: The Last Days of the Confederate Capital* (New York: Penguin, 2002), 166.

13. Lankford, *Richmond Burning*, 163.

14. Winik, *April 1865*, 208. See, however, Lankford's doubts about the authenticity of the Pickett visit, given evidence that Pickett's wife, LaSalle, was a "plagiarizer and forger" (*Richmond Burning*, 242–43). For Lincoln's extensive but discriminating use of pardons with respect to Union soldiers who deserted and were found in dereliction of duty, see William Lee Miller, *President Lincoln* (New York: Knopf, 2008), chapter 17, "Must I Shoot a Simple Soldier Boy."

15. Goodwin, *Team of Rivals*, 719.

16. Admiral [David D.] Porter, *Incidents and Anecdotes of the Civil War* (New York: D. Appleton, 1885). Quoted in John O'Brien, "Reconstruction in Richmond: White Restoration and Black Protest, April–June 1865," *Virginia Magazine of History and Biography* 89 no. 3 (1981), 301–13; and in Lankford, *Richmond Burning*, 165.

17. Miller, *President Lincoln*, 413.

18. Winik, *April 1865*, 214.

19. Winik, *April 1865*, 207.

20. Winik, *April 1865*, 208.

21. Winik, *April 1865*, 218.

22. Goodwin, *Team of Rivals*, 732.

23. Goodwin, *Team of Rivals*, 732.

24. Winik, *April 1865*, 193–94. Goodwin quotes Winik's lovely phrase about the two generals, one "magnanimous in victory, the other, gracious and equally dignified in defeat" (Goodwin, *Team of Rivals*, 725).

25. Goodwin, *Team of Rivals*, 182.

26. "The officers and men surrendered are to be paroled and disqualified from taking up arms again until properly exchanged, and all arms, ammunition, and supplies to be delivered up as captured property" (Goodwin, *Team of Rivals*, 185).

27. Goodwin, *Team of Rivals*, 187.

28. Goodwin, *Team of Rivals*, 187–88.

29. Goodwin, *Team of Rivals*, 188.

30. Goodwin, *Team of Rivals*, 188–89.

31. Goodwin, *Team of Rivals*, 189.

32. Winik, *April 1865*, 170–71.
33. Goodwin, *Team of Rivals*, 190.
34. Winik, *April 1865*, 171.
35. Goodwin, *Team of Rivals*, 182. Throughout his long career Nelson Mandela has exhibited a keen sense of the importance of small and symbolic acts. In wearing traditional Xhosa dress to his treason trial in the 1950s, he made clear that he was a traditional African being tried in white man's court. More than forty years later, as president of postapartheid South Africa, he sought to overcome the deep hostility between his black (and colored) followers and white Afrikaners by securing South Africa as the site of the rugby World Cup and by wearing the jersey and cap of the Springboks, a team that Afrikaners adored and blacks abhorred. See Nelson Mandela, *Long Walk to Freedom* (Boston: Little Brown, 1994) and Carlin, *Playing the Enemy*. However, Mandela would join other democrats in arguing that leaders without active citizens, who challenge and support them, rarely accomplish great things.
36. Winik, *April 1865*, 191.
37. Winik, *April 1865*, 192–93.
38. Winik, *April 1865*, 194.
39. Winik, *April 1865*, 195.
40. Winik, *April 1865*, 197.
41. Bruce Catton, *A Stillness at Appomattox* (New York: Doubleday, 1953).
42. Museum of the Confederacy, Richmond, Virginia, viewed June 25, 2010. Neither a professional nor an amateur historian, I am in no position to say which interpretation of the event came closer to getting it right. But the museum, situated next to Jefferson Davis's Confederate White House, does raise the question of whether Winik has overdone the theme of the reconciling dimension of April 1865 let alone the impact of this month on postconflict America. In a personal correspondence, John M. Coski, Museum of the Confederacy historian and director of library and research, indicates that a new primary source has recently surfaced, one that favors Chamberlain's version. Coski also remarked that the museum's text "is likely to change" as it reckons with this new evidence and more generally tries "to strike a proper balance between the various interpretive disagreements" with respect to postwar harmony and reconciliation (email July 19, 2010). I am grateful to Mr. Coski for his assistance on this matter.
43. Winik, *April 1865*, 314.
44. Winik, *April 1865*, 315–16.
45. Winik, *April 1865*, 316.
46. Winik, *April 1865*, 317.
47. Winik, *April 1865*, 362.
48. Winik, *April 1865*, 362–63.
49. Nelson Lankford, historian of the fall of Richmond, readily acknowledges that this account, like that of Lincoln's visit to Pickett's house, is "filled with a spirit of reconciliation and of hope for the future of the broken country, reunited by force of arms and facing an uncertain road ahead" (Lankford, *Richmond Burning*, 243). But the two stories share "the likelihood of being outright fiction" (243). Lankford argues that the source of the

"touching" communion story is a "misinterpretation" of an aging rebel veteran's 1905 newspaper article, "Recollection of Maj. Thomas Broun," *Richmond Times-Dispatch*, April 16, 1905. In this piece, the Confederate author interprets Lee's action not as one of symbolic reconciliation but rather the opposite: "to show how to deal with the impudence of a black man who dared cross the racial line at Holy Communion . . . by ignoring him as if he did not exist" (Lankford, *Richmond Burning*, 244). Lankford does not hazard a guess as to which account is correct but does say that the 1905 veteran—and presumably Winik—"could not have divined what was in Lee's mind as he knelt to take communion" (244). And Lankford does make the general point that credence should be given to contemporary written testimony rather than to opinions written long after an event. If we follow this methodological rule, however, we have seen that Winik does provide written evidence of Lee as reconciler of North and South. What Winik does not provide is anything that Lee wrote or said about the ideal of black and white equality and reconciliation.

50. Winik, *April 1865*, 318. For an excellent study of the ethical and political aspects of disobeying orders, see Mark Osiel, *Obeying Orders: Atrocity, Military Discipline, and the Law of War* (New Brunswick, NJ: Transaction Books, 2001).

51. Nathan Bedford Forrest, "Farewell Address to His Troops, May 9, 1865," available online at http://the-american-catholic.com/2010/08/06/nathan-bedford-forrest-and-racial-reconciliation. Partially quoted by Winik, *April 1865*, 322.

52. Eric Foner, with illustrations edited by Joshua Broun, *Forever Free: The Story of Emancipation and Reconstruction* (New York: Random House/Vintage, 2005), xxi.

53. Foner, *Forever Free*, xii.

54. William Lee Miller, *President Lincoln* (New York: Knopf, 2008), 411.

55. Abraham Lincoln, Second Inaugural Address, March 4, 1865. Quoted by Miller, *President Lincoln*, 409.

56. Miller, *President Lincoln*, 410.

57. Harry R. Davis and Robert C. Good, eds., *Reinhold Niebuhr on Politics: His Political Philosophy and Its Application to Our Age as Expressed in His Writings* (New York: Charles Scribner's Sons, 1960; reprint (Eugene, OR: Wipf and Stock, 2007); Miller, *President Lincoln*, 412, 413.

58. Abraham Lincoln, Second Inaugural Address, March 4, 1865. Quoted by Miller, *President Lincoln*, 409, emphasis mine.

59. Miller, *President Lincoln*, 338. Miller's quote from John Hay is in Michael Burlingame and John R. Turner Ettlinger, eds., *Inside Lincoln's White House: The Complete Civil War Diary of John Hay* (Carbondale: Southern Illinois University Press, 1997), 64.

60. Miller, *President Lincoln*, 310.

61. Miller, *President Lincoln*, 310.

62. For arguments that fair trials and punishments can contribute to some sorts of reconciliation, see Crocker, "Punishment, Reconciliation, and Democratic Deliberation."

63. Winik, *April 1865*, 380.

64. Winik, *April 1865*, 211.

65. Winik, *April 1865*, 295.

66. Abraham Lincoln, Gettysburg Address, November 19, 1863. Commenting on Phillip S. Paludan's claim that for Lincoln "freeing the slaves and saving the Union were

linked as one goal, not two optional goals": *The Presidency of Abraham Lincoln* (Lawrence: University of Kansas Press, 1994), xv, William Lee Miller wisely remarks as follows: "'saving the Union' had to be, for the oath-bound office-holding president, something more than a 'goal.' It was now his supreme duty. 'Freeing the slaves'—that is, opposing the evil institution of slavery—although indeed for him closely linked in aspiration to the moral essence of the Union that was to be saved, was not a mandatory formal obligation but a profound purpose springing from a deep moral conviction": *President Lincoln*, 266. See also 261 and 269.

67. Winik, *April 1865*, 15.

68. Eric Foner, *Reconstruction: America's Unfinished Revolution, 1863–1877* (New York: Harper, 1988), 70.

69. Foner, *Forever Free*, 3.

70. Foner, *Reconstruction*, 70–71, and *Forever Free*, 3–6.

71. Foner, *Reconstruction*, 71.

72. Foner, *Forever Free*, 5.

73. Winik, *April 1865*, 171, 352, 375, 436, 443.

74. David W. Blight, *Race and Reunion: The Civil War in American Memory* (Cambridge, MA: Belknap Press of Harvard University Press, 2001), 152. Cited by Benjamin G. Cloyd, *Haunted by Atrocity: Civil War Prisons in American Memory* (Baton Rouge: Louisiana State University Press, 2010), 1.

75. Cloyd, *Haunted by Atrocity*, chapters 1–4.

76. Foner, *Forever Free*, xxvii. For the defense of the empirical and ethical significance of individual and communal agency or self-determination, see David A. Crocker, *Ethics of Global Development: Agency, Capability, and Deliberative Democracy* (Cambridge: Cambridge University Press, 2008), especially chapter 5. Among the volume's epigraph is a passage with striking similarity to Foner's from the writings of economist and philosopher Amartya Sen: "In terms of the medieval distinction between 'the patient' and 'the agent,' this freedom-centered understanding of economics and of the process of development is very much an agent-oriented view. With adequate social opportunities, individuals can effectively shape their own destiny and help each other. They need not be seen primarily as passive recipients of the benefits of cunning development programs. There is indeed a strong rationale for recognizing the positive role of free and sustainable agency—and even of constructive impatience": Amartya Sen, *Development as Freedom* (New York: Knopf, 1999), 11.

77. "April 1865," History Channel (A&E television networks, 2003).

78. Winik, *April 1865*, 381, 446.

79. Foner, *Reconstruction*, xxii–xxiii.

80. Foner, *Forever Free*, xx.

81. Winik, *April 1865*, 365–74.

82. Eric Foner, "Ken Burns and the Romance of Reunion," in Robert Brent Toplin, ed. *Ken Burns's The Civil War: Historians Respond* (Oxford: Oxford University Press, 1997), 113.

83. Foner, *Forever Free*, 238.

CHAPTER 9

JUSTICE AFTER WAR

Toward a New Geneva Convention

BRIAN OREND

THE TOPIC OF THE AFTERMATH OF WAR has only recently been getting the attention it deserves. Historically, it was assumed that, as the old saying goes, to the victor go the spoils of war. As a result of this widespread belief, there is actually next to no clear international law regulating the termination phase of war. We have witnessed these struggles, as I describe below, in the contexts of Afghanistan and Iraq. This, however, is a bad state of affairs that needs to be changed. In fact, there are numerous reasons why there needs to be a brand-new Geneva Convention—one devoted exclusively to the vital issues raised by the endings of wars. Why?

First, completion. There are many international laws regulating both the start of war and the middle (or conduct) of war. Moreover, many of these laws make sound strategic and good moral sense.[1] Thus, to complete our analysis of war's many impacts on international life, we need to consider the ending phase of war. Bottom line: If it is important to guide both the start and the middle of war, it is just as important to guide the end.

A second reason for a new Geneva Convention is focus. The practical task of drafting and then ratifying a binding legal document on this issue would focus international attention on doing something constructive and improving about war in general, and take *jus post bellum* (justice after war) out of abstract theory and into the concrete reality of global politics.

Third, guidance. The function of any kind of law is to guide behavior, hopefully in a way useful, advantageous, and improving for all. The laws of *jus ad bellum* (the justice of the start of war) and *jus in bello* (the justice of the conduct of war) are designed to guide the behavior of all belligerents. The rules of *jus post bellum* could likewise guide both the winner and the loser in the aftermath of armed conflict. This is assuming there even *is* a clear-cut winner and loser, which sometimes isn't the case, such as with the Iran–Iraq War of 1979–89 when the belligerents just stopped fighting after eventually realizing that neither of them could win. Contrary to the old cliché mentioned at the start, both winners and losers would gain by there being clear postwar rules. The losers, of course, could be assured that they would not be subjected to cruel, vindictive treatment at the hands of a gloating, arrogant winner. And the winners could get a clear understanding of their rights and obligations during the aftermath of war. In particular, winners would appreciate being able to point to such rules and say that they have done what they are duty-bound to do, and are therefore free to leave. It seems to me that America, for example, would have very much wanted to say this, and benefit from this, earlier on during its difficult, ongoing occupation experiences in Afghanistan and Iraq. Rules provide assurances and expectations for everyone, plus clear ways of proceeding, and all parties benefit from such clarity and can put greater confidence in the process moving forward.

Failure to regulate war termination probably prolongs fighting on the ground; a new Geneva Convention could help end the fighting. Since they have few assurances, or firm expectations, regarding the nature of the settlement, belligerents will be sorely tempted to keep using force to jockey for position. Since international law imposes very few constraints upon the winners of war, losers can conclude it is reasonable for them to refuse to surrender and, instead, to continue to fight. Perhaps they think that they might get lucky and the military tide will turn, and that it is better than just throwing themselves at the mercy of the enemy. Many observers felt that this reality plagued the Bosnian Civil War (1992–95), which had many failed negotiations and a three-year slow burn of continuous violence as the negotiations took place.[2]

A new Geneva Convention will also help restrain winners. Failure to construct principles of *jus post bellum* is to allow unconstrained war termination. And to allow unconstrained war termination is, indeed, to allow the winner to enjoy the spoils of war. This is dangerously permissive, since winners have been known to exact peace terms that are draconian and vengeful. The Treaty of Versailles, terminating World War I in 1918–19, is often mentioned in this connection. It is commonly suggested that the sizable territorial concessions and steep compensations payments forced upon Germany created hatred and economic distress, opening a space on which Hitler capitalized. In effect, the harsh terms permitted the Nazis to vent their rage by attempting to recapture lost lands, rebuild the economy by refusing to pay compensation, and ramp up war-related manufacturing.[3]

Finally, a new Geneva Convention will prevent future wars. When wars are wrapped up badly, they sow the seeds for future bloodshed. Some people, for example, think that America's failure to remove Saddam Hussein from power at the conclusion of the First Gulf War in 1991 prolonged a serious struggle and eventually necessitated the second war, of regime change, in 2003. Would the second war have happened at all had the first been ended differently—more properly and thoroughly, with a longer-range vision in mind? Many historians ask the exact same question of the two world wars and the recent related Serbian wars, first in Bosnia and then over Kosovo (1999).

Peace treaties should still, of course, remain tightly tailored to the historical realities of the particular conflict in question. There is much nitty-gritty detail that is integral to each peace treaty. But admitting this is *not* to concede that the search for general guidelines or universal standards is futile or naïve. There is no inconsistency or mystery in holding particular actors in complex local conflicts up to more general, even universal, standards of conduct. Judges and juries do that on a daily basis, evaluating the factual complexities of a given case in light of general moral and legal principles. We should do the same regarding war termination. The goal of this chapter, accordingly, is to construct a general set of plausible principles to guide communities seeking to resolve their armed conflicts fairly and decently. After that, quick application will be made of these principles to the ongoing cases in Afghanistan and Iraq.[4]

Responding to Objections

Three strong objections are often mentioned to defeat or at least challenge this proposal for a brand new Geneva Convention devoted exclusively to postwar justice. The first is that the existing Geneva Conventions do not get perfectly adhered to anyway, and so what is the point, really, of adding another one to them? The weakness of this pessimistic challenge is shown by analogy. The challenge is akin to saying that because no one adheres to the speed limits on the road, there should be no speed limits at all. Why not let everyone do whatever they want? But the existence of lawbreakers does *not* negate the point of having law: Should we, for example, get rid of the laws on property ownership because there will always be some thieves?

The second challenge has to do with the power of the winner in the postwar moment. The winner is in the position of power: Wouldn't it penalize the winner to restrict what it can do, perhaps leading to a less effective postwar experience for both winner and loser? In reply, the winner does occupy a powerful role, but this objection seems to confuse power (the factual ability to get what you want) with authority (the moral or legal right to use that power). Having won a war does not entitle the winner to do whatever it wants—there is never a moment of total moral vacuum—nor does placing some restrictions on its postwar conduct show disrespect to its power or cause unhelpful interference. To the contrary, as explained above, it is in the selfish interests of war winners to have clear rules guiding everyone's conduct.

The final challenge has to do with how such a new piece of international law might get agreed upon and enforced, especially in the typical chaos and instability of the postwar moment. This is a practical challenge, one confronted by every new piece of international law. There is some reason to believe, though, that if states have already agreed on other, controversial rules of war—and controversial human rights treaties, and difficult trade deals—they can also find common ground on rules of postwar conduct. Once drafted and agreed upon, such a new treaty could be subjected to whichever tools of enforcement states would find useful. There are many such tools in international law, including fines; court cases and trials; the creation of a new international body or bureaucracy whose job it is to ensure compliance; and so on.[5] But the better point is to ensure that the rules to begin with are—to the extent possible—in everyone's interests for, as the realist would tell us, that is the most effective enforcement mechanism of all.

JUSTICE AFTER WAR | 179

Clash of the Models: Revenge versus Rehabilitation

To guide the construction of a new postwar Geneva Convention, we can turn to two dominant, contrasting models of postwar justice: that of revenge and that of rehabilitation. It seems fair to say that the revenge model is older, but that rehabilitation has made a strong showing for itself since the end of World War II. There are, perhaps, some grounds for detecting a pendulum swing between these models over time, and moving into the future. According to the revenge model, and assuming that the so-called good side won and that the aggressive side lost, the basic aspects of a decent postwar peace are the following.[6]

Public Peace Treaty. While it does not need to be nitpicky in detail, the basic elements of a peace agreement should be written down and publicly proclaimed so that everyone's expectations are clear, everyone knows the war is over, and everyone has an idea of what the general framework of the new postwar era will be. By contrast, in medieval Europe, the most crucial parts of a peace treaty were often kept secret from the public.

Exchange of Prisoners of War (POWs). At war's end, all sides need to exchange all the POWs from the armed conflict.

Apology from the Aggressor. The aggressor in war, like the criminal in domestic society, needs to admit fault and guilt for causing the war by committing aggression. Aggression is understood to be the first use of force across an international border, thus violating the rights of political sovereignty and territorial integrity which all recognized countries enjoy. This may seem quaint and elemental, yet it can be quite controversial. For example, Germany has offered many, and profuse, official apologies for World War II, and especially for the Holocaust. Germany to this day still pays an annual reparations fee to Israel for the latter. By contrast, Japan has been nowhere near as forthcoming with a meaningful, official apology for World War II. This reticence enrages China in particular, which suffered mightily from Japanese aggression and expansion in the 1930s.[7]

War Crimes Trials for Those Responsible. The world's first postwar international war crimes trials were held after World War II in 1945–46, in both Nuremberg and Tokyo. The vast majority of those tried were soldiers and officers charged with *jus in bello* violations such as torturing POWs and targeting civilians. But a handful of senior Nazis were also charged with the *jus ad bellum* violation of committing crimes against peace—that is, of launching an aggressive war. In 1998, the international community passed the Treaty of Rome, creating the world's first permanent international war crimes tribunal. Situated mainly at The Hague, in Holland, its ambitious mandate is to prosecute all war crimes committed by all sides in all wars, and to do so using lawyers and judges from countries which were *not* part of the war in question. Recently, this new court has heard many cases from the Bosnian Civil War and from various African wars. It has even put on trial former heads of state, and not just ordinary soldiers: Slobodan Milosevic of Serbia (until his death in 2006); and Jean Kambanda, the former prime minister of Rwanda during the 1994 genocide.[8]

Aggressor to Give Up Any Gains. The thinking here is that the aggressor, as the wrongdoer, cannot be rewarded for its aggression and be allowed to keep any gains it may have won for itself during its aggression. For instance, during its initial campaign in 1992–94, the Serb side of the Bosnian Civil War initially conquered 70 percent of Bosnia, way beyond the area traditionally occupied by ethnic Serbs. More dramatically, during the Blitzkrieg of 1939–40, Hitler's Germany conquered Austria, Czechoslovakia, France, Poland, and the Scandinavian countries. This principle requires that, at war's end, the aggressor give back all such unjust gains.

Aggressor Must Be Demilitarized to Avoid a Repeat. Since the aggressor broke international trust, so to speak, by committing aggression, it cannot be trusted not to commit aggression again (at least in the short term and in the absence of regime change there). The international community is entitled to some added security. The tools the aggressor has to commit aggression must thus be taken away from it, in a process known as demilitarization. This is to say that, often, defeated aggressors lose many of their military assets and weapons capabilities, and have caps placed on their ability to rebuild their armed forces over time.

Aggressor Must Suffer Further Losses. What makes this model one of revenge is the conviction that it is not enough for the defeated aggressor merely to give up what it wrongly took, plus some weapons. *The aggressor must be made worse off than it was prior to the war.* Why? Several reasons. First, it is thought that justice demands retribution of this nature—the aggressor must be made to feel the wrongness and sting of the war that it unjustly began. Second, consider an analogy to an individual criminal: In domestic society, when a thief has stolen a diamond ring, we do not just make him give the ring back and take away his thieving tools. We also make him pay a fine or send him to jail, to impress upon him the wrongness of his conduct. And this ties into the third reason: by punishing the aggressor, we hope to deter or prevent future aggression, both by him (so to speak) and by any others who might be having similar ideas.

But what will make the aggressor worse off? Demilitarization, of course. But two further things get heavily mentioned: reparations payments to the victims of the aggressor, plus sanctions slapped onto the aggressor as a whole. These are the postwar equivalent of fines, so to speak, on all of the aggressive society. Reparations payments are due, in the first instance, to the countries victimized and hurt by the aggressor's aggression and then, secondly, to the broader international community. The reparations payments are backward-looking in that sense, whereas the sanctions are more forward-looking in the sense that they are designed to hurt and curb the aggressor's future economic growth opportunities, at least for a period of time (a sort of probation) and especially in connection with any goods and services which might enable the aggressor to commit aggression again.

While there is no denying the coherent, internal logic of the revenge model—especially if one believes that justice requires revenge, in some sense—it does have significant drawbacks as well. A policy of revenge may create new generations of enemies, as rough treatment is typically resented even by those who objectively deserve it. In this sense, the revenge model can sow the seeds of future wars (see the two examples below in particular). And it is a bad model of postwar settlement if, far from ending a war, it actually creates a new one. As for sanctions, there is compelling historical evidence—say, from post–World War I Germany and post–1991 Iraq—that sweeping sanctions hurt the well-being of civilians, those innocent of the war and who have done nothing to deserve vengeful postwar treatment. This is to say that the revenge model can violate the *jus in bello* principle of discrimination and noncombatant immunity. Next, we might ask philosophically whether justice actually does require revenge in analogy to the criminal justice system. Why not move on—forgiving if not forgetting—and concentrate on bettering things for all in the future? Finally, the revenge model does not confront the continuing existence of the bad regime that caused the war. It merely seeks to punish that regime, and reduce the resources it has to cause future trouble. By contrast, the rehabilitation model attempts to dismantle and reconstruct bad regimes.

Two Examples of the Revenge Model

Two of the most obvious and infamous historical examples of the revenge model in action concern the settlements of World War I and the First Gulf War. The Treaty of Versailles ended World War I (1914–18), and is widely deemed to be a controversial failure that in a clear sense contributed to the conditions sparking World War II. The First World War had been a disaster for perhaps all belligerents except the United States. It cost much more and lasted so much longer than anyone had predicted and, indeed, it only came to an end with victory for the Allied side when America intervened in 1917. Because of all the cost and misery, the European powers were determined to punish Germany for invading Belgium and sparking the war to begin with. So Germany was extensively demilitarized, had all its war gains taken away, and, furthermore, lost some valuable territory of its own as one aspect of punishment. Crushing reparations payments were levied upon Germany, and they would have lasted into the 1980s had the peace terms stuck. But they did not, because essentially these fines bankrupted Germany within only a few years, causing massive economic dislocation, hardship, and, eventually, civil unrest. The victorious powers also tried to force elections upon Germany, but the only result was that the people there came to associate democracy with the economic problems and they began to turn to radical, nondemocratic parties promising simple solutions in a time of complex crisis. Hitler was thus able to come to power; he stopped all reparations payments, canceled all elections and named himself the dictator, and rebuilt the German war machine—growing the economy—and promised to get all the lost lands back. He did, or tried to, thus sparking World War II.[9]

The 1991 treaty ending the First Gulf War was similarly punitive and also paved the way for a second war. The treaty called upon Saddam's Iraq to give up any claims on Kuwait, officially apologize for the aggression, and surrender all POWs. Saddam was left in power, however, and no attempt was made either to change the regime or to bring anyone to trial on war crimes charges. But Iraq was to be extensively demilitarized.

It lost many weapons, and had strict caps put on any rebuilding. Iraq had no fly zones (NFZs) imposed on it, both in the north (to protect the Kurds in Iraq from Saddam) and in the south (to protect the Shi'ites). Saddam also had to agree to a rigorous, UN-sponsored weapons inspections process. This process lasted from 1991 to 1998, and it found and destroyed literally tons of illegal weapons, including chemical and biological agents. After Saddam kicked out the inspectors in 1998, this issue grew into a major factor in favor of war in 2003, as the Americans suspected Saddam still had weapons of mass destruction (WMDs) and, moreover, was plotting to give some to al-Qaeda to enable another September 11–style terrorist strike on America. Finally, Iraq had to pay reparations to Kuwait for the aggressive invasion in 1990 and, moreover, had to suffer continuing sweeping sanctions on its economy, especially on its ability to sell oil. These sanctions devastated Iraqi civilians and did very little to hurt Saddam. There is, in fact, evidence that the sanctions only cemented Saddam's grip on Iraq, as increasingly impoverished citizens grew more and more dependent on favors from Saddam's government in order to survive.[10]

The Rehabilitation Alternative: Reconstructing Germany and Japan

As mentioned, there is no sharp split between the revenge and rehabilitation models. They share commitment to the following aspects of a decent postwar settlement: the need for a public peace treaty; official apologies; exchange of POWs; trials for criminals; some demilitarization; and the aggressor's surrender of any unjust gains. Where the models differ is over three major issues. First, the rehabilitation model rejects sanctions, especially on the grounds that they have been shown, historically, to harm civilians and thus to violate discrimination. Second, the rehabilitation model rejects compensation payments, for the same reason. In fact, the model favors investing in a defeated aggressor, to help it rebuild and to help smooth over the wounds of war. Finally, the rehabilitation model favors forcing regime change whereas the revenge model views that as too risky and costly. That it may be, but those who favor the rehabilitative model suggest that it can be worth it over the long term, leading to the creation of a new, better, nonaggressive, and even progressive member of the international community. To those who scoff that such deep-rooted transformation simply cannot be done, supporters of the rehabilitative model reply that not only *can* it be done, it *has* been done. The two leading examples are West Germany and Japan after World War II.

World War II's settlement was not contained in a detailed, legalistic peace treaty. This was partly because Germany and Japan were so thoroughly crushed and had so little leverage. But World War II's settlement was sweeping and profound, with immense effects on world history. It was worked out, essentially, between America and the Soviet Union at meetings in Tehran and Yalta, but with participation from the United Kingdom, France, China, and other of the "lesser" Allies. Both Britain and France kept control over their colonies, but everyone knew that powerful forces of anticolonialism—abetted by the exhaustion of England and France—would soon cause those old empires to crumble. As for the new empires, it was understood that the Soviet Union would hold sway in Eastern Europe, ostensibly to serve as a barrier between itself and Germany, preventing another Nazi-style invasion. (This also had the effect of providing for the export and spread of communism in the other direction.) The United States, by contrast, would get Hawaii, a number of Pacific Islands, and total sway over the reconstruction of Japan. As for Germany, it was agreed that America, Britain, France, and Russia would split it, into Western and Eastern halves. Ditto for the German capital Berlin, which was otherwise entirely within the Eastern (Soviet) territory. Within this Soviet sphere, police-state communism came to dominate as readily as it did in Russia. But within the West, there was a concerted effort to establish genuine free market, rights-respecting democracies. The same experiment was undertaken in Japan, but there the US military, under the firm leadership of Douglas MacArthur, held more direct control for longer than it did in West Germany.

The Allies, genuinely working with nationals in both countries—more so in Germany than Japan, perhaps—first undertook a purging process, which in Germany came to be known as de-Nazification. All signs, symbols, buildings, literature, and other things directly associated with the Nazis were destroyed. The Nazi party itself was abolished and declared illegal. Surviving ex-Nazis—but not all of them—were put on trial, put in jail, or otherwise punished and prohibited from political participation.[11]

The militaries of both Germany and Japan were utterly disbanded, and for years the Allied military became *the* military and the direct ruler of both Germany and Japan.

After the negative purging process, the Allies in both countries established written constitutions or basic law. These constitutions, after the period of direct military rule ended, provided for bills and charters of human rights, eventual democratic elections, and, above all, the checks and balances so prominently featured in the American system. Since government had grown so huge and tyrannical in both Germany and Japan in the 1930s, it had to be shrunk down and then broken into pieces, with each piece only authorized to handle its own business. Independent judiciaries and completely reconstituted police forces were an important part of this—and they went a long way to reestablishing the impersonal rule of law over the personal whims of former fascists. The executive branches, much more so than in the American system, were made more accountable and closely tied to the legislative branch. The goal, of course, was to ensure that the executive could not grow into another dictator. By design, there were to be no strong presidents. So Germany and Japan became true parliamentary democracies, more in the European than American style.

Western-style liberal democracy was not the only change forcibly implemented. The education systems of both Germany and Japan were overhauled, since they played huge propaganda roles for both regimes and the content of their curricula had been filled with racism, ultra-nationalism, and distorted ignorance of the outside world. Western experts redesigned these systems to impart concrete skills needed to participate in reconstruction, as well as to stress a more objective content favoring the basic cognitive functions ("the three Rs") as well as critical thinking and especially science and technology. The curricula were radically stripped of political content, though of course some lessons on the new social institutions and their principles were required.

The Americans quickly saw that their sweeping legal, constitutional, social, and educational reforms would lack stability unless they could stimulate the German and Japanese economies. The people needed their vital needs addressed, as well as a sense of hope that, concretely, the future would get better. Otherwise, they might revolt and the reforms fail. Instead of making the mistake from World War I of sucking money out of these ruined countries through mandatory reparations payments, the Americans were the ones who poured money into Germany and Japan. America shunned the revenge paradigm and embraced the rehabilitative one. It was a staggering sum of money, too, channeled through the Marshall Plan. Money was needed to buy essentials as well as to clear away all the rubble and ruined infrastructure. It was also needed to circulate in the economy, to get the Germans and Japanese used to free market trading. Jobs were plentiful, as entire systems of infrastructure—transportation, water, sewage, electricity, agriculture, finance—had to be rebuilt. Since jobs paid wages, thanks to the Marshall Plan, the people's lives improved and the free market system deepened. But it was not just the money. American management experts poured into Germany and Japan, showing them the very latest and most efficient means of production. Within thirty years Germany and Japan had not only rebounded economically, they had the two strongest economies in the world after America itself, based especially on quality high-tech manufacturing such as automobiles.

The postwar reconstructions of Germany and Japan easily count as the most impressive postwar rehabilitations in modern history, rivaled perhaps only by America's rebuilding of its own South after the Civil War (1861–65). Germany and Japan today have massive free market economies and politically remain peaceful, stable, and decent democracies. They are both very good citizens on the global stage. In addition, these countries are by no means clones (much less colonies) of America: They each have gone their own way, adding local color and pursuing political paths quite distinct from those that most interest the United States—consider especially Germany's formative role in the European Union. So we have clear evidence that even massive and forcible postwar changes need not threaten a nation's character, or what makes it unique and special to its people. But such success did come at a huge cost in terms of time and treasure: it cost trillions of dollars; it took trillions of man-hours in work and expertise; it took decades of real time; it involved the cooperation of most of the German and Japanese people; and, above all, it took the will of the United States to see it through. It was American money, American security, American know-how, American patience, and American generosity which brought it all into being. Such is the magnitude of commitment needed by any party bent on successfully implementing substantial postwar rehabilitation.[12]

Suggested General Principles for the New Postwar Geneva Convention

Having considered some of the most relevant historical cases and lessons, I would now like to propose one general way in which any new *jus post bellum* Geneva Convention ought to be structured. Any such convention needs to have a sense of the goal to be achieved by the settlement, as well as an understanding of the means needed to secure that goal. I favor the rehabilitative model over the revenge model, for the reasons given above, and I would thus like to suggest that the goal of postwar justice ought to be the construction of something we might call a minimally just regime in any defeated aggressor. A minimally just regime is *not* narrowly a Western one; rather, it is capable of existing and thriving in non-Western contexts as well, as shown by Japan. A minimally just society satisfies three general principles.

First, it is peaceful, nonoutlaw, and nonaggressive. Second, it is run by a government seen as legitimate *both* in the eyes of its own people and in the eyes of the international community. The clearest way to prove political legitimacy—the right and authority to exercise power within a society—is by having the government be selected democratically, by a free and fair public and regular election, based on the principles of one person, one vote and majority rules. Such a process, more than any other, shows the consent of the people. Yet we might imagine more complex alternatives where there is widespread, uncoerced social peace in a society, and acknowledge that such may show consent and legitimacy, too. International recognition is shown by diplomatic recognition and by welcoming that society into membership in all the major international institutions, notably the UN.[13]

Third, the society in question does what it can to satisfy the human rights of its people. The very point of government is to do its part to realize human rights. This is so because human rights are claims we all have to the most basic objects of vital human need—the things without which we cannot live a minimally good life in the modern world. I argue that, abstractly, there are five major objects of human rights claims: personal security, individual freedom, elemental equality, material subsistence, and social recognition as a person and rights-holder. I propose this as a general, abstract, first-level understanding of human rights objects from which we can derive—based on combination and circumstance—particular, concrete, more detailed second-level lists of human rights objects, such as that contained within the Universal Declaration of Human Rights.[14]

The Process

If that is the kind of society to be sought after by pursuing postwar reconstruction, what are the means needed to achieve it? I have structured what I call a ten-step recipe to take us from here to there, and it is based on what we have learned from the historical best cases such as the reconstruction of Germany and Japan. A war winner, striving to achieve the goal of creating in the defeated aggressor a minimally just society, ought to do all of the following:

(1) Adhere diligently to the laws of war during the regime take-down and occupation.
(2) Purge much of the old regime, and prosecute its war criminals.
(3) Disarm and demilitarize the society.
(4) Provide effective military and police security for the whole country.
(5) Work with a cross section of locals on a new, rights-respecting constitution that features checks and balances.
(6) Allow other, nonstate associations or civil society to flourish.
(7) Forego compensation and sanctions in favor of investing in and rebuilding the economy.
(8) If necessary, revamp educational curricula to purge past propaganda and cement new values.
(9) Ensure that the benefits of the new order will be (a) concrete and (b) widely, not narrowly, distributed.
(10) Follow an orderly, not-too-hasty exit strategy when the new regime can stand on its own two feet.

This ten-point recipe for reconstruction is only a general blueprint; clearly, in particular cases, some things will need to be emphasized over others. The best recipes always allow for individual variance and input depending on time and the ingredients at hand. We should also note the heavy interconnectedness of many of these elements. US Major-General William Nash is probably only exaggerating a bit when he declares that "the first rule of nation-building is that everything is related to everything, and it's all political."[15] Further, in spite of the variances among aggressive, rights-violating societies—different geography, history, language, economy, diet, ethnic composition—there has been striking similarity in the kind of regime here in view. Think of the major twentieth-century aggressors and dictatorships: the USSR, Fascist Spain and Italy, Nazi Germany, Imperial Japan, North Korea, Communist China, Pol Pot's Cambodia, Idi Amin's Uganda, Saddam Hussein's Iraq, the Taliban's Afghanistan. In spite of all the differences among them, the regimes shared large affinities: a small group of ruthless fanatics uses force to come to power; it keeps power through the widespread use of violence, both internally and externally; it engages in massively invasive control over every major sphere of life, with no other associations allowed to rival the state's prestige; the rule of law is jettisoned; the military, or dominant party, becomes all-important; human rights are trampled upon; and so on.[16] To a remarkable extent, in spite of all the other differences, it has been the same kind of regime. And this should not, in the end, come as so much of a surprise: They all learned from each other and sought to emulate what worked elsewhere. The modern police state only has so many precedents to draw upon, and might in fact be located ultimately in such early examples as Napoleonic France, or most probably Robespierre's reign of terror during the French Revolution.[17] So, then, we should not be all that shocked, surprised, and skeptical if it turns out that one general recipe can in fact be found for transforming such regimes and societies away from rampant rights violation into ones that are at least minimally just.

Application to Afghanistan and Iraq

Afghanistan has been in a period of postwar reconstruction since early 2002; Iraq since mid-2003. It seems true that the international community as led by America has—more or less—been trying to implement the above ten-step recipe in each instance. It has been a very difficult process in both countries and has seen a mixture of both successes and failures.

The major successes in both nations have been the replacement of aggressive, rogue, or outlaw regimes with new governments. The old regimes have been purged, and these new governments enjoy democratic legitimacy—through multiple elections in both countries (most recently in 2010)—and are based on written constitutions crafted by locals. Civil society—compared to what it was under Saddam or the Taliban—has now blossomed. The gains in terms of personal freedom in both societies have been huge and must be noted. Also, in Afghanistan at least, the gains in terms of gender equality have been very substantial with, for example, the international community building and staffing many new schools for girls and women.

The problem, however, is that the evidence suggests that it is not abstract things like individual liberty and gender equality which matter most when it comes to the success and durability of postwar reconstruction. The historical data suggest instead that it is concrete things that are decisive, in particular security and the economy. Jim Dobbins, probably the leading scholar on the issue, has distilled all this data into one crystal-clear rule of thumb regarding postwar success: The war-winning occupier, and the new local regime, have about ten years to form an effective partnership and to devote themselves in particular to making the average person in that society feel better off—more secure and more prosperous, especially—than they were prior to the outbreak of the war.[18] If they can do this, postwar reconstruction will probably succeed in the sense that there will be a new country which is a) stable, b) minimally just (in the threefold sense described above), and c) run entirely by locals. If not, there will be failure, and a serious risk of backsliding into armed conflict. Using this rule of thumb, we note with concern that the approximate deadline for achieving this in Afghanistan would be 2012, and in Iraq, 2013. While the average person in both nations would no doubt report huge improvement in personal freedoms, what would they say about their security from violence and their economic situation? They would not all say the same thing, of course, but I would suggest that in both countries, five big obstacles stand in the way of timely and successful postwar reconstruction.

The first obstacle is simply the weight of history. Psychologists have, as a maxim of treatment, the rule that the single greatest predictor of future behavior is past behavior. If this is true and can be applied to societies as a whole, then the future does not bode well for these two countries. Both nations have been plagued by devastating, near-constant warfare since 1979, and their deeper histories have seen serious armed conflict and rivalries, inequality and instability, underdevelopment, and foreign power interference and meddling.

The second obstacle is internal divisions. Though both countries have agreed upon new constitutions and ratified them through elections, powerful internal group rivalries, and even bitter hatreds, exist. These call into question whether there is enough trust and willingness to compromise for these new regimes to work once occupying forces leave entirely. In Iraq, there is a powerful threefold division between the Kurds in the north, the Sunnis in the middle, and the Shi'ites in the south. The Kurds want as much autonomy as possible and probably, one day, want their own new and separate country. The Shi'ites are the majority, and tend to be more religiously conservative in their interpretation of Islam; Sunnis are more moderate, but even though they are the minority, historically they are used to being in power. This has created resentment in the other groups. In Afghanistan, there are many more rival ethnic, religious, and tribal groupings, compounding even further the issue of coming up with arrangements that can get everyone on board.

A third obstacle is external interference. With both these countries, there are neighboring nations meddling with postwar reconstruction or, at least, making it difficult. With Iraq, each of the three groups has allies outside their borders who support them. With the Kurds, it is the Kurdish population in Turkey (which itself does *not* want to see Kurdish independence, lest it lose some of its own territory to an independent Kurdistan). With the Sunnis it is Saudi Arabia, and with the Shi'ites it is Iran. All these regional powers have tried to sway or even sabotage US-led reconstruction. Iran has also been involved in meddling with Afghanistan— giving support and sponsorship to terrorists and religious extremists, including al-Qaeda and the Taliban—but the real issue here is Pakistan. The border between Afghanistan and Pakistan is one of the most dangerous places in the world, and is the scene of multiparty scheming and conflict, very often still breaking out into open battles. The players include the Taliban, al-Qaeda, the Pakistan army (which contains internal divisions), the new Afghan army (ditto), and the international allies, especially the United States.

The fourth obstacle is security. The hot war along the Pakistan border means that Afghanistan is not secure. While the capital, Kabul, is quite secure, the same cannot be said for the rest of the nation: There is a deep urban–rural split in this regard. Afghanistan is a highly weaponized society, with nearly all men owning guns and with local tribal leaders protecting their families' farms and crops with their own armed militias. The Taliban—the former government of Afghanistan, overthrown by the United States during the post–September 11 invasion in November 2001—is making a comeback in rural areas by clamping down on these local tribal warlords and promising a return to the very strict, religious law-and-order state they feel they achieved when in power. So would the average Afghan feel they are more secure now than back when the Taliban were in power? Probably not, and this is one reason why President Barack Obama has ordered a new surge of US troops into Afghanistan over the next few years. He has done this with the aim of bringing security, turning the tide against a resurgent Taliban, and dealing more effectively with the border area to ensure that radical Islamic extremists do not use it to rebuild and potentially strike America once more.

Things were so bad in terms of security in Iraq during 2005–6 that experts spoke openly of there being a civil war between the three groups. At the time, President George W. Bush ordered a big surge of more US troops into Iraq and, as led by General David Petraeus, they have succeeded beyond anyone's expectations in cutting down group-on-group violence and in keeping the peace. (This success is what inspired Obama to order the same for Afghanistan, with Petraeus likewise in charge.) But is it enough? Dobbins would remind us that more security now than in 2006 is not the same thing as more security back when Saddam was in power in 2003. Saddam was a brutal tyrant, but he did keep law and order. So would the average Iraqi say they feel safer and more secure than before the war? My sense is not quite yet, in spite of real recent progress.

The fifth obstacle is the economy. Would the average Afghan or Iraqi say they are more prosperous than prior to the war? Thankfully, the Americans did not implement the revenge model in either case, and instead have sent investment flowing into both countries. Iraq probably has a better shot here, as at least it has the oil and gas resources, as well as a large and reasonably educated workforce. Yet huge challenges remain.

The near-constant war since 1979, plus the effects of the sanctions from 1991 to 2003, devastated Iraq's basic infrastructure and well being. So much rebuilding needs to be done. Unemployment, estimated at half the workforce, remains a terrible problem. One solution would seem to be to pay the unemployed to perform all the rebuilding, but the costs would be enormous—in the dozens of billions, or more—and the Americans have been reluctant to pay the bill all on their own.

Afghanistan is one of the world's poorest countries, where two-thirds of the population lives on the equivalent of two US dollars per day. The same proportion of the population is thought to be functionally illiterate, and unemployment is also thought to afflict half the workforce. Afghanistan faces the same issues of ruined infrastructure and the brutal consequences that constant warfare has inflicted on the economy. These consequences can be condensed as follows.

Would you open a business in a war zone? Afghanistan's economy is a toxic mixture of war and drugs. Poppies grow well there, and farmers can earn much more growing them than legal crops like wheat or corn. It is estimated that one-third of Afghanistan's economy comes from poppy production, and the heroin and opium trade which comes out of it. Transforming Afghanistan's economy from one of war and drugs to a peaceful and legal economy rooted in broad-based, healthy economic growth is proving terribly difficult. The local tribal warlords sell drugs and use the money to induce the farmers into growing poppies instead of potatoes. They also use the money to pay officials to look the other way, creating widespread corruption in the Afghan government. Moreover, the warlords get into turf wars with each other, trying to capture each other's markets or to steal drugs or crops. Thus, the drugs fuel the violence, and the violence perpetuates underdevelopment. Afghanistan is dangerously close to being what political scientists call a narco-state, with similarities to Colombia and even Mexico. And this cycle of violence and underdevelopment only deals with the drug side of the equation; the same cycle exists due to the religious and political instability and factionalism that sparks violence, which in turn hampers development. Somehow stopping these two terribly strong and interlinked vicious cycles is a top concern as the international community tries to prevent Afghanistan from becoming a failed state.[19]

Conclusion

Though history shows that successful postwar reconstruction has been and can be done, it is a separate issue whether it will be done in Iraq and Afghanistan. Such are the problems in those countries that it may well produce a backlash effect against the rehabilitation model itself, causing the pendulum of public and elite opinion to sway back to the revenge model, which might be seen as simpler and less costly. That would be a shame, as we have seen that the revenge model has substantial flaws. Systematic debate and reflection on these difficult issues seems the only way out of this cycle, and such debate and reflection would be enhanced enormously by the creation of a brand new Geneva Convention, one devoted exclusively to justice after war.

Notes

1. See especially the Hague Conventions (1899–1907), the UN Charter (1945), and the Geneva Conventions (1877 and 1949). See also Geoffrey Best, *War and Law since 1945* (Oxford: Clarendon, 1994).

2. David Rieff, *Slaughterhouse: Bosnia and the Failure of the West* (New York: Simon and Schuster, 1995).

3. Manfred F. Boemeke, ed., *The Treaty of Versailles* (Cambridge: Cambridge University Press, 1998). We shouldn't make the mistake, however, of believing that the treaty exonerates the German people from allowing Hitler to come to power. The treaty may have been *a* factor in laying the groundwork for World War II but it can hardly be considered the only one. The failure of rival German elites to challenge Hitler, the ruthless thuggery of the Nazis, and the electoral appeal of simple solutions in a time of complex crisis were all important domestic factors in Germany. For an excellent study, see Margaret MacMillan, *Paris 1919* (New York: Macmillan, 2003).

4. Stephen J. Cimbala, *Strategic War Termination* (New York: Praeger, 1986); Paul R. Pillar, *Negotiating Peace: War Termination as a Bargaining Process* (Princeton, NJ: Princeton University Press, 1983); Stuart Albert and Edward C. Luck, eds., *On the Endings of Wars* (London: Kennikat Press, 1980); and Fen Osler Hampson, *Nurturing Peace: Why Peace Settlements Succeed or Fail* (Washington, DC: US Institute of Peace, 1996).

5. Thomas Buergenthal and Harold G. Maier, *Public International Law in a Nutshell* (St. Paul, MN: West, 1990).

6. The following section draws upon my "Justice after War," *Ethics and International Affairs* (2002): 43–56 and my *The Morality of War* (Peterborough, ON: Broadview, 2006), 160–89.

7. John Keegan, *The Second World War* (New York: Vintage, 1990).

8. Joseph E. Persico, *Nuremberg* (New York: Penguin, 1995); Tim Maga, *Judgment at Tokyo* (Lexington, KY: University of Kentucky Press, 2001); William Schabas, *An Introduction to the International Criminal Court* (Cambridge: Cambridge University Press, 2001).

9. Macmillan, *Paris 1919*; John Keegan, *The First World War* (New York: Vintage, 1994).

10. Geoffrey Leslie Simons, *The Scourging of Iraq* (New York: Macmillan, 2nd ed., 1996).

11. Some especially useful ex-Nazis were provided safe havens in the West, particularly those who were working on Hitler's rocket program.

12. Leon V. Sigal, *Fighting to the Finish: The Politics of War Termination in America and Japan* (Ithaca, NY: Cornell University Press, 1989); Howard B. Schonberger, *Aftermath of War: Americans and The Remaking of Japan* (Kent, OH: Kent State University Press, 1989); Michael Schaller, *The American Occupation of Japan* (Oxford: Oxford University Press, 1987); and Eugene Davidson, *The Death and Life of Germany: An Account of the American Occupation* (St. Louis: University of Missouri Press, 1999).

13. John Rawls, *The Law of Peoples* (Cambridge, MA: Harvard University Press, 1999).

14. See my *Human Rights: Concept and Context* (Peterborough, ON: Broadview, 2002).

15. William Nash, quoted in James Traub, "Making Sense of the Mission," *New York Times Magazine* (April 11, 2004), 35.

16. Jonathan Glover, *Humanity: A Moral History of the Twentieth Century* (New Haven, CT: Yale University Press, 2001).

17. Lynn Hunt, ed. *The French Revolution and Human Rights* (London: Bedford, 1996).

18. Jim Dobbins, et al., *America's Role in Nation-Building: From Germany to Iraq* (Washington, DC: RAND, 2003); Jim Dobbins and Seth G. Jones, eds., *The United Nations' Role in Nation-Building* (Washington, DC: RAND, 2007).

19. Material for this section comes from Stephen Tanner, *Afghanistan: A Military History* (New York: De Capo, 2009); Toby Dodge, *Inventing Iraq* (New York: Columbia University Press, 2003); and Dobbins et al., *America's Role in Nation-Building* and *The United Nations' Role in Nation-Building*.

CHAPTER 10

"JUST PEACE"

An Elusive Ideal

MARK EVANS

ABSOLUTELY CENTRAL TO THE CASE for a theory of *jus post bellum* that has garnered support only relatively recently is the ideal of a just peace. This centrality is evident in both types of context in which we may invoke the tenets of such a theory. The first is where *jus post bellum* is added to the traditional bipartite structure of just war theory, which holds that the ultimate goal of a just war must be a just peace. This addition is needed in at least three ways. First, some sense of what this goal means is needed not only in the original justification of a just war but also, where possible and appropriate, to orient its conduct. Second, it matters greatly to the achievement of a just peace how a just war is ended. Third, insofar as a just peace is not secured simply by silencing the guns, the ideal must govern the processes of peace building, especially (because this might be overlooked in the triumphalism of victory) with respect to specifying the responsibilities as well as the rights of just victors.

The second context is the ending and aftermath of a war that had no initial moral sanction, or lost whatever sanction it started with. This is because the immorality of an unjust war does not free its participants from morality's obligations in rectifying the initial wrong, or alleviating the harm and repairing the damage it has caused.[1] A just peace is still desirable, and may still be possible, even after such a war: The ideal should thus, where possible, govern planning and conduct in such circumstances (and, in instances of noncompliance, it is what would rightly inform criticism of postconflict behavior). Thus, it makes sense to talk of *jus post bellum* for agents other than just victors and in circumstances other than the ending/aftermath of a just war.[2]

What these aspects of *jus post bellum* are aiming to address are nothing more than the aspirations of all those who have lived through war and long for a better future: Who among them would ideally want, other things being equal, anything other than a just peace? It is thus remarkable that it has taken so long for the ideal to receive the kind of scholarly scrutiny it is now generating.

Or is it? One could readily agree with the above observations about its importance but argue that just peace is an *elusive* concept, a characteristic that might help to explain the relative lack of attention paid to it. There are two senses in which the claim that it is elusive can be intended: (i) as a state of affairs it is in general unobtainable; (ii) as a concept it eludes clear and coherent exposition. It evades attempts to define it adequately such that, while we may agree that it is an important ideal, we cannot say much to illuminate what it actually denotes.

In this chapter I will pay more attention to the second sense (conceptual) as I believe it poses more of a threat to the very point of theorizing just peace and hence to a significant extent *jus post bellum* itself (thus suggesting that there may have been valid reasons, if unrecognized at the time, as to why it did not figure in just war debates until recently). The elusiveness of just peace as a concept arises in part from the way in which a particular style of philosophy approaches such ideals, and the contribution (or lack of it) that such philosophy makes to this debate must therefore be considered. Before I move to this discussion, however, I shall comment briefly and incompletely on the first sense—just peace as a state of affairs—which, of course, generates important reservations on its own account that are potentially very damaging to the theory of *jus post bellum*.

Saying that just peace is unobtainable is obviously to assume that we know what the ideal stands for, so just peace as a state of affairs clearly departs from the thrust of just peace as a concept. In short, this first sense can depict the mooted unobtainability of just peace in distinct ways, three of which I shall identify here.

First, some might say that justice itself is unobtainable in the radically imperfect real world we inhabit, the imperfections of which are typically exacerbated in postconflict situations not least because even a just war is a response to an initial injustice (a threatened or actual aggression) and has caused even those on the side of justice to do many bad things.[3] So, with the best will in the world, we can grasp the meaning and import of just peace only in thought, not in the relevant scenario for its practice. The conjunction of justice and peace is therefore a piece of conceptual wishful thinking, which is of no use when thinking about what should be done in war's aftermath.[4]

This claim is closely related to a familiar objection to just war theory, which denies that justice could ever be what might justify the terrible things one has to do in war, even if other considerations *might* justify them.[5] Now, I think that we can begin to resolve the controversy over the place of justice in the morality of war by distinguishing two concepts of justice that are often incoherently conflated in the debate. The first regards justice as what I call a pristine virtue and it is, very generally stated, what we would expect to find as (partly) constitutive of the ideal world. This ideal world is what is described in ideal theory and, though it need not, strictly speaking, describe a perfect world, such theory does offer an account of how things should be ideally with no significant ills to address or hard compromises to be hammered out.[6] Thus, those who deny that war can be just might do so on the grounds that there is nothing ideal about having to wage war (there is no war in the ideal world and, if justice is a constituent of that world, there can be no justice in war). Those who use the pristine concept of justice in support of the claim that just peace is unobtainable are therefore making an empirical assumption about the irremediable nature of the so-called nonideal world's imperfections that block the possibility of a just peace.

The second concept of justice does not treat it as a matter for our utopias (realistic or otherwise), though it need not deny (as we shall shortly see) that it is intelligible and useful sometimes to utilize the pristine concept as well. Instead, it posits justice as a remedial or rectificatory virtue. It is what we invoke to right a wrong, and would not therefore be needed if there were no wrong in the first place. It is the sense of justice we find in conceptions of punishment, for example: Just punishments are inflicted on wrongdoers as morally appropriate responses to their wrongdoing which may partly have the function of restoring things to the way they ought to be.[7] Put differently: The first concept treats justice as pure and unalloyed in the sense of not being a response to a wrong, whereas the second concept treats justice as precisely such a morally appropriate response. To be sure, the two are related in the sense that morally appropriate rectificatory justice is necessarily inspired at some level by the pristine view of the way the world ought to be.[8] But the former becomes no less a matter of justice in its understanding of the concept, to any extent that it falls short of an unqualified reiteration of pristine justice.[9]

Second, one might agree with the position above that pristine just peace is currently unobtainable, but argue that the latter's justice is largely rectificatory in character. Even that might not be achievable in certain situations, of course, and this is the second version of the unobtainability problem for just peace. Proponents of this view need not believe in the perpetual inevitability of war. Instead, they may say that whatever theoretical reconciliation may be effected between justice and peace, in practice and regrettably the two typically pull away from each other. Peace, for example, is so often difficult enough to achieve in itself, let alone bringing it into line with the demands of rectificatory justice, that we simply should not posit such ambitious goals in the ending of war.

The third argument is a variant of the second, and I call it the Beilin objection, for it was Yossi Beilin (an Israeli diplomat and politician) who articulated it in one of the comparatively few works devoted to just peace.[10] He calls just peace a dangerous objective: To make justice an essential condition of the peace that is sought in ending a war is more than likely going to extend the war's duration, with all the additional horrors and tragedies that will bring. Not only does justice make the desired objective more demanding, it is also a concept open to manipulation. In general, everyone who fights does so using justice as their cause, and conflicting understandings of what it means generates more excuses for prolonging the conflict:

> The great danger in the term Just Peace is, naturally, legitimizing the term "unjust peace." It is not a big stretch from its academic use to a political use and may justify opposition to peace by claiming that it is unjust. Since no peace treaty can address the needs of both sides in their entirety, a newly legitimized excuse may be provided for those opposing it.[11]

I do not deny that just peace can be a strenuous objective—though this point should not be overgeneralized—and we must indeed be careful not to become so obsessed with it that it counterproductively prolongs the sufferings of war. On my reading of just war theory, peace generally takes precedence over justice, and one may often need an ideal of an acceptable peace that falls short of justice's requirements, to define the most satisfactory possible outcome of a particular conflict.[12]

Substituting acceptable for just peace merely displaces the problem of how to define the desired end-state, of course. And if the second or third variants are dogmatically adopted as general maxims on the disutility of just peace, rather than as possibilities that may need to be carefully explored in specific situations, then the door is opened for moral backsliding: an incentive to settle for less than what is actually possible from the perspective of justice. Similarly to how rectificatory justice looks to pristine justice for inspiration, so does acceptable peace look to justice (rectificatory and thus pristine) to help one work out what is indeed acceptable.

So much, in the present discussion, for the first sense of just peace's elusiveness as a state of affairs. The second, conceptual claim that we cannot in general adequately say what just peace *is* can also be rendered in various ways. Not all of them are compatible with each other, though more than one could be invoked in the same argument to explain and justify the conceptual claim. Five of them are:

(1) What just peace actually means and requires can shift during the course of a war: It is a moving target in analysis even in a single situation;

(2) Justice and peace are essentially contested concepts, varying in meaning and implications across time and space and can only therefore be understood on a bespoke, case-by-case basis;

(3) Even if we can talk about justice and peace in general, universalizable terms, thus eschewing the more thoroughgoing relativism suggested by (2), their full meaning and, especially, their practical implications can only be understood in context. Abstract from particular situations, which are themselves very distinct from each other, and just peace evaporates as a substantive concept;

(4) Insofar as just peace is an objective of excombatants to construct, there is no definitive way of identifying what should and should

not count as constitutive of it such that we can say its construction had been achieved;

(5) Insofar as just peace is a balance of justice and peace, we cannot know when that balance is adequately struck to deliver the ideal because its two constituents are incommensurate. There is no accepted common standard by which the two can be weighed and their requirements traded off against each other.

Those who are persuaded by this form of the elusiveness charge against just peace are therefore prone to treat talk of just peace as being little more than a rhetorical slogan, sounding noble but either denoting nothing or, in fact, dignifying whatever less edifying aims and objectives its users have in mind. Any attempt to develop it into a concept that could resist the objections would, in these critics' view, be futile. It would be crushed under the weight of impossible expectations and internal contradictions.

I shall not pretend to be able fully to satisfy critics of just peace, from whatever direction their skepticism is mounted, that I can vindicate the ideal as something that can be meaningfully expounded and analyzed. This is partly because I do not think their reservations are wholly without foundation. I shall map some (but not all) sources of the conceptual elusiveness in this chapter, but I want to begin mounting the counterclaim that all need not be silence in elucidating just peace.

A Note on Philosophy

It will be evident that what I am seeking is a concept of just peace which can stand back from the intricate particularities of specific contexts to posit generalized (and, I would say, universalizable) guidelines as to the form a just peace must take. In other words, I want to see how far just peace can function as a regulative ideal which does not seek by itself to provide a comprehensive blueprint for a just peace everywhere, but instead helps to establish the normative framework within which the details are appropriately worked out on a more case-sensitive basis.

An important problem with the notion of a regulative ideal is what is sometimes called the magnification problem. On the one hand, its construction becomes so sensitive to the nuances and qualifications prompted by the idiosyncrasies of each specific case to which it may be applied that it loses any recognizable general character: It has focused too closely on each relevant particular case, losing sight of the forest for the trees. On the other hand, it may reduce its magnification too much, stepping back from the particular so far that the resulting generalized product is too abstracted from any specific instance or application to be of much use in comprehending the latter. (It becomes too indistinct to identify substantive detail.) In light of previous remarks, it is the latter aspect of the magnification problem that one may be tempted to think is an entirely predictable outcome of the kind of philosophical approach I am using here. The charge, then, is that just peace becomes elusive only when one erroneously employs such a method. As my contribution to this volume is about philosophical approaches, and as one which utilizes this particular methodology, it is incumbent on me to say something about what I think it can and cannot contribute to these debates.

The approach I use, which is characteristic of analytic philosophy, wishes to abstract from the complexities of individual concrete situations because they are typically messy, conflicting, and confusing. In the face of this, we wish to seek order and consistency in our moral judgments by employing general points of principle as and when we can, even if only as regulative (and hence incomplete) ideals. The method of reflective equilibrium, which is frequently employed in this process of abstraction, proceeds from individual judgments about specific situations, proposes the general principles that may be informing them, and then seeks to modify both the individual judgments and the mooted principles until they are brought into mutually supportive equilibrium with each other.[13]

To be sure, by starting from *given* individual intuitive judgments, the process may appear to be conservative, thus potentially giving its opponents one more argument against it. Wouldn't such an approach merely relate what one already thinks, the problems with which are precisely what prompted to philosophy in the first place? But the appeal to intuition is meant to work by trying to get arguments and conclusions to connect to what authors are assuming to be certain widely shared or shareable basic normative intuitions among their audience. Quite apart from the trivially true fact that I can't see how any argument will sway an audience without appealing to *something* they are already thinking, it is incorrect to assume that the method just reinforces what we already think *in sum*, not least because—again—what we already think often is multiply deficient: confused, contradictory, incoherent, incomplete. Indeed, one way of doing philosophy of this type well is to start off with familiar and widely accepted premises and then, by dint of its various techniques, infer or deduce conclusions that are unfamiliar and surprising. Thus, our moral thinking is typically too flawed at the outset to expect this method to exhibit great degrees of conservatism with respect to initial belief systems.

Still, the reservations about this methodology are widely entertained and many who hold them think that what is at stake is no mere philosophical triviality. A common and powerful criticism of certain peace building projects, where the concept of just peace is clearly at issue, says that their mistakes have arisen from precisely this kind of abstractive methodology on the part of policymakers: stepping back too far from the all-important details of context to attempt the imposition of an abstractly conceived blueprint that, precisely because of its context-insensitivity, was doomed to fail. If the defense of just peace as a regulative ideal is to succeed, then, it has to show how it can avoid the problem of overabstraction.

A vivid contemporary way of illustrating the challenge is to ask what would count as a just peace in Iraq and, especially, Afghanistan. But in my estimation, thinking about these two situations generates powerful intuitions on both sides of the argument. On one hand, it seems bewilderingly difficult to imagine a *possible* settlement that could count as sufficiently just. Yet on the other hand, it is not difficult to formulate some clear ideas about what would count as an *unjust* settlement: Many critics of what has gone in these two states very obviously have found it a straightforward business to do so. By contraposition, then, we can begin to piece together some idea of what justice would require.

Relatedly, I claim that it is misleading to dismiss just peace as merely a rhetorical slogan. Even if it were sufficiently open to introduce a degree of crucial indeterminacy, it is not, for most of us, utterly inert: It nudges us, sometimes quite forcefully, in certain normative directions. Nobody would say that the peace of imperial conquest, or the internal condition of prewar Nazi Germany, was just. If, as I believe to be the case, it is justice that is the more problematic of the two elements of just peace in the present context (which is not to say what counts as peace is always straightforward), most of us have at least a bare sense of what the concept denotes such that we can begin to apply it competently.[14] Those for whom just peace matters—just combatants, peace workers, and the like—do not begin their engagement with their specific tasks with no orienting idea of what it is that they are aiming for. Philosophy can certainly seek to describe, clarify, and analyze such starting points, and guide one beyond them. But how well might it really help to address the five criticisms listed above?

Just Peace and the Just Society: To Restrict or Extend?

The rest of this chapter is a partial attempt to answer this last question, and I begin by addressing the question of scope: What is it that we wish to exhibit the characteristics of a just peace?

Obviously, because each war is in some sense unique and there are very many different types under which we can nevertheless group them, we must not look for a one-size-fits-all account of to what it is that just peace as an ideal must apply. To illustrate simply, one type of interstate war might be satisfactorily concluded from the just peace perspective simply by restoring the right kind of relationship between the two, without raising any concern with the internal domestic constitution of the states in question. This can be contrasted with a war that is concluded with the occupation of one state by another. Here, just peace is very likely (perhaps always) going to have as at least part of its focus the internal condition of the occupied state (and possibly even a justly victorious state). Civil wars, and other wars not of the state-state type, will differ again on this score.

For this reason, if we are to say anything in general about what just peace might entail, to guide our thinking about and application of the ideal, it will largely take the form of what kind of specific concern is relevant to a just peace, rather than any overly specific location account of which kind of political relationship, institution, and so forth to which the ideal applies. Nevertheless—and this is the particular indeterminacy on which I am focusing at this point—there could at times be significant dispute over the appropriate scope of just peace in a single postconflict situation. Put slightly differently, there may be reasonable disagreement over what are the appropriate concerns and objectives of *jus post bellum* for any one postconflict scenario. Sometimes it may be relatively easy to agree that the understanding of just peace in a particular war has shifted during its course. For example: A war might justly begin on the assumption that to restore a just peace after X has unjustly invaded Y, the restoration of Y's sovereignty through the expulsion of X alone is what is required. Thereafter, however, it might subsequently become necessary, in order to prevent such aggression again, to invade X as well in order to remove the aggressor regime. But it could be highly contentious as to whether just peace has indeed shifted thus (have the just peace objectives changed?).[15] And even if there is no disagreement on this score, the question of the extent of appropriate responsibility on the part of just victors as far as *jus post bellum* should be concerned may well be highly contentious.[16]

I characterize the broad structure of this dispute in terms of a distinction between restricted conceptions of *jus post bellum*, so named because they restrict their concerns to the ending and relatively immediate aftermath of war, and extended conceptions, so named because they expand their concerns to broader or deeper issues, and thus in all probability extend the time frame during which *jus post bellum*'s objectives are to be pursued.

Brian Orend's seven-point model of *jus post bellum*, referred to in this volume, is representative of the restricted variant:

> *Proportionality and Publicity.* The peace settlement should be both measured and reasonable, as well as publicly proclaimed. To make a settlement serve as an instrument of revenge is to make a volatile bed one may be forced to sleep in later. In general, this rules out insistence on unconditional surrender.
> *Rights Vindication.* The settlement should secure those basic rights whose violation triggered the justified war.
> *Discrimination.* Distinction needs to be made between the leaders, the soldiers, and the civilians in the defeated country one is negotiating with. Civilians are entitled to reasonable immunity from punitive postwar measures.
> *Punishment # 1.* When the defeated country has been a blatant, rights-violating aggressor, proportionate punishment must be meted out. The leaders of the regime, in particular, should face fair and public international trials for war crimes.

Punishment # 2. Soldiers also commit war crimes. Justice after war requires that such soldiers, *from all sides of the conflict*, likewise be held accountable to investigation and possible trial.

Compensation. Financial restitution may be mandated, subject to both proportionality and discrimination. . . . There needs to be enough resources left so that the defeated country can begin its own reconstruction.

Rehabilitation. The postwar environment provides a promising opportunity to reform decrepit institutions in an aggressor regime. Such reforms are permissible . . . but they must be proportional to the degree of depravity in the regime. They may involve: demilitarization and disarmament; police and judicial retraining; human rights education; and even deep structural transformation toward a minimally just society governed by a legitimate regime.[17]

In some conceivable circumstances, this set could well suffice as a specification of just victors' rights and responsibilities. But there are some respects, and other conceivable scenarios, in which it might prove to be inadequate. For example, and perhaps despite the tenor of proportionality and publicity in particular, there may be too much of a sense of victor's justice—of what the justly victorious can do *to* their vanquished opponents—in the framing of its requirements. One may legitimately argue that there could sometimes be much more to peace building than this, going beyond the immediate aftermath of the war and its necessarily rather punitive phase in terms of, for example, properly repairing the relationships between the former enemies. (It may be a rather more two-way, mutually supportive and transformative process.)[18]

Further, in occupation scenarios one may wonder whether just occupiers have rather more extensive, and hence potentially longer-term, responsibilities than is suggested by rehabilitation.

If we grant that just victors have some responsibilities for peacebuilding, we may identify the following three general areas of potential focus:

(1) Reconstruction of the physical infrastructure of the defeated society;
(2) Appropriate redistribution of material resources (which may go some way beyond reparations);

(3) Appropriate reestablishment of sociocultural institutions, practices, and relationships.

And if peacebuilding is about more than putting the defeated society back on its feet and in the right kind of relationship with the just victor, if that alone may not be sufficient to establish a stable peace somewhat more widely for the former enemies, then we might add:

(4) Pursuit of diplomatic initiatives to institutionalize peace more widely (or, at least, to develop conflict-prevention or containment measures).

Hence, in my extended alternative to the restricted conception, I offer a more thematic list of concerns which is designed to provide a covering statement of *jus post bellum* in general, the full understandings and implications of which (including possible trade-offs) have to be worked out *in situ*:

To secure justice in the ending and aftermath of war, one must be prepared to:
(a) Set peace terms which are proportionately determined to make that peace just and stable as well as to redress the injustice which prompted the conflict;
(b) Take full responsibility for their fair share of the material burdens of the war's aftermath in constructing a just and stable peace;
(c) Pursue those national and international political initiatives for war prevention (and/or, suboptimally, conflict containment and postwar reconstruction);
(d) Take full and proactive part in the ethical and sociocultural processes of forgiveness and reconciliation that are central to the construction of a just and stable peace;
(e) Where just combatants occupy the defeated unjust aggressor, and/or are present in another territory in the aftermath of a humanitarian intervention, they have a duty to restore sovereignty/self-determination to the territory as soon as is reasonably possible.[19]

The broader, more onerous concerns and responsibilities which we are prompted to contemplate by an extended conception of *jus post bellum* arise insofar as it is the case that justice in the peace sought at war's end may not be achieved simply through punishment and rehabilitation narrowly understood. However, and focusing for clarity in the argument again on the question of what just occupiers can do in (and to) a justly occupied society, it is vital to stress that extended *jus post bellum* is not setting out to collapse the distinction between a just peace and a just society, the latter denoting a society which is socially just in at least a partly pristine sense (however that might be conceptualized). It cannot be the objective of a just war to make another society just, and it would be both too onerous and anyway inappropriate to make that the responsibility of the occupiers.[20]

But it would be far too quick to conclude from this important point of principle that in fact we should settle for something like a restricted *jus post bellum* after all. Earlier, I noted how rectificatory justice takes its cue from and is inspired by pristine justice, and, while the justice of just peace is rectificatory in general, it cannot dispense with some view of what constitutes a just society in a pristine sense. It cannot be the responsibility of just occupiers to restore all the egregious injustices of an occupied society regardless of their contribution to the starting of the conflict. Still less can occupiers have any right, let alone a responsibility, to institute anything that does not meet some threshold standard of social justice. Three examples from an occupation scenario can help to illuminate this claim.

First, the socioeconomic and political reconstruction in postwar West Germany went well beyond the removal of peace-threatening phenomena and institutions and practices that compromised the standards of minimum justice. The inappropriateness of the briefly mooted Morgenthau Plan may have been primarily rooted in the danger of its replication of Versailles-type resentment, but it was also a socially unjust arrangement for a people with ultimate rights of self-determination, social development, and so forth.

Second, feminist scholars have recently stressed how some instances of postconflict reconstruction have not paid sufficient attention to gendered inequalities in occupied societies. These raise rectificatory questions not simply because of how their redress may aid in the pacification of a society and its relations with others.

Third, the neo-liberalization of the postinvasion Iraqi economy as a result of the diktat of Paul Bremer and the Coalition Provisional Authority raises clear—and very traditional—justice issues about forms of economic organization and the distribution of wealth.[21] The dispute over its legitimacy can invoke perspectives that, though they can be linked, are also distinct and emerge from highly divergent views about the character of a just society. To what extent was the policy to the detriment of Iraqi self-determination, for example? What counts as exploitation is a hotly contested issue that has great bearing on how the policy is to be characterized. The general point is that the debate about what counts as a just society in more than mere postconflict rectificatory terms is impossible to avoid when thinking about what the occupiers have put into the place of the Ba'athist state's structures.[22] The state's longer-term future, after all, is what is being constructed.

So just peace in general does broach questions that would be asked when we consider the nature of the just society, and there are rival conceptions of social justice that are thus likely to prompt divergent conceptions of just peace. Yet I do want to maintain that most of us can begin this debate with widely shared ideas of what would count as unjust, which a generalized conception of just peace can describe and political philosophy can help to guide and shape the ensuing discussion toward certain substantive general conclusions, informed with appropriate contextual sensitivity, without pretending that a full-blown universal model of social justice is desirable or that consensus on key issues will be possible.[23]

Two other concepts in particular from my version of extended *jus post bellum* also seem liable, like justice, to generate rival conceptions: forgiveness and reconciliation. I do not think it is too difficult to argue at least a prima facie attractive case for their inclusion in this theory: It does look like a potentially serious deficiency in those accounts of *jus post bellum* that seem to neglect the obvious and widely acknowledged sociocultural dimensions of postconflict reconstruction, as if it was always enough to rebuild a country, punish criminals, and institute the rule of law. But these two concepts are yet more examples of important ideals that nevertheless can mean very different things, and about which a generalized theory may consequently be able to say rather little. Indeed, when we engage with certain specific conceptions of them, we begin to encounter arguments that one or both of them may not be possible or necessary for a just peace.

Once again, I do not think it is fruitless to state them as general considerations for any viable version of just peace.[24] For these concepts are to be understood in the first instance in very thin, minimal terms that allow us to identify them as necessarily present if peace (let alone just peace) is to be achieved at all. Forgiveness I treat as an attitude or mind-set that allows the process of reconciliation to begin, and Andrew Schaap conceptualizes it in a way that expresses the thinness:

> Forgiveness undoes the meaning of a wrong by bringing to an end the story that continues to implicate the other in an original transgression. In doing so, it leaves the meaning of the event in the past. Trust is ventured in this moment, since it involves a suspension of judgment . . . not . . . of the wrongness of the act, but the judgment that this confirms the other as one's enemy in the present. Trust is ventured for the sake of establishing a new relation based on mutual recognition of each as cobuilders of a common world.[25]

This idea of setting aside to begin anew does not conceptually require any ethical negation or canceling out of the past wrong; that is what only certain, more specific conceptions of forgiveness will demand and it may be that in some postconflict circumstances, this would not be desirable or even necessary. Similarly with reconciliation: Thinly understood, it refers only to the business of developing means by which former enemies can live on the same planet without fighting each other. There is no necessary requirement that their relations should become amicable. Again, that kind of thicker reading may well be what one identifies when thinking through what reconciliation means in a specific situation. But criterion (d) in my version of *jus post bellum* only insists that forgiveness and reconciliation are necessary *in some form* for postconflict justice generally, and it enjoins people to think about their implications for their specific situation.[26]

My interim proposal here, then, is that just peace can be characterized in general form using thinly universal concepts and values which offer initial moral guidance and framing, identifying what needs to be fleshed out more thickly in context and engaging with the divergences in conception that typically emerge when we try to convert thin into thick concepts.[27] The ideal need not be elusive even in its general form, and thus need not be so once theorists and practitioners have set out to substantiate it for their own circumstances.

Just Peace: Democratic, Perpetual

I now want to turn to a second type of theoretical indeterminacy that might appear to render just peace elusive in the conceptual sense. To grasp its nature, we need briefly to consider the idea of an essentially contested concept that I have mentioned but not clarified. It has been used here somewhat loosely to convey the idea of radical disagreement, and I am as yet venturing no great claim about the nature of concepts and conceptual dispute: My contention about the possible elusiveness of just peace is probably compatible with a range of views about this matter. But it is now appropriate to venture a little more about essential contestability.

By suggesting that justice, for example, may be an essentially contested conception I have been implicitly following the understanding of this notion that is found in Steven Lukes's work.[28] He contends that there are concepts over which it is possible to have basic, highly generalized agreement about their meaning but which are inherently liable to rival interpretation due to normative principle: the values, and the priority we ascribe to those values (moral principles or interests), by which we substantiate the concepts can radically differ. I certainly believe that this is one source of deep-rooted conceptual conflict and one source, therefore, of the elusiveness of just peace that I am exploring here.

But I accept that this normative understanding of essential contestability's roots is not the only account of what can cause the essential-contestability phenomenon: Theories about the nature of social and political reality can also be in radical conflict and disagreement with each other for reasons other than conflicts over values. Theorists may share the same normative commitments but have different interpretative frameworks by which they attempt to comprehend the social world (a difference which can lead to normative dispute, of course, but which is neither wholly rooted in, nor necessarily guaranteed to lead to, such).

This is the kind of dispute we find over the democratic peace thesis and the related perpetual peace thesis, a dispute that is another source of elusiveness over just peace's content and implications. These are essentially theory-laden disputes over what it is in terms of socioeconomic and political form, as a matter of *fact*, that will be most inimical to the outbreak of war. I shall not rehearse here how these theses may be stated but I will begin by denoting that democratic peace theory, for example, splits very readily into two versions: the dyadic, which says that democracies do not in general go to war with each other (and which is perhaps the more venerable form of the argument), and the monadic, which says that a democracy is less likely than any other form of regime to go to war with anyone else, democratic or otherwise. The theses are thus almost immediately open to conflicting versions before we have even started to unpack their claims further.

One might agree that democratic peace theory is an important thesis but also argue that in the context of *jus post bellum*, they are not ones that have any great bearing on just peace. This position comports with a restricted conception of *jus post bellum*, where the just peace to be pursued is generally limited in its scope to a righting or rebalancing of the relations between former enemies. Restricted *jus post bellum* disavows any wider commitments to peace building that are implied by efforts to pursue the peace-promoting implications of the two theses.[29]

I argue, however, that there are good reasons to prise *jus post bellum* from this narrow focus and incorporate some recognition of the bigger picture painted by democratic peace theory, even if we *thereafter* disagree along the lines suggested above. A just peace must be a stable peace of some kind if possible, and the ending of a just war surely brings with it the hope (certainly shared by those who hope for just peace) that there will be no more war *tout court*.[30] This entails a commitment to conflict prevention (which I interpret as a *pro tanto* responsibility). And, especially in our increasingly interconnected world, it is difficult to pursue meaningful conflict prevention in isolation from the wider supranational contexts within which intrastate and other wars are waged. Of course it may sometimes be difficult to pursue any kind of prevention after certain kinds of conflict, and we may never be able abstractly to quantify what would count as adequate discharge of the conflict prevention responsibility. But there is an obligation, *ceteris paribus*, to try.[31] This, then, is the basis of my claim that democratic peace theory does have a bearing on just peace in this context.

In just occupation scenarios, the question of whether postconflict political reconstruction should be democratic—whether just occupiers have the right, perhaps even the responsibility—to construct a democratic order even where there was none before is particularly pertinent, and has recently been very much so.³² If one believes that democracy is most conducive to peace, the case for it in the postwar domestic order of the occupied state could be compelling.³³ (Very obviously, there are implications here for the appropriate domestic political form of any genuinely just occupier too, but I shall leave them aside for now.)

But here are some indications of where essential contestability in its variegated forms can really take hold of the debate. First: democracy, used deliberately vaguely thus far. Of course, the vast majority of people understand by this concept a rather specific conception of liberal, representative, capitalist democracy (a descendant of what was once more frequently called republicanism). And it is fair to say that in general democratic peace theory relies upon appeal to the various socioeconomic and political features of liberal democracy in explication and justification of their claims. Yet throughout the age of democracy, there have been powerful challenges to the democratic credentials of liberal democracy. A socialist model of democracy, which argues that democracy must be direct and participatory in form and has to extend to control of economic activity, certainly does so. Now, the dispute over whether to prefer a socialist or liberal conception of democracy can reflect normative disputes in terms of interpreting and balancing principles, and thus be essentially contested in *that* sense. But it can alternatively exhibit the other version of contestability in terms of an empirical dispute over, for example, where power actually lies in society and what institutional forms are required to enable it to be exercised democratically.

To continue with this example: In thinking through what domestic political forms may be conducive to a just peace, the socialist democratic peace thesis can challenge its liberal variant on at least three counts. First, it can deny its democratic credentials, at least to an extent, but agree that it nevertheless incorporates peace-promoting features (whatever it is that inclines it to peace are nevertheless not democratic features). Second, it can deny its claims to be maximally peace-promoting (for example, its capitalist nature inclines it rather more to war than it would like to admit) and affirm that a properly democratized society is to be preferred on this score.³⁴ Third, it can deny liberal democracy's claims to be both democratic and pacifistic, and contend that what would promote peace is something other, or substantially in addition to, democracy.

Similar and related controversies attend the question of what form of international order is required by just peace. For example, there is considerable disagreement over the justice of the international order that was constructed by the Allies after World War II. Against the prevailing view in those states who have permanent representation on the Security Council, many argue that the peace (such as it has been since 1945) has been heavily and unjustly skewed in favor of the big powers, who seem to be able to act with impunity even when they flagrantly ignore the norms and laws they officially avow.[35] Although this dispute can reflect conflicts of normative principle, it can also arise from empirical disputes about the actual nature of the order in question.

To illustrate this general point from a different direction: If *jus post bellum* is concerned to try, where possible, to eliminate from the international order the sources of conflict, or at least to develop suitable mechanisms of conflict containment, it must obviously have (or encourage its adherents to develop) some view of the nature and causes of violent conflict and some conception of the means by which it may be prevented or contained. And we can identify two very different types of perspective on this matter, each likely to have its own highly distinctive variants:

(1) The moderate (which liberal democratic peace theory is likely to prefer) takes the given balance of power largely for granted and assumes that the relevant parties in that context will wish to see their interests as currently conceptualized upheld and enhanced where possible; and
(2) The radical (likely to be preferred by the socialist democratic peace theory) which problematizes that balance of power insofar as it may itself be suboptimal with reference to just conflict prevention even if it is unrealistic to expect the beneficiaries of the existing situation to respond positively to the prescriptions which may emerge from this perspective.

The moderate position thus defines just peace in terms that make it possible to conceive of it being realized in the existing world order. The radical view defines just peace in terms that make it unrealizable without considerable— perhaps revolutionary—reform. The differences in the two will probably reflect theoretical disputes on both normative and empirical matters.

Conclusion

All of us who have witnessed or experienced war aspire for a better future: a just peace. Nonetheless, I have argued that both in the popular imagination and in scholarly writing the concept is at the least elusive, and perhaps even unobtainable. The problem is that we seem to assume that we know what the ideal stands for; often we do not. This is both due to the inscrutability of some of our theories and to the intractability of the conflicts around us. This chapter is a call for more thinking on an expansive agenda of *jus post bellum* that links our aspirations, our ideals, and our realities to policy programs in pursuit of that elusive ideal.

Notes

1. This is why I think that *jus post bellum* is logically independent of *jus ad bellum* and *jus in bello* in just war theory, although this independence does not, I believe, clearly cut both ways.

2. *Jus post bellum* could, then, specify rights and responsibilities for excombatants when a just war has been lost, or has ended in stalemate, as well. The implications of this argument for what justice means are discussed shortly.

3. For exposition of this claim concerning the injustices within a just war, see Evans, "Moral Responsibilities and the Conflicting Demands of *Jus Post Bellum*," *Ethics & International Affairs* 23, no. 2 (2009): 147–64.

4. This position is rendered more robust when it claims that the point of moral and political theorizing is entirely action-guiding. I would not endorse this position myself, but it would be foolish to deny that *much* of the value of such theorizing is action-guiding, especially in the context of *jus post bellum*.

5. Those who make this claim are inclined to talk of justified as opposed to just war. What I say in this paragraph helps to explain my response to this, to wit: If not justice, then what could ever justify war?

6. My use of the concept of ideal theory differs slightly from its apparently more common usage in contemporary moral and political philosophy, though in the rather general sense employed here it seems to me perfectly acceptable.

7. And, hence, just war theory should be treated as a matter for nonideal theory.

8. So one way of resolving the justice and war debate is to say that a just war aims for a just peace, with the latter understanding justice in the pristine sense, and invokes principles of justice in the remedial sense to specify how the desired outcome, when war is necessary, ought to be pursued. As will become clear, I think the issue is more complex than this attempted resolution allows.

9. This debate about the nature of justice is of course familiar and quite venerable in political theory, most recently entered into by G. A. Cohen, who believes that justice is

pristine and hence distinguishes himself from orthodox Marxism, for example, in which justice is something essentially to be transcended along with class society. See Cohen, *Rescuing Justice and Equality* (Cambridge, MA: Harvard University Press, 2008).

10. Yossi Beilin, "Just Peace: A Dangerous Objective," in Allan and Keller, eds., *What Is Just Peace?* (Oxford: Oxford University Press, 2006), 130–48.

11. Beilin, *Just Peace?* 148.

12. The general argument in support of this claim is that there are so many conditions that require satisfaction for the resort to war to be justified that peace, even when significantly suboptimal in certain ways, is the theory's obvious default position. It is departure from peace that has to be (strenuously and rigorously) justified. For discussion of acceptable peace, see Evans, "Balancing Peace, Justice and Sovereignty in *Jus Post Bellum*: The Case of Just Occupation," *Millennium* 36, no. 3 (2008).

13. This methodology is, of course, most famously associated with John Rawls, *A Theory of Justice* (Cambridge, MA: Belknap Press, 1972), 48–50.

14. I shall say more on this in a revised draft. The issue about what counts as peace revolves around (a) what counts as violence and its absence: (b) what degrees of violence, however it is conceptualized, can be compatible with societal peace? Where is the threshold beyond which one could no longer say there is peace?

15. I am aware that many have thought that this was the case with the 1991 Gulf War, the dispute being over whether a just peace was restored with the expulsion of Iraqi forces or whether it was in fact necessary to invade Iraq itself. I personally would argue that international law rightfully has the last word in this instance.

16. For clarity, I shall hereafter focus only on that part of *jus post bellum* that considers what just victors should do after victory in their just war.

17. Brian Orend, *The Morality of War* (Peterborough, ON: Broadview, 2006), 169.

18. For example, many civil society organizations in former Allied and Axis states undertook friendship reconciliation events in the years after World War II. One way of understanding the suggestion here is that these may not have been purely supererogatory activities with respect to just peace, even if they had proven to be more difficult to undertake than in fact sometimes seemed to have been the case.

19. See Evans, "Balancing Peace, Justice and Sovereignty" and "Moral Responsibilities."

20. The inappropriateness of such arises from the sovereignty/self-determination tenet (e) in the extended conception.

21. Traditional in the sense that, until comparatively recently, social justice focused on distributive/economic issues such as this.

22. It could also be argued that it would be too hasty to assume that no questions from the extended perspective could be raised about the behavior or make-up of just victors, as if they were unimpugnable. A just victor may nevertheless have something in its character unconducive to just peace—and if we have an extended just peace conception such that, qua occupying power, it has the right and/or responsibility to promote justice in the occupied state, then it can only do so from the basis of sufficient internal justice itself.

23. I aim to say more about how this sensitivity may be generated or enhanced in philosophical reflection in future versions of this work.

24. The next two paragraphs replicate sections from Evans, "Moral Responsibilities," 155, and will be reworked in future versions.

25. Andrew Schaap, "Political Grounds for Forgiveness," *Contemporary Political Theory* 2, no. 1 (2003): 77–87.

26. It should hardly need adding that forgiveness and reconciliation will typically be two-way processes. For example, there will have been mistakes for which just combatants will ask forgiveness and even what they have justifiably done to their former enemies should yield a regret which must shape the relationship they seek to reconstruct with them. (I leave aside here the more controversial argument in Evans's "Moral Responsibilities" concerning atonement by just victors, which has no bearing on the present discussion.)

27. I say more about the idea of thin universalism in Evans, "Balancing Peace, Justice and Sovereignty."

28. See Stephen Lukes, *Power: A Radical View* (New York: Palgrave, 1974).

29. Which is emphatically not to say that restricted *jus post bellum* must reject the theses. All I think it says here is that we do not have to go as far as they logically take us in building the just peace that satisfactorily or adequately resolves the specific conflict in view.

30. A qualification which does not rule the need at times to trade justice for stability in what would therefore be a suboptimal if necessary outcome. See Evans, "Moral Responsibilities."

31. On my reading, prompted by this analysis, the establishment of the United Nations by the Allies in 1945 represents, no matter how imperfectly, a discharge of the peace-building responsibility by just excombatants.

32. I separate this possibility from the quite distinct and dangerous claim that says that one just cause for war is to institute a democratic order in a currently nondemocratic state, a perversion of the democratic peace theory that has recently had deleterious foreign policy influence.

33. I think that just war theory in general, of which *jus post bellum* can be a part, exhibits a not necessarily decisive bias toward democracy in other ways, primarily through its commitment to the principle of self-determination (violation of which generates a venerable just cause for war). For consider: there is something odd about the 1991 war to restore self-determination to the Kuwaiti state and then simply put back into place a regime that denied domestic democratic self-determination to the Kuwaiti people. To be sure, an occupied people have the right to determine their own form of government and so on, but that in itself assumes some kind of democratic mechanism by which to exercise that right, even if they choose not to have a democratic government. Furthermore, there is a strong pragmatic argument for democracy of some kind: wars can fragment societies so radically (if they were not already divided) that only a form of government that accommodates all of the factions somehow will actually work. (The oft-heard claim that certain societies need an authoritarian strong-man government to hold them together typically overestimates the longer-term ability of such a form of government to do so.) And perhaps we should not *always* be so wary of the imposition of democracy: the West German and

Japanese people were given no choice in this matter by their occupiers in the later 1940s but very few, I wager, now or then, consider that to be a *problem* for the legitimacy of their postwar reconstruction.

34. Pessimistic leftists may agree with socialism's critics that the mooted ideal is not feasible, but they need not on this count reject either the claim that liberal democracy is not any less prone to war than other forms or regimes or that a socialist democracy would be maximally pacifistic in character.

35. Which, of course, is a very limited or qualified peace, to put the point very mildly. This viewpoint is one that would attribute much of the ensuing conflict to the iniquities summarized in this passage. A very recent statement of this view is Danilo Zolo, *Victor's Justice: From Nuremberg to Baghdad* (New York: Verso Books, 2009). He claims that even the punishment of Nazi and Japanese war criminals, which a restricted version of *jus post bellum* would presumably endorse, was victors' justice in its pejorative sense not in the fact that they were punished at all (they deserved to be) but in the manner in which they were tried in particular.

CONCLUSION

Toward a Twenty-First Century *Jus Post Bellum*

ERIC PATTERSON

IN MAY 2009 the national military of Sri Lanka convincingly smashed the Liberation Tigers of Tamil Eelam (LTTE) after nearly three decades of war. The conflict was particularly bloody, killing many thousands of civilians, landmines contaminating vast swathes of agricultural regions, terrorism haunting major cities, and introducing black widows (female suicide bombers) to the global lexicon. However, the end was decisive: The Tamil Tigers were bested on the battlefield and their senior leaders were killed, and at the time of this writing—two years later—there is no question that the government won and the LTTE has essentially ceased to exist. Unlike many other contemporary conflicts, this one ended definitively with a horizon open to peace, security, economic development, and political representation, although it is unclear whether the national government is committed to working through the dilemmas of justice and conciliation. These principles—order, justice, and conciliation—were broached in the introduction of this book as a threefold framework for conceptualizing the overlapping issues inherent in any discussion of the ethics of postconflict. Order is the environment of security and rule of law necessary for a society to get back on its feet: domestic security (stopping the bullets), governance (basic institutions for law and order), and international security (freedom from direct external threat). The second and third elements of the framework, justice and conciliation (or reconciliation), spark considerable debate about their conception and implementation when applied to real-world cases. In order to get at some of the issues raised as well as the points of controversy that need further research, this chapter compares key themes from the volume's contributors along the three dimensions of order, justice, and conciliation.

Order

When it comes to the need for some form of postconflict order and security, there is no disagreement between the contributors to this book: order is necessary. Michael Walzer, for instance, argues that the immediate postconflict environment will require provision (meeting the survival needs of human beings) and reconstruction (infrastructure, homes, livelihoods). Certainly provision and reconstruction are critical dimensions of the postconflict order; otherwise, the populace will starve and the region will be prey to internal and external security challenges. Nonetheless, from the perspectives of policy and ethics, a number of issues immediately come to the fore. First, *who* has an obligation to do *what*? Some form of political authority assumes an obligation to provide for the postconflict order, from law enforcement to provision for the survival needs of the populace to protecting the borders. But how far does that obligation extend in practice? Providing potable water? Combating disease? Pensions for military veterans? Pensions for senior citizens? University education?

The what is challenging to define without getting at the who. Obligation implies relationship—there is a benefactor and a beneficiary. How do these relationships form in contemporary postconflict? The issue is further problematized, as Walzer suggests, because many of the contemporary wars that the West has engaged in are armed humanitarian interventions rather than classic conflicts between state governments. In classic warfare, the roles of the protagonists were clear and there was little sense of moral obligation at war's end.

In contrast, for much of the past quarter century the West has chosen a different postconflict approach, one where there is not a winner and a loser, victor and vanquished but rather aggressors, victims, and the international community. The Balkan wars of the 1990s are cases in point: aggressor Serbs, victimized Bosnian Muslims, and the international community to the rescue. The international community (i.e., NATO) did not claim the mantle of victor in Bosnia or Kosovo, but neither did it absorb the loser or simply go home. Instead, following a precedent set after World War II but neglected for much of the Cold War, the intervening powers—at great expense to themselves and with little sense of vital interests—chose to not only provide provision and reconstruction, but provided billions in an attempt to transform Bosnia and Kosovo into capitalist democracies, as well as East Timor, Afghanistan, and a half dozen other cases.

James Turner Johnson argues that all of this discussion occurs, in part, because of what has been lost by the wider just war tradition. Historic just war theory was rooted in much wider moral structures that we today call political philosophy, questions and answers about the rightly ordered society and the conventions of statesmanship and chivalry. Founders of just war theory such as Augustine and Aquinas wrote a few pages about the ethics of war nested in massive tomes on law, justice, and political authority. All of this suggests that we need more scholarly and policy attention to whether or not there actually are ethical obligations to provision, reconstruction, and transformation; on the nature of the moral agents involved; and on the ethical obligations of winners, losers, aggressors, victims, and especially interveners. Walzer in particular noted the oxymoron of humanitarian intervention: governments who do not intervene take on no responsibility; those who make a citizen's arrest and intervene take on obligation for ending the conflict and for its aftermath—the proverbial concept of no good deed going unpunished.

This suggests at least three additional order issues. Robert Royal and Michael Walzer discuss the first, the trade-off between capabilities and the victor or intervening power's obligation. The United States or European Union need not go bankrupt to make provision for and reconstruct Afghanistan or Kosovo, because their first priority must be the lives and livelihoods of their own populations. But by getting involved they have taken on some obligation—more thinking needs to be done on the depth and breadth of this obligation. Some of the authors in this volume point to calls from the NGO community for postconflict reconstruction. Another order issue raised by Brian Orend is whether the intervening power or victor has the authority or the obligation to return the postconflict situation to the status quo *ante bellum* or, as noted above, transform the situation in some way—such as deposing the Nazis (or Baathists) or empowering Japanese (or Afghan) women. The third remaining order issue is what Jean Bethke Elshtain calls the ethics of exit: When should the victorious intervening power leave and allow domestic institutions full autonomy over their affairs?

Many of these order issues are hinted at in this volume, but they suggest that a far more ambitious *jus post bellum* research agenda is necessary that considers the moral issues involved in the context of real-world war and peace. Furthermore, the order issues are inextricably linked to deeper philosophical issues about how we define the good life, morally satisfying definitions of government and security, notions of what it means to be a citizen, and the explicit links between order and justice.

Justice

A second set of considerations raised by this volume has to do with justice. Issues of justice permeate every part of war: Was the decision to go to war just? Was the war fought according to the ethical principles of the laws of armed conflict? Is the postconflict settlement just? The contributors to this volume agree that although justice is linked across all three phases of war, nonetheless justice in each phase is also distinct. For instance, even a war with a just cause (self-defense) can be fought unjustly (bombing orphanages); conversely, insurgents and nonstate actors (lacking legitimate authority) can fight within the laws of armed conflict. Victims of aggression who somehow win in the end can impose harsh postconflict conditions, as occurred in Afghanistan: The *mujaheddin* fought a legitimate war against the Soviet aggressor, but when elements of the insurgency imposed the Taliban's version of postconflict order it was certainly not in tune with international norms of justice.

Elsewhere I have defined postconflict justice in the most modest of terms: getting what one deserves. However, the various overlapping literatures on postconflict such as conflict resolution theory and transitional justice problematize justice as retributive, distributive, and restorative. These distinctions are raised in the present volume by David Crocker, Brian Orend, Mark Evans, and others. How one defines justice as a moral principle and ethical obligation is critical to a policy-relevant approach to postconflict.

However, what all of the contributors agree upon is that *post bellum* justice links *jus ad bellum* (the decision to go to war) and *jus in bello* (how war is fought) to *jus post bellum*. George Lucas calls this the temporal circle of just war thinking: the idea that postconflict, hot war, and postconflict are not a continuum, but rather are a cycle or a circle. Indeed, as Pauletta Otis asserts in her chapter, in places like Sudan, Africa's Great Lakes, and Central Asia it seems that these postconflict phases are actually simply the next preconflict phase; savvy and morally responsible political and military leaders conceive and implement postconflict settlements in ways that seek to avoid this cycle of insecurity and warfare.

Just war analysis must consider the ethical and policy links of all of war's phases. More specifically, the ethics of the decision to employ force include critical distinctions regarding legitimate authority, just cause, and right intent—all of which have important ramifications for justice in war's aftermath. For instance, the violent actions of nonstate actors across borders or the unprovoked *blitzkrieg* of one government against its neighbor suggests postconflict punishment of criminal aggressors or the set of political leaders responsible for the decision to go to war. Likewise, violations of the war convention such as torture or indiscriminate attacks on civilian hospitals and houses of worship should be linked to justice considerations in the postconflict settlement.

However, Robert Williams and others in this volume point to the imperfect nature of postconflict justice. Punishment of senior leaders responsible for the decision to go to war, however morally satisfying, does not turn the clock back. Punishment does limit future aggression by the same party and it does vindicate victims in some ways, but it does not restore those who have died. Similarly, reparations are a method of acknowledging loss and approximating compensation for the destruction of life and property, but again they simply cannot restore all that was lost or damaged.

Furthermore, justice may paradoxically be impossible in some cases due to political instability. A fragile conflict settlement may require that the postconflict deal involve amnesty, a return to the political status quo, a cooling-off period, or the outright suspension of justice claims. This may be necessary to get all parties to agree to lay down their arms and found a new political order, particularly in cases of civil war or violent regime transition. Indeed, putting the past behind may be a healthy step toward establishing an enduring political order, as David Crocker illustrates in his chapter on the US Civil War.

In sum, justice is a critical principle for postconflict that links what happened before and during the war to conflict's aftermath. The principle of justice keeps in mind how lingering senses of grievance and injustice can smolder, ultimately resulting in a return to conflict, but justice also recognizes its limitations in real-world policy and the potential for massive claims for justice can undermine the postconflict order. This is what seems to have happened at the end of the First World War: Legitimate claims for justice, often informed by a desire for revenge, decimated Germany and eventually sowed the seeds for a second, more terrible world war.

With all of these challenges in mind, Brian Orend argues that one way to solve the uncertainties of postconflict justice is to employ positive law. Orend argues for policies of rehabilitation rather than revenge, suggesting a new Geneva Convention on postconflict that would outline the roles of belligerents and specify in detail the forms and mechanisms appropriate for postconflict justice. An internationally binding agreement between state parties on postconflict would not only outline obligations but also concretize in law the expectations and avenues for postconflict justice, thus dispensing with the controversies and inconsistencies associated with ad hoc tribunals (e.g., the International Criminal Tribunals for Yugoslavia and Rwanda) and the International Criminal Court.

Conciliation

Conciliation means coming to terms with the past. Conciliation is future-focused in that it sees former enemies as partners in a shared future. Sometimes, particularly in intrastate conflict, it is reconciliation—building bridges between parties that have some shared past. In international conflict, it is more likely that the goal is modest conciliation, the mutual effort of both sides to overcome past hostility and reframe the relationship as one of partnership. In either case, conciliation is rooted in evolving collective interests and it can expand and enhance order and justice under the right conditions.

However, as the contributors to this volume note, conciliation is difficult to apprehend and quite rare in the aftermath of war. The literature on reconciliation often seems to blithely assume that both sides to a conflict realize that it is in their interests to reconcile—a far cry from reality.

Indeed, there are many reasons that former belligerents would not want to reconcile: hatred, a sense of injustice, unresolved grievances, the political power that derives in part from taking a strong stance against the other, and so on. Moreover, it is one thing to speak of individual reconciliation; it is another thing entirely to imagine collective, political expressions of conciliation.

Some of the authors in this volume dealt with these difficult issues. David Crocker looked at the US Civil War—the rare civil war that definitively ended without a return to violence. Crocker notes that political leadership was critical to national reconciliation. Abraham Lincoln continually exhorted political and military elites to let them up easy, and this view was internalized by his successors and established in policy through a series of amnesties. Crocker observes that a spirit of conciliation is necessary on the losing side as well—Robert E. Lee's admonition to end the war and return home peaceably was in direct violation of Jefferson Davis's call to guerrilla warfare. Fortunately, the South's remaining military leaders in the field heeded Lee's call to lay down their arms and peaceably reconcile.

Jean Bethke Elshtain also points to moral leadership in reconciliation, such as Nelson Mandela, Desmond Tutu, and religious figures on all sides of Northern Ireland's Troubles, focusing more explicitly on taking account of the past without it predetermining the present. She calls this knowing-forgetting: acknowledging the violence and injustice of the past but deciding not to allow the past to imprison the present and future. Elshtain's work suggests multiple questions for future research, such as the difference between the knowing-forgetting of an individual (e.g., a rape victim) and that of a society (e.g., Rwanda) and whether social scientists and social psychologists can identify pathways to collective conciliation. For instance, are some cultures more likely to reconcile than others? Are there internal cultural or religious mechanisms for postconflict conciliation that can be utilized domestically or across state borders to reconcile former adversaries?

Both Elshtain and Crocker intimate that future research is needed on the role of time in conciliation. Crocker demonstrates the potency of decisions made for the postconflict while the war was waging, but he also notes the many unresolved issues of the US Civil War, be it Southern quasi-nationalism or race relations. Elshtain likewise points to how the distance provided by time can help soothe the wounds of violence. But how do we quantify the role of time in conciliation? Does time heal all wounds? Why did Americans and Vietnamese find it easy to reconcile less than two decades after the end of that war, yet people in the Lebanon conflict point to three-hundred-year-old grievances that torment them? Again, the intersections of time and culture in reconciliation and how they apply to postconflict ethics need much more scholarly research.

Finally, the idea of reconciliation brings up one of the major disagreements among the volume's contributors. There are those who argue for a modest approach to postconflict that is highly restrained. Contributors Walzer, Elshtain, and Royal seem deeply concerned with allowing domestic institutions to take responsibility for themselves and outside powers—whether they are termed victors or interveners—to exit as quickly as reasonably possible. Others, such as Robert Williams, are concerned that a postconflict order that does not explicitly deal with human rights violations (justice) is likely to lack stability over the long run. However, Mark Evans's approach calls for an expansive role for postconflict policies that deliberately transforms the scenario to a new status quo, requiring major commitments to and investments in justice, reconciliation, human rights resolution, transitional justice, conflict resolution, and representative government.

All of this suggests that a great deal of work needs to be done on the ethics of and policy ramifications for conciliation and reconciliation. Under what conditions can collectives find it in their interests to work toward conciliation? What moral imperatives reside in specific cultures or international norms that can underpin efforts at conciliation? What are the trade-offs between reconciliation and justice or conciliation and order? What role does time play, and can it be measured? What roles can agents outside of government such as religious institutions and third-party mediators play, and how can we understand their role as moral agency? Are there links between conciliation and just war principles such as right intention and legitimate authority?

Conclusion

The twentieth century witnessed, in the words of Michael Walzer, "the triumph of just war theory."[1] Just war principles about the decision to go to war and how war is fought were concretized as legally binding in the Geneva, Hague, Torture, and Genocide Conventions. More importantly, just war thinking moved from the fringe of theological and philosophical debate to the basis for restraint in Western military doctrine and common nomenclature from op-ed pages to collegiate debate societies to President Obama's 2009 Nobel Prize address.

However, the twenty-first century has its own challenge for just war thinking: developing a comprehensive approach to ethics at war's end. The cyclical nature of violence in many parts of the globe in the Cold War's aftermath has garnered the attention of Western publics and their leaders, and forced a conversation at the global level about shared notions of order, justice, and conciliation. Many aspire toward a world with less war, more security, and rising standards of living, but at times their visions are dashed by the realities of mistrust, insecurity, violence, and social collapse that populate the headlines.

So, there is work to be done. Just war thinking will continue to engage the difficult decisions of going to war and how war is fought: against nonstate actors in the mountains of Central Asia, against rogue states with weapons of mass destruction, against organized criminal syndicates in the jungles of South America, against pirates on the high seas, by nontraditional actors such as corporate contractors and mercenaries, and in consideration of advanced forms of technology such as lasers, nonlethal weaponry, and robots. Furthermore, a twenty-first century just war theory will take into account postconflict factors, specifically how to establish an enduring order, how to employ political forms of justice, and how to cultivate and harvest collective forms of conciliation. Just war theory is not an artifact of the past—it is a framework for the future.

Note

1. Michael Walzer, "The Triumph of Just War Theory," reprinted in his *Arguing about War* (New Haven, CT: Yale University Press, 2005).

CONTRIBUTORS

David Crocker is senior research scholar at the Institute for Philosophy and Public Policy and the School of Public Policy at the University of Maryland. Crocker specializes in sociopolitical philosophy, international development ethics, transitional justice, democracy and democratization, and the ethics of consumption. In May 2009, he shared with Herman Daly the school's award for outstanding faculty member. After three degrees from Yale University (MDiv., MA, and PhD), Crocker taught philosophy for twenty-five years at Colorado State University. He was a visiting professor at the University of Munich, twice a Fulbright Scholar at the University of Costa Rica, held the UNESCO chair in development at the University of Valencia (Spain), and taught in the Faculty of Philosophy at the University of Chile. He has been an officer of the Human Development and Capability Association and was a founder and former president of the International Development Ethics Association (IDEA). Among his publications are *Ethics of Global Development: Agency, Capability, and Deliberative Democracy* (Cambridge University Press, 2008).

Jean Bethke Elshtain is the Laura Spelman Rockefeller Professor of Social and Political Ethics, Divinity School, the University of Chicago, with appointments in political science and the Committee on International Relations and holder of the Leavey Chair in the Foundations of American Freedom, Georgetown University. Among her many books are *Democracy on Trial* (a New York Times notable book for 1995); *Just War against Terror: The Burden of American Power in a Violent World* (named one of the best nonfiction books of 2003 by *Publishers Weekly*);

and *Sovereignty: God, State, and Self* (her Gifford Lectures, published 2008); all are published by Basic Books. She is a fellow of the American Academy of Arts and Sciences, a Guggenheim fellow, a fellow at the Bellagio Center of the Rockefeller Foundation, holder of the Maguire Chair in Ethics at the Library of Congress, and a fellow at the Institute for Advanced Studies, Princeton, where she also served on the board of trustees. Professor Elshtain also currently serves as cochair of the Pew Forum on Religion and Public Life, and chair of the Council on Families in America.

Mark Evans is reader in politics in the Centre for the Study of Culture and Politics, and director of the Graduate Centre in the School of Arts and Humanities at Swansea University. He is the author of numerous articles on just war theory and other topics in contemporary political philosophy, and the editor of *The Edinburgh Companion to Contemporary Liberalism* (Routledge, 2001) and *Just War Theory: A Reappraisal* (Macmillan, 2005). He is currently writing a book-length analysis of *jus post bellum*.

James Turner Johnson is professor of religion and associate of the graduate program in political science at Rutgers–The State University of New Jersey, where he has been on the faculty since 1969. His research and teaching focus principally on the historical development and application of moral traditions related to war, peace, and the practice of statecraft. Johnson has received Rockefeller, Guggenheim, and National Endowment for the Humanities fellowships and various other research grants and has directed two NEH summer seminars for college teachers. His most recent books are *The War to Oust Saddam Hussein* (Rowman & Littlefield, 2005), *Morality and Contemporary Warfare* (Yale, 1999), and *The Holy War Idea in Western and Islamic Tradition* (Penn State, 1997). Johnson is a trustee, editorial board member, and former general editor of *The Journal of Religious Ethics*, coeditor of *The Journal of Military Ethics*, and a member of professional societies in the fields of religion and political science. He has lectured to academic, military, and general audiences in the United States and abroad.

George R. Lucas Jr. is professor of philosophy at the US Naval Academy, where he holds the Class of 1984 Distinguished Chair in Ethics at the VADM James Stockdale Center for Ethical Leadership. He is also professor of ethics and public policy at the Naval Postgraduate School in Monterey, CA. His most recent book is *Anthropologists in Arms: The Ethics of Military Anthropology* (AltaMira Press, 2009).

Brian Orend is the director of international studies and global engagement and a professor of philosophy at the University of Waterloo in Canada. He is the author of five books: *On War: A Dialogue* (Rowman & Littlefield, 2009); *The Morality of War* (Broadview, 2006); *Human Rights: Concept and Context* (Broadview, 2002); *Michael Walzer on War and Justice* (McGill-Queens University Press, 2000); and *War and International Justice: A Kantian Perspective* (Wilfrid Laurier University Press, 2000). He is currently writing *An Introduction to International Studies* for Oxford University Press as well as a book on happiness. He is perhaps best known for his work on *jus post bellum*, arguing for an inclusion of human rights into postwar reconstruction plans. His PhD is from Columbia University in New York City.

Pauletta Otis is professor of security studies in the Command and Staff College at Marine Corps University. She served as the senior research fellow for religion in international affairs at the Pew Forum in Washington, DC, in 2005–6. She previously taught at Colorado State University-Pueblo from 1989 to 2004. She has held other positions, including distinguished visiting professor of international security studies at the Joint Military Intelligence College (1998, DOD), visiting scholar at the National Security Education Program (1999, NDU), and professor of international security studies (2002–4, JMIC). She has served as a member of the Defense Intelligence Advisory Board, Defense Science Policy Board Summer Study on Homeland Security, and in a senior advisory capacity for the US military chaplains. Dr. Otis has special expertise in the study of subnational violence and combines both theoretical and operational experience and expertise. Her current research focuses on issues concerning cultural factors that impact military strategy and operations, religious factors in violence, and irregular warfare/insurgency analysis. She received her PhD and an MA from the Graduate School of International Studies at the University of Denver in 1989.

Eric Patterson is associate director of the Berkley Center for Religion, Peace, and World Affairs and has a visiting appointment in the Department of Government at Georgetown University. He is the author or editor of eight books, including most recently *Politics in a Religious World* (Continuum, 2011), *Debating the War of Ideas* (coedited; Macmillan, 2009) and *Just War Thinking: Morality and Pragmatism in the Struggle Against Contemporary Threats* (Lexington, 2007). Prior to coming to Georgetown University, Patterson spent three years working for the federal government as a White House fellow and special assistant to the director of the US Office of Personnel Management (2007–8), and before that he was on university leave of absence as William C. Foster fellow in the State Department's Bureau of Political and Military Affairs.

Robert Royal is president of the Faith and Reason Institute in Washington, DC. He is a frequent speaker and writer on questions of ethics, culture, religion, and politics. His recent books include *1492 and all That: Political Manipulations of History* (University Press of America, 1992) and *Reinventing the American People: Unity and Diversity Today* (Eerdmans, 1995). Royal holds a BA and MA from Brown University and a PhD in comparative literature from the Catholic University of America. He has taught at Brown University, Rhode Island College, and the Catholic University of America. He is a regular columnist for *Crisis* magazine and his articles have appeared in numerous scholarly journals and other publications, including *First Things, Communio, The Wilson Quarterly, Catholic Historical Review, Washington Post, Washington Times, National Review, The Wall Street Journal*, and *The American Spectator*.

Michael Walzer is professor emeritus of social science at the Institute for Advanced Study at Princeton University. As a professor, author, editor, and lecturer, Walzer has addressed a wide variety of topics in political theory and moral philosophy: political obligation, just and unjust war, nationalism and ethnicity, economic justice and the welfare state. His books—among them *Just and Unjust Wars* (Basic, 2006), *Spheres of Justice* (Basic, 1984), *The Company of Critics* (Basic, 2002), *Thick and Thin:*

Moral Argument at Home and Abroad (University of Notre Dame, 2006), and *On Toleration* (Yale, 1999)—and essays have played a part in the revival of practical, issue-focused ethics and in the development of a pluralist approach to political and moral life. Walzer is a contributing editor for *The New Republic* and coeditor of *Dissent*, now in its fifty-sixth year. His articles and interviews frequently appear in the world's foremost newspapers and journals. He is currently working on the toleration and accommodation of difference in all its forms, and also on the third volume of *The Jewish Political Tradition*, a comprehensive collaborative project focused on the history of Jewish political thought.

Robert E. Williams Jr. is associate professor of political science at Pepperdine University. He is the coauthor, with Dan Caldwell, of *Seeking Security in an Insecure World* (Rowman & Littlefield, 2006) and the coeditor, with Paul Viotti, of a two-volume encyclopedia of arms control published by Praeger. Williams also writes on international human rights.

INDEX

Abu Ghraib, 11, 110, 111
Adenauer, Konrad, 67
Afghanistan War: and economy, 193; goals of, 69; and humanitarian crisis, 15; as irregular war, 49, 50; and *jus ante bellum*, 59; and *jus in bellum*, 52; and *jus post bellum*, 11, 68–69; just peace in, 204; *mujaheddin* control at end of Soviet war, 224; NATO strategy in, 59; Orend's view of, 52; reconstruction and rehabilitation of, 14, 75, 189–94, 223; regime change in, 39; sovereignty of Afghanistan to be maintained during, 28; US ways to terminate, 74–75
aftermath of war, 23–27, 35–46. *See also jus post bellum* (justice after war)
aggressors, treatment after war. *See* Geneva Conventions, proposal for new Convention; reconstruction and rehabilitation; revenge; war criminals, punishment of
Algerian war, 45
al-Qaeda, 75, 183, 191
Ambrose of Milan, 4, 125
Amin, Idi, 41
amnesty, 161–63, 226, 227
Amnesty, Reintegration, and Reconciliation (AR2), 13, 146
Andersonville prison atrocities (US Civil War), 165
Angell, Norman, 83
Angola, 12
antiterrorist wars, 39. *See also* Afghanistan War; Iraq War
apology from aggressor, 179, 182
Appleby, Scott, 115
Appomattox (surrender in US Civil War), 147, 151, 152–56
Aquinas, Thomas: and *jus ad bellum*, 73, 80; and just war tradition, 4–10, 18–19, 33nn5–6, 73, 223

Arendt, Hannah, 130–31, 133, 135
Argentina, 13, 145
Aristotle, 7, 79, 80, 93
armies: growth of, 23, 24; individual responsibility of soldiers, 49; international coalition of, 58; military preparedness of, 55–60; postwar treatment of, 54, 74; view of Muslims after September 11, 2001 terrorist attacks, 108. *See also* demilitarization of aggressor
"arrow of time," 47, 54
Arusha Accords (1992), 8
Augustine (bishop of Hippo): on justice and order, 10, 21; and just war tradition, 4, 33nn5–6, 125, 223; on peace, 21, 79–80; and postwar thinking, 5–6; and right intention, 20

backlash effect against rehabilitation, 194
Bass, Gary, 38
Beilin, Yossi, 200
black Freedmen's Bureau, 167
black suffrage, 160, 163, 168
Blair, Tony, 85
Blight, David, 147, 165
Blitzkrieg (1939–40), 180
Bonhoeffer, Dietrich, 143n16
Bosnia, 8, 101, 124, 176, 177, 180, 222–23
Bremer, Paul, 210
Bull, Hedley, 93n2
Burns, Ken, 169
Bush, George H. W., 36–37, 71
Bush, George W., 63n34, 85, 106, 128, 192

Cahoone, Lawrence, 133
Cambodia, 13, 39–40, 41, 145
Camus, Albert, 135
Canby, Edward, 157
Carnegie Endowment trustees, 82

| 237 |

Carr, E. H., 90
Catton, Bruce, 155
Central Asia, political disorder in, ix, 225
Chamberlain, Joshua, 155, 172n42
chaplains, military, 112
charity in terms of Civil War combatants, 160–61
Cheney, Richard, 110
Chesterton, G. K., 68
Chile, 13, 145
China: and Cambodia genocide, 39–40; as war threat, 105, 106; and World War II, 179, 184
Christian Democrats of Europe, 67
Churchill, Winston, 1–2
citizen-militia, 56
City of God (Augustine), 10, 12, 21, 79, 125
civilians. *See* noncombatants
civilian violence, 114–15
civil war: as dominant form of contemporary wars, 79, 86–88; *jus post bellum* principles applied to, 12, 88, 90, 91, 93; and just peace, 87–88, 205; most difficult type of war to conclude, 12; reconciliation after, 226; recurrence after settlement, 79
Civil War, US, 13–14, 145–70; amnesty after, 161–63; causes of, 88, 169; and racial justice, 146–47, 151, 157, 160–61, 163–64, 167–68; reconciliation achieved in, 14, 147–59, 160, 227; reconstructing society after, 159–70; rejection of idea of punishing Confederate soldiers, 151–52, 153, 162; restoring law and order in Southern states, 152; terms of surrender, 153–54; treatment of prisoners in, 153, 162, 165. *See also* Appomattox; Lincoln, Abraham; *specific generals*
classical war theory, 4
Clausewitz, Carl von, 89
Clinton, Bill, 85
Cloyd, Benjamin C., 147, 165
Coady, Antony, 54–55, 63n29
Coalition Provisional Authority (Iraq), 210
Cobden, Richard, 83
Coburn, Tom, 117
Cohen, G. A., 216–17n9
COIN manual *(US Government Counterinsurgency Guide)*, 50, 51
Coker, Christopher, 106
Cold War, 8, 67, 106, 128, 129, 223
collective punishment of reparations, 42
Collier, Paul, 87, 96n54
common good, 19–20, 30, 32

communism, 184
Concert of Europe, 83
conciliation or reconciliation, x, 3, 10, 146, 147–59, 208, 210–11, 217n18, 218n26, 221, 226–28
Confederacy. *See* Civil War, US
conflict containment, 208, 215
conflict prevention, initiatives to secure, 208, 213, 215
conflict resolution (phase 5), 12, 100, 115–18, 224
"conflict trap," 87–88
Congo, 12, 125
Congress of Vienna (1814–15), 83
Constitution, US. *See specific Amendments*
constructivist approach to stable peace, 84, 85
Contra Faustum (Augustine), 20
Convention against Torture (UN), 92, 124, 229
Cook, Patricia, 143n16
Correlates of War Project, 87
Coski, John M., 172n42
Crimean War (1853–56), 83
criminal activities, 114
Crocker, David A., 13–14, 145, 224, 225, 227
culture: and ethical interoperability, 58, 59; and knowing-forgetting, 227–28; mixed with religious factors for war, 100, 102, 105
Czechoslovakia, 137–38, 180

Daly, Cahal, 136–37
Darfur, 8, 38, 56, 125
Davis, Jefferson, 150, 151, 153, 156, 227
de Bueil, Jean V., 111
Decretum (Gratian), 18
Defense Department, US (DOD), 99, 103; budget, 117; Joint Operating Concepts, 61n7; Joint Publication 1-05, 102, 112; Joint Publication 3-0, 100, 113
demilitarization of aggressor, 128, 146, 180, 181, 182–83, 185, 226
democracy: creation of democratic regime, 44–45, 187; democracies do not wage war against other democracies, 85, 213; and just war thinking, 11; liberal model of, 214, 219n34; in post-WWII Germany and Japan, 130, 185; socialist model of, 214, 219n34; spread of, 82, 87
democratic peace thesis, 212–16, 218n32
de-Nazification, 184
despoiling of beaten enemy, 25
deterrence as ethical responsibility, 128

Deutsch, Karl, 84–85
dictatorships, 127, 189. *See also* regime change
diplomacy, 88, 208
Disarmament, Demobilization, and Reintegration (DDR), 146
disarmament, responsibility of occupying power, 128. *See also* demilitarization of aggressor
divine retribution, 161
Djibouti, 87
Dobbins, Jim, 190, 192
DOD. *See* Defense Department, US
double effect, doctrine of, 50
Douglass, Frederick, 160
Dover Air Force Base, caskets arriving at, 110
drug economy of Afghanistan, 193
duration: defined, 120n19; of *jus post bellum* (justice after war), 44, 46; of warfare, 112

East Asia, 145
Eastern European governments after World War II, 43, 184
East Timor, 223
economic reconstruction, 26, 193, 210
Eddington, Arthur, 47
education systems, overhaul of, 185
Eichmann, Adolph, 135
Eichmann in Jerusalem (Arendt), 135
Eliot, T. S., 66
Elshtain, Jean Bethke, 13, 123, 224, 227–28
emancipation, 160, 163, 165, 167
Emancipation Proclamation, 150, 167
empirical approach to stable peace, 84–85
Epelbaum, Renée de, 141
Eritrea, 87
essential contestability phenomenon, 212
ethical interoperability, 58, 59
ethics in times of war, 12–13, 99–119, 225; challenges, 99–101; phase 0: religious role in time of near peace, 101–3; phase 1: road to war, 12, 100, 103–5; phase 2: mobilizing for war, 12, 100, 105–8; phase 3: full spectrum war, 12, 100, 108–13; phase 4: stability and support, demobilization, 8, 12, 100, 113–15; phase 5: peace and conflict resolution, 12, 100, 115–18; religion and just war theory, 98–99
ethics of responsibility, 13, 124–30
ethnic cleansing. *See* genocide
Europe: debellicization of, since World War II, 84; and humanitarian intervention, 124; rebuilding after World War II, 15. *See also* Marshall Plan; World War I; World War II

European Union, 67, 85, 186, 223
Evans, Mark, 14, 54, 197, 224, 228
"evil" terminology, 106
ex bello efforts in irregular war, 50
exit strategies, 74, 142, 188, 224, 228

failed states, 127, 128
The Faith of the American Soldier (Mansfield), 111–12
fault, 31, 55
feminist views, 134, 209
Fifteenth Amendment, 168
Fifth Amendment, 110
firearms, introduction of, 23
First Amendment, 110
First Gulf War (1991): conclusion leading to Iraq War, 177, 182–83; as humanitarian intervention, 27; and just war criteria, 71; negative effects of sanctions after, 181; *post bellum* justice of, 39, 217n15; reparations after, 36–37, 183
Foner, Eric, 147, 160, 164, 167–68, 169
Forde, Gerhard, 143n13
forgetting. *See* knowing-forgetting of history
forgiveness, 123, 130–41, 208, 210–11, 218n26
Forrest, Nathan Bedford: and ending of Civil War, 145, 146, 152, 156, 158–59, 163; and Ku Klux Klan, 158–59, 165
Fort Pillow massacre (US Civil War), 158
Fourteenth Amendment, 168
France, 45, 143n19, 180, 184
Franco-German relationship, x, 3, 65–67
French Bishops' Declaration of Repentance (1997), 143n19
full spectrum war (phase 3), 12, 100, 108–13. *See also jus in bello* (justice in war)

gains to be forfeited by aggressor, 180, 182
gender equality in Japan, 43
General Assembly (UN), 40–41
Geneva Conventions: adoption of (1949), 3; and ethics of responsibility, 124; first Convention, 24
Geneva Conventions, proposal for new Convention, 14, 175–94, 226; human rights in, 187–88; legitimate government in, 187; minimally just regime as goal of, 187–88; objections to, 177–78; principles of, 187–88; process for, 188–89; reasons for, 175–77; rehabilitation alternative to, 183–86; revenge models, examples of, 182–83; revenge vs. rehabilitation, 179–82, 226

genocide, 11, 56, 101, 124, 135. *See also* Bosnia; Darfur; Holocaust; Rwanda
Genocide Convention, 8, 92, 125, 229
Germany: bankruptcy caused by reparations of World War I, 182; constitution, 185; Franco-German relationship, x, 3, 65–67; reconstruction and rehabilitation of, 14, 26, 63n29, 69, 123, 183–86, 188, 209; and regime change, 14, 38, 130; Sudetenland and revenge of Czechs, 137–40. *See also* World War I; World War II
Gettysburg reunions, 169
good behavior, obligations attached to, 39–40
Goodwin, Doris Kearns, 150, 152
Gordon, John B., 155
Grant, Ulysses S., 145, 149, 151, 152–56
Gratian, 18, 19
Great Britain, 136, 184
The Great Illusion (Angell), 83
Grotius, Hugo, 4, 6, 18–19, 25, 31–32, 80
Guantánamo, 110
Gulf War. *See* First Gulf War (1991)

Hague Conventions, 61–62n9
Hague Declaration (1899), 24
Hardin, Russell, 90
Hatzfeld, Jean, 101
Havel, Vaclav, 138
Hay, John, 162
Hebrew prophets on end of war, 82
Hegel, G. W. F., 47, 61n2
history, likelihood of repetition of, 133
history of aftermath of wars, 23–27, 223
Hitler, Adolph. *See* Nazis; World War II
Hobbes, Thomas, 6, 16, 128
Holocaust, 38, 135, 143n19, 179
humanitarian intervention: by armed force, 8, 26–27, 28–29, 51, 208; differentiating citizens from enemy actors, 53; as ethic of responsibility, 124, 223; goal of, 38; lingering obligations of, 45, 222; and rebuilding after invasion, 41; and social justice, 102
human rights: commitment to, 9, 91–93, 228; and just peace, 207; in new Geneva Convention, 187–88; responsibility to protect, 27, 29, 43
humility, 66, 76
Hundred Years War, 19
Hussein, Saddam, x, 36–37, 39, 71, 107, 142, 177
hybrid war, 48–56. *See also* irregular war

ideal theory, 199, 216n6
IGOs. *See* intergovernmental organizations
immunity of noncombatants, 50, 52, 53, 181
Indian invasion of East Pakistan, 41
intelligence community: employees in Washington, DC, 120n15; and religion, 107, 111
intensity, 120n19
intergovernmental organizations (IGOs), 70, 113, 115, 116
International Commission on Intervention and State Sovereignty, 26
International Criminal Court, 8, 180, 226, 229
international human rights law, 91–92
International Military Tribunal (1945), 3
interstate wars: conclusion of, 205; decline in, after World War II, 79, 87
intervention. *See* humanitarian intervention
intrastate war. *See* civil war
"invention of peace," 86
IRA. *See* Irish Republican Army
Iran, 72, 105, 176, 191
Iran–Iraq War (1979–89), 176
Iraq invasion of Kuwait. *See* First Gulf War (1991)
Iraq War: American unreadiness to take responsibility in, 44; armed force in aftermath of, 8, 22, 126; and civil war, 126; deterrence as US responsibility in, 128; exit problems, 74, 142; First Gulf War conclusion leading to, 177, 182–83; goals of, 71; as irregular war, 49; and *jus post bellum*, 11, 68, 69; just peace in, 204; limits on US responsibility in, 28; and military chaplains, 112; Orend's view of, 52; reconstruction and rehabilitation, 123, 189–93; sovereignty of Iraq during, 28; and surge, 126, 192; and United Nations, 70
Irish Catholics, 136
Irish Republican Army, 136–37
irregular war, 48–56, 61n7; as dominant form of war, 49; and *jus in bello*, 53; linearity erased by, 53–54, 59; proportionality and double-effect of, 50; purpose of, 60; vacillation between routine combat and security operations, 50
Islam, 107, 120n16, 191
Israel, 7, 37, 42, 179

Jackson, Robert, 3
Japan: American writing of constitution for, 43, 130, 185; official apology for World War II, reticence on, 179; Pearl Harbor attack, 106;

reconstruction and rehabilitation of, 15, 26, 52, 123, 183–86
John Paul II (pope), 131
Johnson, Andrew, 168
Johnson, James Turner, 10, 17, 223
Johnston, Joe, 145, 152, 156–57, 163
Jones, Dorothy V., 85–86
Jones, Greg L., 131
jus ad bellum (justice of start of war): aim of peace as right intention for, 54; and Aquinas, 80; ethics of, 8, 66; and human rights, 92; and humility, 76; and just war tradition, 21, 91, 146; and moral war aims, 12; multilateral *ad bellum* decisions, 40–42; overlap with *jus post bellum*, 35, 42, 51–54, 69, 89, 224–25; principles of, 4, 73; purpose of laws of, 176; and rehabilitation, 14; and religious grievances, 101; success of, 9; and World War II, 179
jus ante bellum (just military preparedness), 55–60
jus in bello (justice in war): asymmetry in behavior and intentionality in, 55–56; historical development of, 17–21; in irregular war, 49, 53; juridical instruments for, 8–9; and just war tradition, 21, 146; limitations and constraints on, 48; and military chaplains, 112; and noncombatant differentiation, 55, 181, 206; overlap with *jus post bellum*, 35, 42, 51–54, 66, 69, 101, 146, 224–25; principles of, 4–5, 73; purpose of laws of, 176; and rehabilitation, 14; and religion, 101; and revenge, 181
jus post bellum (justice after war), 11, 49–64; asymmetry in behavior and intentionality in, 55–56; and civil wars, 88, 91, 93; and Coady's model, 54–55; collective punishment of reparations as part of, 42; and conciliation, 226–28; criteria for, 70–76; criticism of terminology, 32; and deterrence, 128; duration of, 44, 46; forgiveness and reconciliation in, 211; formation of principles for, 90–93; Geneva Convention proposed for, 175–96; and Gulf War (1991), 36–37; and immunity of noncombatants, 52–53, 181; in irregular war, 53; just peace as goal of, 197; in just war theory, 35, 146, 197, 216n1, 218n33; Kant's proposals on, 56; neglect of, 5–7, 51; obligations of, 39–46, 55, 179–82; and order, 222–24; and Orend's model, 48, 51–52, 206–7; overlap with *jus ad bellum* and *jus in bello*, 51–54, 66, 89, 224–25; and peace as purpose of war, 79–81; research agenda for, 224, 229; "restoration minus," 75; "restoration plus," 71, 75; restricted conception of, 213; and stable peace, 77–93; and status quo *ante bellum*, 130, 223, 226; and unjust war, 197–98; and victors' rights, 207–8; and wars that engender war, 86–88; and wars to end wars, 81–86
Just and Unjust Wars (Walzer), 90–91
just cause, 4, 12, 80, 104, 224
justice: destabilizing effect of pursuit of, x, 68, 225; importance as link of phases of war, 226; just peace taking precedence over, 201; in morality of war, 199, 224–26; process of, 221; and rehabilitation, 183–86; as remedial or rectificatory virtue, 199–200, 209; simultaneous ostensible justice, 31–32; and sovereignty, 20; at World War II end, 2–3
just outcome, 11, 35–36, 44
just peace, 14, 197–216; as dangerous objective, 200; democratic and perpetual peace theses, 212–16; elusiveness of, 14, 198–202; and forgiveness, 211; and human rights, 91; and international order, 215; "just a peace" as opposed to "a just peace," 37, 45; and moral sanctions, 197–98; philosophical approach to, 202–5; precedence over justice, 201; and racial justice at end of US Civil War, 163; and reconciliation, 211; restriction vs. extension, 205–11; role of, 89
just punishment, 13, 141
just society, 11, 45, 169
just war theory, 10–11, 17–33, 91–99; *bellum justum*, defined, 19; categories of, 51; and civil wars, 88; conceptual circle of, 11, 56, 60, 225; elements of, 17; and ethics of responsibility, 124–30; evaluating start and end of wars, 145–46; historic view vs. current view of, 223; history of, 4, 18–19; and human rights, 92; and lessons from the past, 66–70; and military preparedness, 56, 60; and neutral states, 40; new approach to *jus post bellum*, 35–39; overview, 4–9; and peace, 28, 77; and political forgiveness, 123, 130–41; and postconflict principles, 75; and punishment, 13; purpose of, 30–31, 89, 216n8; and religion, 98–100. *See also* right intention

Kagan, Donald, 61n3
Kambanda, Jean, 180

Kant, Immanuel, 11, 48, 51, 56, 83, 84
Kegley, Charles W., Jr., 83
Keynes, John Maynard, 89–90, 96*n*45
Klaus, Vaclav, 138
knowing-forgetting of history, 133, 135–36, 143*n*16, 227
Korea. *See* Korean War; North Korea; South Korea
Korean War, 37, 71
Kosovo, 70, 127, 177, 222–23
Krulak, Charles C., 62*n*17
Ku Klux Klan (KKK), 158–59, 165, 168
Kurds, 39, 183, 191
Kuwait, 27, 36–37, 182–83, 218*n*33. *See also* First Gulf War (1991)

Lankford, Nelson, 171*n*14, 172–73*n*49
last resort, war as, 104
Law of Armed Conflict (LOAC), 49, 92
League of Nations, 41, 66, 70
Lee, Robert E., 145, 152–55, 156–57, 163, 173*n*49, 227. *See also* Appomattox
Left Behind (LeHaye), 107
legalist paradigm, 7
legitimate authority: and political order, 125; restoration of, after war, 128; to wage war, 104
LeHaye, Tim, 107
Leviathan (Hobbes), 128
lex talionis, 135, 141
liberal model of democracy, 214, 219*n*34
Liberation Tigers of Tamil Eelam (LTTE), 221
Liddell-Hart, B. H., 5, 80
Lieber Code, 24, 61*n*9
Lincoln, Abraham: and amnesty, 161–63, 227; assassination of, 156; and Emancipation Proclamation, 150, 167; and ending of Civil War, 145, 146, 148–52; preservation of union as goal of, 88; and racial justice, 163–64; and reconciliation, 147, 154–55, 227; and Reconstruction, 157–63; Richmond visit of, 149–50, 151; River Queen Doctrine of, 148–49, 151, 153, 157; and Wenz trial, 165
Lloyd George, David, 89
LOAC. *See* Law of Armed Conflict
loi d'armes (law of arms/law of war), 19
Los Angeles Police Department, 58
Lucas, E. V., 89
Lucas, George R., Jr., 11, 47, 225
Lukes, Steven, 212
Luther, Martin, 123

MacArthur, Douglas, 184
magnification problem, 202–3
major combat operations (MCOs), 61*n*7
Mandela, Nelson, 170*n*8, 172*n*35, 227
Mandelbaum, Michael, 86, 96*n*45
Mansfield, Stephen, 111–12
Mao Zedong, 81
Margalit, Avishai, 37
Marshall Plan, 3, 52, 66, 67, 186
Marxism, 217*n*9
Mexico, 105, 193
Middle Ages, nature of war in, 23
militaries. *See* armies
military chaplaincy, 112
Military Ethics Education Network (MEEN), 57
military operations other than war (MOOTW), 49, 61*n*7. *See also* irregular war
military preparedness, 55–60
Miller, William Lee, 130, 162, 174*n*66
Milosevic, Slobodan, 180
minimally just regime, 187–88, 207
mission creep, 68
Mitrany, David, 90
mobilizing for war (phase 2), 12, 100, 105–8. *See also jus ad bellum* (justice of start of war)
Mojze, Paul, 100–101
Morgenthau Plan (post-World War II Germany), 209
Mueller, John, 85, 106
Muhammad, 107
mujaheddin, 224
multilateral *ad bellum* decisions, 40–42
Museum of the Confederacy (Richmond, Virginia), 155, 172*n*42
Myers, Richard, 106–7

Napoleonic wars, 24, 83
narco-states, 193
Nash, William, 189
National Security Presidential Directive 44, 113
NATO. *See* North Atlantic Treaty Organization
natural disasters, 30, 55, 56
natural law, 29, 49
Nazis, 38, 138–39, 184, 194*n*3. *See also* World War II
negotiated agreements to end armed conflicts, 26
neutral states, 40
NGOs. *See* non-governmental organizations
Nichomachean Ethics (Aristotle), 79

Niebuhr, Reinhold, 161
noncombatants: deaths of, 109; differentiation from enemy combatants, 53, 55, 181, 206; immunity of, 50, 52, 53, 181; limiting harm to, 5, 19, 23, 74, 181; reconciliation of, 164; rights of, 53, 58
non-governmental organizations (NGOs), 115, 223
North Atlantic Treaty Organization (NATO), 2, 3, 50, 59, 99, 222–23
Northern Ireland, 101, 136, 227
North Korea, 72, 106. *See also* Korean War
nuclear weapons, 7, 24, 33*n*11, 57, 129
Nuremberg trials, x, 3, 7, 38, 45, 179–80

Obama, Barack: and just war thinking, 229; ordering troop surge in Afghanistan, 192
occupiers, responsibilities of, 11, 39–46, 51, 213–14; and Coady's model, 54; in disarmament, 128; and law of postwar occupation, 91; restoration of sovereignty, 208; and social justice, 209. *See also* reconstruction and rehabilitation; *specific wars*
OGAs. *See* other government agencies
On the Laws of War and Peace (Grotius), 25
order, 10, 21, 75, 221, 222–24. *See also tranquillitas ordinis* (tranquility of order)
Orend, Brian, ix, 14, 48, 51–54, 175, 206–7, 223, 226
Otis, Pauletta, 13, 97, 225

Pakistan, 41, 72, 75, 86, 191–92
Palestine, 105
Paludan, Philip S., 173–74*n*66
pardons of US Civil War soldiers, 162, 171*n*14
Paris Declaration (1856), 24
passive states, 40
patriotism, 110
Patterson, Eric, 1, 51, 142*n*6, 221
peace: AR2 framework for, 146; defined, 21; developing and implementing of, 10; "invention of peace," 86; "just a peace" as opposed to "a just peace," 37, 45; oppressive peace, 78; as purpose of war, 79–81; stable peace as goal, 77–93; through transitional justice, 146; war to end war and bring lasting peace, 81–86. *See also* just peace
peace and conflict resolution (phase 5), 12, 100, 115–18. *See also jus post bellum* (justice after war)
Peace of Westphalia (1648), 24, 83
peace protests, 115

peace treaties, details of, 177, 179, 208
Pearl Harbor attack (1941), 106
Péguy, Charles, 68
The Peloponnesian War (Thucydides), 123
Perpetual Peace (Kant), 83
perpetual peace thesis, 212–16
"perpetual perishing," 47
Petraeus, David, 192
phases of warfare: phase 0: religious role in time of near peace, 8, 12, 100, 101–3; phase 1: road to war, 12, 100, 103–5; phase 2: mobilizing for war, 12, 100, 105–8; phase 3: full spectrum war, 12, 100, 108–13; phase 4: stability and support, demobilization, 8, 12, 100, 113–15; phase 5: peace and conflict resolution, 12, 100, 115–18
Philippines, 13, 86
Pickett, George, 150, 171*n*14
Plato, 80
police states, 189
Political Community in the North Atlantic Area (Deutsch), 84–85
political forgiveness, 123, 130–40
political legitimacy, 43, 44, 187
political order, 125. *See also* order
political revolution, 36
Porter, David, 149, 150
positive law, use of, 226
preemptive use of force, 125
President of Good and Evil (Singer), 106
presumption against war, 22
prevention of conflict. *See* conflict prevention, initiatives to secure
preventive use of force, 125
prisoners of war: exchange of, 179; in US Civil War, treatment of, 153, 162, 165
Proclamation of Amnesty and Reconstruction (US 1863), 162
Project for Perpetual Peace (Abbé de Saint-Pierre), 82
proportionality, 50, 72, 109, 111, 206
protractedness, 120*n*19
provisions from victors, 43–44, 73, 222
punishment of aggressors. *See* reparations; war criminals, punishment of
puppet governments, 43, 44

R2P. *See* Responsibility to Protect
racial justice, 146–47, 151, 157, 160–61, 162–64, 167–68
Radical Congressional Reconstruction (1870–77), 168

radical fundamentalism, 100
Ramsey, Paul, 7, 33n11
Rawls, John, 45
Raymond, Gregory A., 83
realism, 126, 142n5
reasonable chance of success, 12, 67, 104
reconciliation. See conciliation or reconciliation
reconstruction and rehabilitation: as alternative to revenge model, 14, 183–86; backlash effect against, 194; burden on aggressors, 127; and Coady's model, 54, 55, 63n29; economic reconstruction, 26; and fault, 31, 55; and humanitarian intervention, 41; as *jus post bellum* principle, 207; motivation for, 69–70; parties obligated in, 31, 222, 223; and political legitimacy, 43, 44; realistic limits of, 42–43; "restoration minus," 75; "restoration plus," 71, 75; US State Department's responsibility for, 113. See also Marshall Plan; occupiers, responsibilities of; World War II
Reconstruction period (US), 146–47, 159–70
reflective equilibrium, 203
regime change: and humanitarian intervention, 38–39; and *jus post bellum*, 38; and local norms, 43; and revenge model, 181–82; when appropriate, 72
regular warfare *(guerre réglée)*, 49
rehabilitation. See reconstruction and rehabilitation
Religion and Ethics (Coker), 106
religion and just war theory, 98–100; full spectrum war (phase 3), 12, 100, 108–13; mobilizing for war (phase 2), 12, 100, 105–8; peace and conflict resolution (phase 5), 12, 100, 115–18; in peace times (phase 0), 12, 100, 101–3; road to war (phase 1), 12, 100, 103–5; stability and support, demobilization (phase 4), 8, 12, 100, 113–15
Religious Affairs in Joint Operations (DOD Joint Publication 1-05), 102, 112
religious wars, 23–24, 32, 83
reparations: after First Gulf War, 36–37, 183; and Coady's model, 54; collective punishment of, 42; imperfect nature of, 36, 38, 225; as punishment for aggressors, 25, 181, 207; Sudetenland and expelled Germans, 137–39. See also *specific wars*
responsibility after armed conflict, 27–32; to both sides of conflict, 29; Coady's view of, 55; and *jus post bellum* principles, 39–46. See

also occupiers, responsibilities of; reconstruction and rehabilitation
Responsibility to Protect (R2P), 124
The Responsibility to Protect (ICISS), 26
restorative justice, 140–41
restraint: defined, 5; on Iraq after Gulf War (1991), 37; and *jus post bellum* principles, 53, 66, 75; just cause and tradition of restraint, 129; and just war thinking, 7; legal and moral efforts for, 25
revenge, 73, 111, 164, 179–83, 194
revolution and concept of just war, 36
Richmond, Virginia, 149–50, 151, 156, 165–66
right intention, 4, 11, 20, 54, 60, 67, 73, 80, 104
right religious allegiance, 24
River Queen Doctrine (Lincoln), 148–49, 151, 153, 157
road to war (phase 1), 12, 100, 103–5
rogue states, 128
Rome Treaty (1998), 180
Royal, Robert, 11–12, 65, 223, 228
rule of law: and *jus post bellum*, 11, 51; and justice, 114; necessity for, 140, 210, 221; reestablishment of, 185
Rwanda: genocide in, 8, 56, 101, 180; humanitarian intervention in, 26, 38; and International Criminal Tribunal, 45, 226; justice system established in, x; religion's role in conflict, 101; and Responsibility to Protect (R2P), 124

St. Paul's Episcopal Church (Richmond, Virginia), 156
St. Petersburg Declaration (1868), 24
Saint-Pierre, Abbé de, 82, 84
Santayana, George, 133
Saudi Arabia, 191
Savannah Colloquy, 164
Schaap, Andrew, 211
Schumann, Robert, 67
security communities, 85
Security Council (UN), 40, 215
self-sacrifice, 29
Sen, Amartya, 174n76
separation of church and state, 100
September 11, 2001 terrorist attacks, 75, 105, 106–7, 128–29, 183
severity, 120n19
Sherman, William Tecumseh: and ending of Civil War, 145, 149, 157–59; and ending of slavery, 163–64; on more perfect peace, 77,

82; and Savannah Colloquy, 164; and Special Field Order No. 15, 164
Shi'ite Muslims, 191
simultaneous ostensible justice, 31–32
Singer, Peter, 106
Six Day War (1967), 37
slavery, ending in US, 150, 160, 161–62, 163, 165. *See also* emancipation
Smith, Adam, 83
socialist model of democracy, 214, 219n34
Somalia, 26, 75, 86
South Africa, 13, 101, 140, 145, 148
South African Truth and Reconciliation Commission (TRC), 140, 141, 146, 170
South Korea, 171
sovereigns' wars, 24
sovereignty: authority of, 20, 72, 80; concept of, 27; of Germany, 38; in Iraq–Kuwait war, 27–29; of Iraq under Hussein, 39; and *jus post bellum*, 205–6; in just war tradition, 5; neutrality and passivity linked to, 40; restoration of, 208; rights of, 29, 40, 72, 208
Soviet Union, 130, 184, 224. *See also* Stalin, Joseph
Spanish American War (1898), 105
Special Field Order No. 15 (Sherman issuance), 164
spoliation, 25
Sri Lanka, 101, 221
stability and support operations (phase 4), 8, 12, 100, 113–15
stabilization, security, transition and reconstruction operations, 61n7
Stalin, Joseph, 1–2, 130
Stanton, Edwin M., 152
State Department, US, 113
status quo *ante bellum*, restoration of, 129–30, 223, 226
Sudan, 12, 15, 86, 225
Sudetenland, 137–39
Summa Theologica (Aquinas), 18, 80
Sunni Muslims, 191

Taliban. *See* Afghanistan War
Tambiah, S. J., 101
Tamil Tigers, 221
Tanzanian invasion of Uganda, 41
Taylor, Richard, 157
telos, 21
third-party nations' responsibility to help rebuild, 55

Thirteenth Amendment, 150
Thirty Years War, 24, 83
Thomas Aquinas. *See* Aquinas, Thomas
threat exaggeration, US reaction to, 106
Thucydides, 123
Tokyo war crime trials, x, 3, 7, 179
torture: as consideration in justice of postconflict settlement, 225; use in interrogation, 110–11. *See also* Convention against Torture (UN)
tranquillitas ordinis (tranquility of order), 10, 21, 80, 125
transitional justice, 9, 13, 15, 145–46, 169, 224, 228
TRC. *See* South African Truth and Reconciliation Commission
treason charges not brought against Confederates, 153, 154, 162, 163
treaties. *See name of treaty*; peace treaties
trials of war criminals. *See* Nuremberg trials; Tokyo war crime trials; war criminals, punishment of
trusteeship, 41–42
Turkey, 191
Tutu, Desmond, 148, 227
Twain, Mark, 105, 119n10
tyranny, revolution as defense against, 36

ubuntu (South African term), 148
Uganda, 13, 41, 145
United Nations, 40–41, 59, 70, 124, 127, 218n31
United Nations Charter, 3, 83, 124, 194
United States: humanitarian intervention by, 124–25; military preparedness of, 57–58; post-World War II territories, 184; threat exaggeration, US reaction to, 106. *See also* Civil War, US; *specific wars in which US participated*
United States Marine Corp, 99, 102
Universal Declaration of Human Rights, 124, 125, 188
unjust war: and just peace, 197–98; just war found unjustly, 224
Uppsala Conflict Data Program (UCPD), 86, 87
US Institute of Peace, 116
USMC. *See* United States Marine Corp
US National Conference of Catholic Bishops, 22, 33n11

Vattel, Emer de, 49, 61–62n9
ven der Linden, Harry, 56–58, 64n37

vengeance. *See* revenge
Verkamp, Bernard, 20
Versailles Treaty (1919), 8, 25–26, 31, 65, 177, 180, 182, 194*n*3
victims' heirs receiving reparations, 42
victors' costs to be borne by defeated enemy, 25, 27, 181. *See also* reparations
victors' obligations. *See* reconstruction and rehabilitation
Vietnam and Cambodia genocide, 39–40, 41
Vietnam War, 7, 24, 33*n*11, 45, 68, 126
Villa-Vicencio, Charles, 140
vindication, 206
violence in aftermath of war, 114–15
Vitoria, Francisco de, 31, 36
von Moltke, Helmuth, 74

Walzer, Michael, 7, 11, 33*n*11, 35, 49, 51, 71, 90–91, 95*n*41, 222, 223, 228
"war convention," 7, 49, 50
war criminals, punishment of, 13, 26, 179–80, 206–7, 225. *See also* Civil War, US; Nuremberg trials; Tokyo war crime trials
warfare, phases of. *See* phases of warfare
The War Prayer (Twain), 105, 119*n*10
wars: aims of, 11, 12, 66; antiterrorist wars, 39; approaches to ending well, 10; begetting new wars, 47–48, 78, 86–88, 181; causes of, 88–93; despoiling of beaten enemy, 25; duration of, 112; history of aftermath of, 23–27; irregular war, 48–56; and justice, 42–46; as last resort, 104; Napoleonic wars, 24; number ongoing globally (1989–2008), 86; religious wars, 23–24, 32, 83; sovereigns' wars, 24; wars to end wars, 81–86; without clear winners and losers, 176. *See also* civil war; phases of warfare
The War That Will End War (Wells), 81

weapons of mass destruction (WMDs), 69, 71–72, 106, 183
Weinberger-Powell doctrine, 63*n*34
Weitzel, Godfrey, 149–50, 151
Wells, H. G., 81–82
Wenz, John, 165
Wertheimer, Roger, 56–57
whistleblowers, 111
Whitehead, A. N., 47, 60–61*n*1
Williams, Robert E., Jr., 12, 77, 225, 228
Wilson, Woodrow, 77, 79, 81–84
Winik, Jay, 14, 145, 146–59
WMDs. *See* weapons of mass destruction
women: gender equality in Japan, 43. *See also* feminist views
World War I: lessons learned from, 66–67; problems created by reparations and settlement of, 2, 25, 31, 65, 77–78, 177, 181, 182, 226; revenge model of settlement of, 182; as war to end war, 81–82
World War II: Allies' approach to post-war issues, 1–3, 184–85, 215; just peace in terms of, 38; lessons learned from, 66–68; rebuilding vanquished after, 26, 52, 66, 183–86; reparations paid by Germany, 42, 179; return of conquered countries after, 180; settlement at end of World War I leading to, 2, 25, 65, 77–78, 177, 182, 194*n*3, 226. *See also* Nuremberg trials; Tokyo war crime trials

Yemen, 75
Yorubaland, 81
Yugoslavia (former), 8, 26, 45, 226

Zolo, Danilo, 219*n*35
zones of peace, 12, 84–85, 87
zones of turmoil, 85, 87